CROSSING WAIYAKI WAY

CROSSING WAIYAKI WAY

A True Story of Poverty, Prayer, and Politics in Kenya

Robin Okumu
&
Gordon Okumu

Copyright © 2024 by Robin Okumu and Gordon Okumu

All rights reserved. No part of this publication may be reproduced in any form or by any means without the prior written permission of the copyright holder, except as permitted by U.S. copyright law. For permission requests, contact the publisher.

Published in the United States by Angels of Africa Press, a division of Angels of Africa, a registered nonprofit organization with 501(c)3 status in the United States. Angels of Africa receives all net proceeds from the sale of this book.

Library of Congress Control Number: 2024940537

ISBN (hardback): 979-8-9905124-0-5
ISBN (paperback): 979-8-9905124-1-2
ISBN (ebook): 979-8-9905124-2-9

www.angelsofafrica.org
info@angelsofafrica.org

Printed in the United States of America on acid-free paper

Cover Photo: *View from Ananda Marga* (2018) by Robin Okumu
Interior design and maps by Robin Okumu
Photographs by Robin and Gordon Okumu

To Selmina Gor and Mary Auma:
for being extraordinary mothers who raised an extraordinary son.

To Fr. Jonathan Landon:
for your guidance and trust that have made all the difference.

CONTENTS

The Kaunda Suit	**3**
Mwendo wa ngamia: the way of the camel	**13**
1. Beginnings	15
2. Rural Rituals	45
3. Mary Auma	56
Mwendo wa kobe: the way of the turtle	**93**
1. To Luo Land	95
2. Grandpa	118
3. Grandma	123
Mwendo wa chui: the way of the leopard	**145**
1. Return	147
2. Ananda Marga	157
3. Come and See	168
Mwendo wa nyoka: the way of the snake	**191**
1. Karibu Tanzania	193
2. Poverty, Chastity, and Obedience	198
3. All that Glitters	211
Mwendo wa ngarama: the difficult way	**227**
1. The Bottom Again	229
2. Mr. President Sir	236
3. The Campaign for Suna West	253
Acknowledgments	277
About the Authors	281

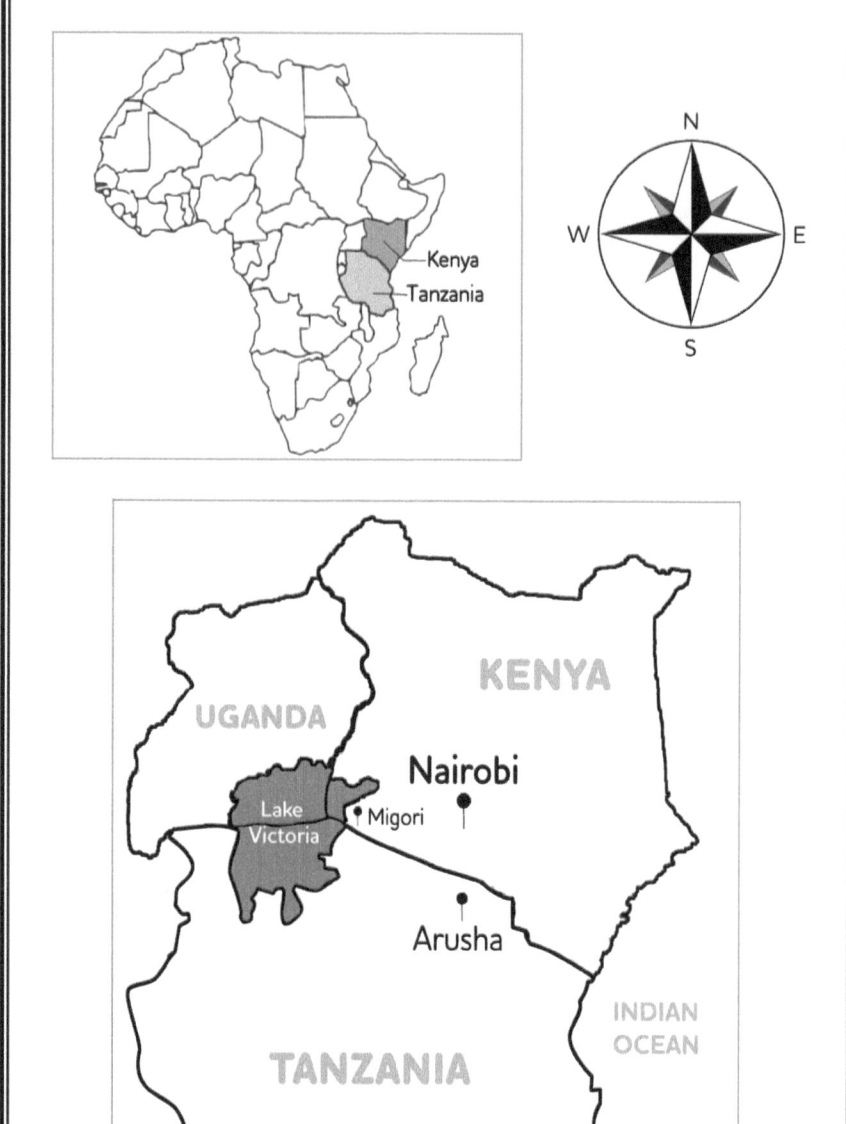

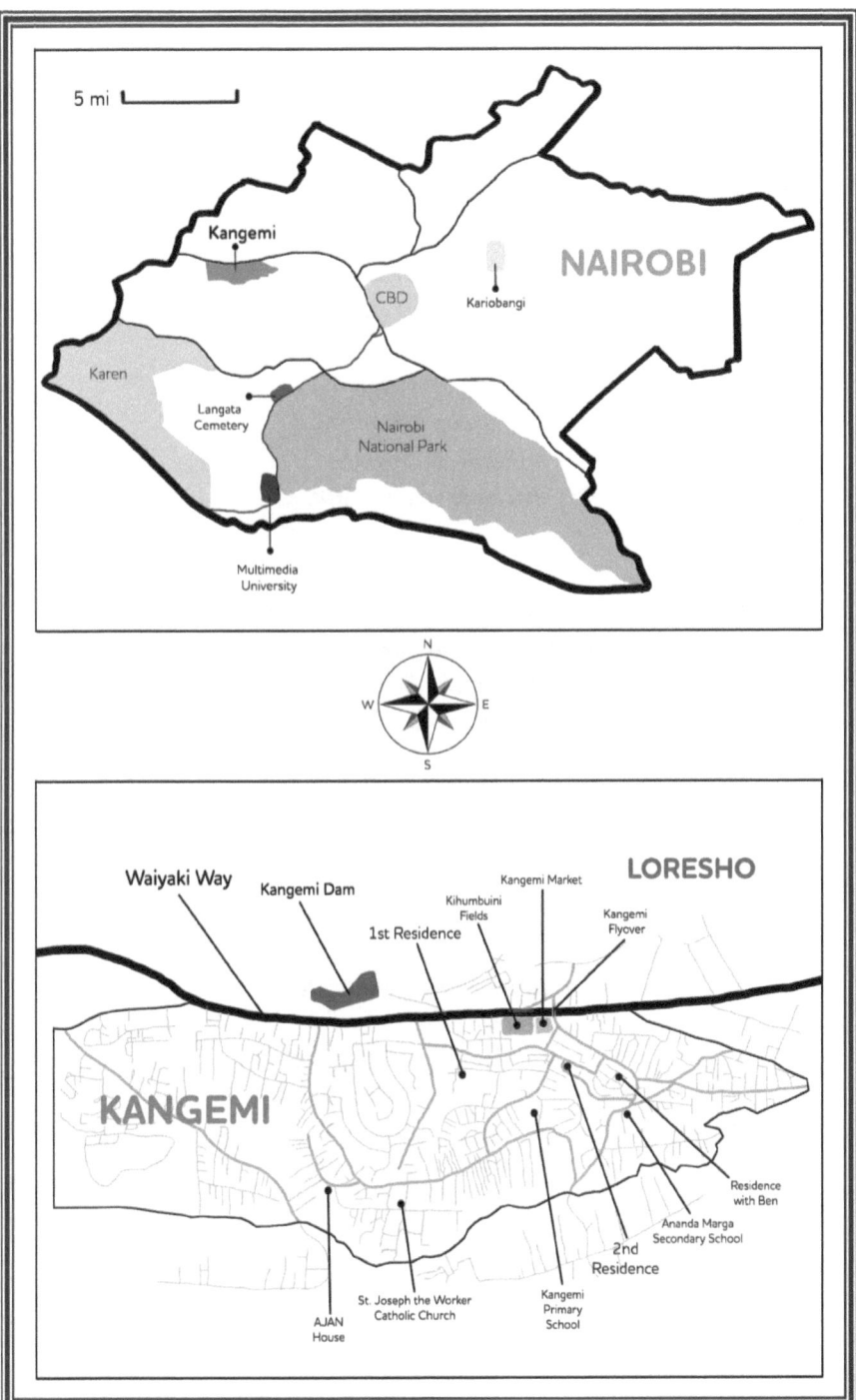

Oh mwanangu dunia ina mambo,
sikia maneno, nakwambiaga,
mpe roho yako Mola wako,
heshima kwa wazazi eee mwanangu.

Dunia hii mama
lukumba lukumba,
dunia ina mambo
mwendo wa ngamia.
...

Mwendo wa kobe *maele maele,*
mwendo wa chui *kuwinda winda,*
mwendo wa nyoka *lukumba lukumba,*
mwendo wa ngarama *ah njia ya faradhi.*

Dunia hii mama
lukumba lukumba,
dunia ina mambo
mwendo wa ngamia.

Tabu na raha inakungojea,
inategemea akili yako,
tafutaaaa eh utapata eh,
kumbuka maneno nakwambiaga.

(Lyrics of a Swahili song,
popular in East Africa in the late twentieth century.
Our emphasis)

O my child the world has issues,
listen to the words I'm telling you,
give your soul to your God,
and respect to parents, my child.

This world, mama
meanders and meanders,
the world has issues,
like **the way of the camel.**
...

The way of the turtle is slow, step by step,
The way of the leopard is driven, ever hunting,
The way of the snake meanders, side to side,
The difficult way – right – it cannot be avoided.

This world, mama
meanders and meanders,
the world has issues,
like the way of the camel.

Suffering and pleasure await you,
depending on your intellect,
search – yes – and you will find – yes,
remember the words I'm telling you.

(Our translation and emphasis)

I
The Kaunda Suit

Msema pweke hakosi.
(A Swahili proverb, or *methali za Kiswahili*)

Literal Translation:
He who speaks to himself cannot be wrong.

Our Paraphrase:
No one can contradict you if you only talk to yourself.

In 1995, near the shores of Lake Victoria in rural western Kenya, the residents of Migori county were anticipating a visit from the Honorable Dalmas Otieno Anyango with a palpitating mixture of excitement and reverence fit for the arrival of a long-awaited savior. On the morning of the visit, people packed into a local church to attend mass before the MP (an elected member of Parliament) was scheduled to make his grand arrival there. Others lined the roadside, hoping to catch a glimpse of the MP as he passed by. He arrived in humble Migori town by car, accompanied by a fleet of vehicles and a police escort. No one knew where these police had come from since Migori didn't even have its own police force. As the line of black, shiny Cadillac Escalades drove through town, the city's main dirt road crunched and cracked under a weight it had never born before. The motorcade stopped at certain points, and the MP emerged from the sunroof, holding a microphone. He greeted the cheering onlookers and made *roadside declarations*, or unofficial promises to construct this road, fix this school, and bring electricity to this area.

For some of the residents, the combination of flashing lights and sirens and hullabaloo from the unprecedented spectacle ignited hope for possibility and development. For others, it raised only fear, for being so close to power was like being close to fire. It could warm, but it could also burn and blacken, leaving only ashes in its wake. In addition to being an MP, Otieno had been appointed Minister of Transportation by President Daniel Arap Moi. Since this was before the revised 2010 Kenyan Constitution, the President still enjoyed unbridled, almost dictatorial power. While the people of Migori did not dare even speak the name of President Moi within their houses *because the walls had ears*, Otieno's name and the figure behind it were only slightly less formidable. One *could* speak of this important man in quick whispers, but only of course, to praise his achievements and character.

While the procession still inched through town and the MP made declarations, over at the church, the mass had ended. Those in attendance then carried the church's wooden pews out onto an adjacent field. They arranged the pews on the grass in a semi-circle facing a short stage. A high-backed, wooden chair of honor stood at the center of the stage, and this lone chair enjoyed a sliver of precious shade from a large tree behind the stage. One long piece of plastic tape set far back from the stage demarcated the start of the area where people were to sit and acted like police tape roping off a crime scene. Everyone was to sit behind the tape—adults in the pews and children in front of them on the ground. No one was supposed to go past that tape.

On this typical warm, sunny afternoon in Migori, the air was thick with the smell of dusty earth and commingled sweat. People had put on their Sunday best, or even better than their best, for if ever there was an occasion to showcase one's finery, this was it. They had walked from their houses to the church in new *vitenge* tunics and dresses bought specifically for this day. The heavy fabric of the brightly-batiked clothes accentuated the women's curves (for there was no stretch in these fibers) and it cut straight, serious silhouettes of the men. The swirling mix of bright colors and patterns expressed the collective exuberance for Otieno's visit. Thickly outlined flowers, feathers, and fans tessellated through fields of fuchsia set atop indigo and turquoise backgrounds, alternatively contrasting with flashes of citrus or blending into cool blues and purples. Most of the women wore matching head decorations. They wrapped long scarves in a series of clearly defined, ever-enlarging creases, which culminated in a voluminous halo of color.

In the middle of this finely dressed, fidgeting audience, a nine-year-old boy sat on the grass in the row of children. He was on the left side facing the platform, directly in front of his mother in the pew behind him. He wore a navy-blue *kaunda* suit-for-boys—(pronounced cow-oonda), a specific two-part men's fashion named after the former president of Zambia, Kenneth Kaunda, who popularized the style by constantly wearing it. The look consisted of long pants and a short-sleeve jacket with four large pockets, two on the chest and two on the waist, each with a pleated seam down the middle and a pointed cover flap. The jacket had four bronze-colored buttons that led up to a double-pointed collar, which resembled the bottom four points of a star. The boy felt like a million dollars in his stiff, fancy suit.

He listened to speeches and watched the groups of dancers and singers that filled the time while everyone anticipated the real event, but he didn't understand exactly who this important man was or why people showed him such respect. He only knew that this man was a boss, the type who people addressed with titles like *sir* and *mister*. The boy had seen pictures, and he admired the man's big belly—he must be so rich. The man probably got to sit behind a desk in a big office in Nairobi, where he made important decisions that affected all the people of Kenya.

Amidst the noise and festivities, the distant sound of a siren interrupted the speeches, signaling that the MP was *close*, probably only about five miles away. Nervous energy rippled through the seated crowd. The boy watched a group of people unfurl a red carpet, stretching it from the wooden chair on the stage down the few steps and onto the grassy area, until it almost reached the tape. The same group positioned themselves along the side of the red carpet as a receiving line. The sirens slowly got louder and louder until their shrill high and low pitches overlapped and blended together into one continuous blaring scream. All other noise stopped and everyone seemed to hold their breath, no moving, whispering, or even blinking. The MP had finally arrived.

The line of large black vehicles turned off the road onto the grass and made their way toward the stage. They drove on the field through the space in front of the seated crowd, one car following another until one of them stopped, with the left-side passenger door perfectly aligned over the red carpet. A bodyguard in the passenger seat got out first, opened the back side door, and stood by as the man himself, Dalmas Otieno Anyango, then stepped out onto the carpet. The Area Chief introduced Otieno to each person in the line of waiting VIPs (the local school principals and priests and other important people of the town). Otieno shook each person's hand before moving to the next, one by one, until he made his way to the steps and walked onto the stage to take his seat of honor. Then the priest said an introduction and a prayer, not any normal prayer but a unique, special one to thank God for this day and this man and this momentous event. All the important people who had shaken the MP's hand moved to the side. A row of policemen stationed themselves behind the MP. As Otieno took his seat and looked out over the gathered crowd, the best-of-the-best, *crème de la crème* entertainment that had been saved for last officially started off the event.

 The boy watched as a group of women dancers took their positions in the grassy area around the red carpet between the audience and the stage. Drumming started, and the dancers slid their feet back and forth on the grass. They started by bouncing their hips up and down to the beat, shaking one side and then the other, so that the *owalo* skirts around their waists shimmied to the rhythm. The drumming became faster. The women shook the pastel-dyed strands of *sisal* (dried agave fibers woven together to form their skirts) in double-time, then triple-time, swinging fast and frantic flurries of color. Other women began to chant along with the drums and make that high pitched, ululating sound that is reserved for the highest of celebrations and thanksgivings—*eeeehhhhiiiiyyyayayayayaya*. They punctuated it with a series of even higher-pitched exclamations—*ya ya YA YA!* The boy felt the rhythm pounding in his chest and the chants ringing in his ears. He thought about those important people who had greeted Otieno, and he decided that he too wanted to shake the man's hand.

He turned to his mother and said simply, "I'm going to go shake his hand."

She looked at him for a second with a mixture of confusion and disbelief as if she didn't understand his words, like he had spoken a foreign language. Her eyes got wider than he'd ever seen them before.

"No—you can't!" She leaned forward and looked right into his eyes. "You'll put me in trouble!"

He nodded slowly and turned back around in his seat. He had heard her words, but now he felt confused. He thought that she just didn't want to be embarrassed by her son. But why would she be embarrassed? Other people had shaken the man's hand, so why couldn't he do it too?

While he pondered, his mother thought about the invisible web of class, status, and socially conditioned decorum that they had been born into. She, like most people of their community, believed in and lived by unspoken rules and silent fears. She knew the reality of real consequences for acting out of turn under the Moi government. You couldn't just approach important men, and you didn't want to even *imply* the tiniest hint of a threat to the government. If they even *thought* you did, they were right, since they were prosecutor, judge, and jury. It was common for people to just disappear. People probably ended up in untraceable torture chambers beneath the bowels of Nairobi, or their bodies mysteriously appeared, dead and disfigured beyond recognition, in ditches outside the city. The mother wondered if the boy would ruin everything, in front of the police and the priest and all the people of the town. What if Otieno and his men thought that she had sent her son to sabotage the celebration? What if they thought he was a child spy, or that she had sent him wearing a homemade bomb? He couldn't step out of place. How could he even *think* of something like that? Oh Lord God in heaven have mercy! It was unthinkable, impossible.

As his mother sat there with these fears filling her mind like smoke expanding from a fast-flaming fire, the boy continued to weigh her words against his own desire. He didn't see himself as any different from anyone else, any less able or any less deserving. And he was not afraid.

He decided that he would do it.

He stood up and heard his mother's loud gasp behind him, but he didn't turn to look at her. He stepped past the other seated kids around him, ducked under the tape, and headed straight toward the stage.

Everyone was watching the dancers, and the music continued, uninterrupted. The boy walked up on the stage by the stairs on the side. He approached the seated man. No one stopped him or came after him—not his mother, not the police, not any of the other important people. It was like everyone and everything was frozen in time. The boy walked up to the MP and didn't say anything but confidently extended his whole arm, with his fingers wide apart and his tan palm facing the seated man.

The man didn't say anything at first, either, and just turned his gaze to look at the boy. It was hard to tell if he was surprised or amused or offended—or maybe a combination of all of those. The man's expression was stern, with his lips pressed together, somewhere between a frown and a smile. He inhaled through his wide nostrils and squinted his eyes. He then extended his own hand, big enough to completely engulf the boy's, and he shook it firmly. He didn't smile, but he pulled the boy in close.

"What's your name young man?" he asked.

"Oduor Okumu," the boy replied.

"Oduor," the man repeated, nodding. "What grade are you in?"

"Third, at Kangemi Primary."

"Very good." Otieno smiled. He let go of the boy's hand and turned back to watch the dancers, as if to signal that the interaction was done. The boy smiled too, flashing the gap between his two front teeth, and he turned to walk back toward his spot in the audience.

He headed down the side steps the way he had come. He held his chin high and his shoulders back, swinging his arms, feeling the reverberations of that handshake surging through his whole body. He stepped onto the grass and walked majestically—milking five full, luxurious syllables out of that word. He felt like everyone was marveling at him in his kaunda suit. He was the only child who had shaken the MP's hand. He had done the unthinkable. What's more, he had proved to himself and to everyone that it was not, in fact, impossible.

When he reached his seat, he sat down quickly and didn't look at his mother. He didn't want to see her disapproval. For the rest of the event, she didn't say anything about it, and when they got home, he expected her to punish or cane him, but strangely she didn't do either. He just overheard her talking with her friends later that evening and her only comment was, "I don't know where his courage comes from."

II
Mwendo wa ngamia: the way of the camel

Mavi ya kale hayanuki.

Translation:
Old droppings do not smell.

Paraphrase:
Everything becomes less unpleasant with the passage of time.

1. Beginnings

When he was one month old, the boy was baptized as *Gordon Odiwuor Okumu* at St. Paul's Catholic Cathedral in Homabay (since Migori didn't have a cathedral church). The word *Okumu* was his father's middle name, and in accordance with Luo custom, it became Gordon's last name. In the Luo language, it means "a child born during hardship." The *kumu* part of Okumu comes from the Luo verb *kumo*, which means to sit with your chin in your hand and your cheek resting on your palm. This is an expression of sadness, or of sitting in sorrow.

Since this baby was born a boy, his surname began with an O, and it would have been changed to an A if he were a girl, as *Akumu*. His mother chose "Gordon" for his English name because she liked the way it sounded, and Odiwuor for his middle name because, again keeping with custom, the name tells what was happening when the baby was born. Odiwuor means "a child that was born at night." In contrast to the related and more commonly used *Otieno*, (to get technical), Odiwuor specifies that the child was born in the second half of the night, or the middle of the night, somewhere between the hours of 11:00 p.m. to 3:00 a.m. The earlier Otieno spans the period where evening becomes night (from 7:00 p.m. to 11:00 p.m.) and implies the movement into darkness. Odiwuor, on the other hand, begins in the darkness and implies the movement toward dawn, or toward the coming of the light.

Six months after this specific Odiwuor came into the world, his father, who worked as one of the rare taxi drivers in Migori, died in a car accident. The man had taken other wives and had fathered other children (as was the custom in this polygamous culture). His death left Gordon's mother to fend for herself and raise her newborn son. She was his third wife (of three), and Gordon was her first and only child. Since there was now no possibility of producing additional Okumu sons to contribute in the only "valuable" way she could to the clan, the Okumus disowned her. She was, bluntly, of no further use to them. Faced with this total retraction of familial support and the sudden need to make an income, she took her son and left Migori in search of a better life.

*

They began again in the Kangemi slum in the Westlands district of Nairobi. Situated on the northwestern border of the capital city, just south of the Nairobi-Nakuru highway, Kangemi was called the West Gate into the city. There was even a sign at the western entrance to the neighborhood that read "Welcome to Nairobi." For Gordon's mother, this was a convenient choice because her younger sister lived there, so at least she knew one person. In the hierarchy of Nairobi slums, Kangemi was regarded as an "uptown" slum, meaning that it was a little more expensive than others like Kibera and less filthy. Kangemi was a little decent because it had electricity available in certain parts and even had security streetlights that came on at night. It contained a variety of housing sizes and shapes, with multi-unit apartment buildings mixed in with rows of connected single-room shanty houses. It was smaller than most other slums too, and the neighborhood was bordered on all sides by green leafy suburbs. These wealthy estates with their large houses and orderly plots of land cast a shadow of their dignity back onto Kangemi's jumbled labyrinth of ersatz structures. The leafiest of these adjacent expensive suburbs sat to the north of Kangemi across the stretch of highway called Waiyaki Way, which defined Kangemi's northern border. When you crossed Waiyaki Way into the Loresho Estates, it was like night and day. You stepped up into another world.

Although there were some stretches of trees and scant greenery scattered throughout Kangemi, the neighborhood was overwhelmingly a combination of browns, oranges, rusty reds, and grays. The foundation of this earthy palette was the pothole-laden dirt roads that billowed abundant dust behind passing *matatus* (small minibuses that somehow squeezed up to fourteen people inside). There were also single *boda boda* motorcycles that streamed little trails of dust and smoke as they darted back and forth ferrying passengers and weaving through the constant flow of pedestrians. Cars slowly pushed their way through these full streets, and in Kangemi you didn't so much *drive* a car as you *danced*. This meant bumping and shaking in your seat to the rhythm of your tires hitting rocks and holes, accompanied by the grating music of the exposed underparts of your vehicle scraping against those rocks and hitting those holes. You basically just hung on and hoped that you weren't leaving a trail of little shreds of your car behind you. With all that bumping and scraping, it really was miraculous that the streets of Kangemi were not littered with fallen car parts.

The dust from all this activity settled on everything, most of all on the iron-sheet shanty roofs. When it rained, the water packed this dust into a sort of clay, causing it to stick there and retain the moisture, further rusting the roofs and rendering them their distinctive burnt orange color. The Kangemi streets were lined with rows upon rows of these corroded *mbati* structures—corrugated iron sheets pieced together against and on top of each other, to form all manner of houses and shops. Sometimes the ridges on the sheets ran vertically and sometimes horizontally, as the structures had been patched and extended and reshaped, and pieces were just added when necessary. With houses so close and people packed so tightly together, there was always noise. Everyone heard everyone's everything, all the time, and this constant cacophony was the soundtrack of their poverty.

In Kangemi, Gordon's mother secured for them one of these 10' x 10' "houses," or dust-covered single-room shanty structures, to rent for 1,000 Kenyan shillings (Ksh), or about $10 per month. On the first night in their new home, they didn't yet have any furniture, so she laid down a few sheets of found cardboard, and she and her infant son slept side by side on the floor. Her only goal now was to support herself and her son, and she was determined to do anything and everything she could to give him a better life.

To afford their shanty home, she found work as a house help (a housekeeper or maid) in one of the nearby estates, earning a total monthly salary of 3,000 Ksh or $30. Out of her $30.00 per month income, she first paid the rent for their home and then bought food, which was easy to find in Kangemi since farmers from the nearby rural areas would bring their produce to sell in Nairobi through Kangemi. They'd sell the best, washed produce first—three pristine tomatoes for 20 Ksh (20 cents). At the end of the day, they'd offer all the misshapen, unwashed, unsold produce at cheaper prices—$1 for a 3-pound bucket of tomatoes. This same process applied to everything, like potatoes, onions, kale, avocados, corn, and cabbage. Gordon's mother also had to buy corn flour to make *ugali*—Kenya's nonnegotiable, always tasteless, and ever-present staple food. Occasionally she bought meat, once or *maybe* twice a week, which she would get fresh from the local slaughterhouse. A quarter pound of pork went for 50 Ksh and one-pound of *matumbo* (intestines or tripe) went for 15 Ksh or (15 cents). The rest of their expenses were for cooking oil and soap, clothing, shoes, bus tickets, and of course, a necessary monthly tithe to their local Catholic Church. With her $30 per month, they balanced on the edge of this most meager subsistence, and life persisted in Kangemi, *pole pole* (slowly slowly).

*

When it came time for Gordon to start the equivalent of kindergarten at public elementary school, his mother now had the additional burden of school fees since there was no free primary education at that time. The school charged $20 per term in addition to $5 or $10 more for books and materials, but thankfully this could be paid in monthly installments. If the school fees weren't paid (which they often weren't), children simply weren't allowed to go, and the children usually didn't mind.

Gordon knew where the school was and would walk past and hear the children reciting the alphabet or singing songs about the days of the week, but when he knew he was supposed to start soon, he didn't want to go. Whenever he heard the other kids, all he could think was how they knew so much more than he did. They knew everything in that school, and he knew nothing.

Once when his mother perceived the fear behind his eyes as they passed Kangemi Primary, she said simply, "That's where you're going to be taught."

"I don't know anything," he said. "The kids will laugh at me."

"You'll learn, and then they won't laugh at you." She said matter-of-factly.

Her words made him feel even worse. He was going to feel embarrassed, and he was going to make a fool of himself. He just *knew* he would. At least when he wasn't in school, he could hide his stupidity, but at school he was going to have to publicly demonstrate it. It was going to be awful.

"I don't want to go." He told his mom.

"You have to go," she replied as they continued walking. "You have to get an education, and this is how you begin."

For Gordon, the lofty concept of "getting an education" seemed far removed from the experience he imagined sitting in that crowded schoolroom chanting the alphabet with other kids.

"I don't want to go." He repeated.

She stopped walking and turned to face him.

"Gordon, to have success in life, you have to get an education. I never got to finish school because I was a girl and Grandpa didn't pay for me to go. But you can, and you are going to go. Men have success because they are educated. You will have success too, and you will make a way for yourself."

"But all those kids are smarter than me. They know how to read. They know how to write. I know nothing."

"That's *because* they go to school. You will learn how to do those things at school. You'll be able to read and write. If you want to do it, you can."

Gordon looked down at the street and nodded. He still didn't want to go and he was not convinced, but he knew there was no use arguing.

In anticipation of that fateful day, his mother bought him clothes that aligned with the school dress code. It was a uniform of sorts, composed of a white, short-sleeved button-up shirt and navy-blue shorts. Since money was tight, it was common for parents to buy shorts that boys could grow into, meaning large enough that they could wear them all the way through high school. As a 6-year-old wearing shorts that could have fit a grown man the size of his dad, Gordon's bottom half disappeared into the navy-blue fabric that billowed down past his knees.

When the morning arrived, Gordon got dressed and prepared the small backpack that his mother had bought for him, which was just large enough to fit one composition notebook. His mom prepared a thermos for his lunch. It had two stacking compartments, and she filled the bottom section with black tea and milk and a slice of white bread in the top—this combination was commonly referred to with a mix of Swahili and English as *chai na bread* (*chai* meaning tea). This phrase also sounded like "China Bread" and played into a running joke in Kangemi that everything imported was made in China, even bread.

As he was walking to the school with his mom, wearing the backpack and carrying the thermos by its handle in one hand, the impending embarrassment weighed upon Gordon. They got closer and closer to the school, and it got heavier and heavier, until he stopped.

"I don't want to go to school." He said firmly, as he slipped the backpack off his shoulders and placed it on the dirt street, still holding onto the thermos.

"You have to go." His mother said. She grabbed his wrist and pulled him in the direction of the school.

"No, I won't go."

He wrestled his wrist out of her grasp. He had made his mind up.

"Yes, you will go. We have to go now or we'll be late."

She grabbed his wrist again in her left hand as she took off her right sandal with other hand.

"No!" Gordon squirmed in her grasp.

She smacked the sole of her sandal against his bottom, causing a small puff of dust and leaving a tan mark on his navy-blue shorts. It stung and he winced, but he didn't budge. She hit him a second time, and still holding onto the thermos in his right hand, he tried to push away from her.

"You have to go!" She punctuated this pronouncement with another smack. They were in the middle of the street, and people continued to pass. This was a normal sight—children were always fighting their parents, and parents were always fighting their children. It happened everywhere. It was what everyone did and what culture encouraged everyone to do. The mother who caned her children (meaning, she spanked them and beat them with a stick or a sandal or whatever she wanted to use) was respected for knowing how to discipline and correct her children's behavior. There was even peer-pressure among mothers to cane children strictly and swiftly. Sometimes you'd see children in the street or at school fighting their parents like animals, scratching and screaming. Maybe people didn't even care and didn't notice, but if they did, no one ever stopped. It was people's personal business after all.

"I won't go." Gordon yelled back at his mom, as his eyes began to well up. He was angry at her, first for making him go when she too knew that he was going to be humiliated, and second for how his shorts were now dirty from the struggle. He'd gotten dust on his white shirt as well. His backpack was dusty, and he'd shaken the thermos so much that it had littered stray drops of tea onto the dirt street. Everything was getting worse.

He weighed his opinions in his mind, and it seemed like there was no way to win this fight. So, he gave in and stopped struggling.

"I'll go." He mumbled.

"Now hurry up." His mother slipped her sandal back on, dusted off his shorts, patted him down.

He didn't care about the actual act of being caned, but now he was also going to be late. The school year had started a few days earlier anyway, and it was customary for new students to wait a few days to begin. The returning students all knew each other already, and when he walked in late, all the other kids were going to make fun of him. He didn't want to look like some backwards boy from the bush, with dirty wrinkled clothes like they'd just been chewed and wrestled out of the cow's mouth.

When they reached the school, his mother led him to the classroom. There was one teacher and a whole room already full of children. He felt like everyone knew that he didn't know anything. His mother passed him off to the teacher, and then she left. Gordon stood in the front corner of the room looking out at all the other kids' faces, imagining all the mean thoughts they were thinking. The teacher made him sit at the first desk in the front corner, and now he felt like they were all looking at him from behind. The kids didn't say anything though and they didn't laugh. There were no introductions, and they were already in the middle of a lesson. The teacher returned to the blackboard and instructed the students to "write the alphabet." Gordon looked around, confused. He didn't know how to write—what was he supposed to do?

He saw other kids open their composition books, so he took his out of his backpack and opened it to the very first page. He took out his pencil and stared at the empty lined paper. He tried to look around covertly with his peripheral vision. He didn't want to obviously gawk and single himself out. He saw the kids writing, making marks in their books, and he tried to do that too. He clutched the pencil in his palm, wrapping his entire fist around it and started making lines on his page. He drew diagonal lines and squiggled some smaller lines in between. Then the teacher came over. She stopped him by holding his hand with both of hers and moved the pencil from his palm to between his thumb and first two fingers. She kept her right hand around his right hand as she guided him to make the letter A. One diagonal mark down, another diagonal mark down, and a straight connector in the middle. He couldn't believe it—he was writing! It was just lines that you had to align in the right way.

When the teacher walked away, he continued. He tried making the shapes of other letters of the alphabet. It felt easy. He heard his mother's words echo in his mind: "If you want to do it, you can." He thought to himself, *I do want to do it. I want to be good at it. I want to be the best.*

After that rocky start, that first day of school went very well, and Gordon actually had fun. He realized that although he was starting at the beginning, that meant he had everything to learn and he could progress quickly. He liked singing the songs about the days of the week and he memorized the letters of the alphabet. Counting numbers during math time was easy for him. He quickly acclimated to the routine of school— you write in your notebook, you go to the bathroom, you eat lunch, you take a nap. Although that first day's *chai na bread* became a soggy mess from the morning tussle, at least it was food, and he was glad to have something to eat on that first day when most of the other kids took out their somethings too.

Gordon began to write on everything at home—on all the little scraps of newspaper that they kept pinned to the wall to take as toilet paper for the public latrines. He sang the school songs nonstop, and soon he knew all the numbers and the letters. If he received top marks in the class, the prize from the teacher was half of a composition notebook. Since the notebooks were just sheets of paper folded in half and stapled in two places, the teacher would cut the book horizontally between the staples and give the two pieces out as prizes for good grades and behavior. That half of a brand-new notebook was more than enough motivation for Gordon to work harder and learn all he could.

When Gordon got into the routine of attending school, he walked there and back on the unpaved roads in his sandals, which were cheaper than actual shoes. When it rained, the dusty roads turned into muddy roads, and by the time he reached the school his feet and his sandals were covered in mud. When it was time for lunch break, the school didn't provide anything and all the kids in the later grades had to leave the grounds—presumably to go home—but if there wasn't any food at home, they could just walk around or go wherever they wanted with their friends until the break was over. As time went on, Gordon and his mother usually didn't have food at home for lunch, and chai na bread even became a rarity, so if he could bum a few peanuts or something to snack on from one of his friends at school, that was a bonus. If not, it was just another day. He got so used to this that he didn't even feel hungry until dinner time rolled around, since that was his one consistent and reliable meal. There was no point in feeling hungry when there was no possibility of getting food—why make yourself miserable wanting something you can't have? Why not just forget about it and go on with your day? That was the logic of life in Kangemi.

*

There was one water faucet for their block in the slum, and the city only turned it on once per week. Every household was allowed to fill three 5-gallon jerry cans, or plastic yellow jugs. Gordon and his mother used this cleaner water from the neighborhood faucet for cooking and drinking (after boiling it). To get more water than that, they had to walk to the so-called "Kangemi dam," which was in Loresho to the north-west of Kangemi across Waiyaki Way. In the evening after school, Gordon's mother tasked him with the job of going to fetch water. Gordon would walk to the dam (only about a mile away) carrying one of those yellow jugs in each hand. They would use this water for cleaning the house and bathing. It was not for drinking since you couldn't be sure what was in it. Sometimes, though, if there really wasn't any option—if *absolutely* necessary—they would have to drink the dam water.

There was only one bridge that crossed Waiyaki Way, called *The Kangemi Flyover*, and it was on the east side of the neighborhood, while the dam sat just north of the center section of Kangemi. Often, like many Kangemi dwellers, Gordon would wind further down in the Kangemi side before crossing over to the Loresho side near the dam. At that time, Waiyaki Way was a split highway that consisted of two lanes going each way, separated by a large dirt median filled with tall trees. Locals knew how to wait for the right size breaks in the traffic and then run across each side of the highway, but you could always tell when visiting country kids tried to cross, because they weren't used to the split structure. Since rural towns almost exclusively had unmarked two-lane roads at most, the country kids didn't know which way to look at the second highway piece, and some would get hit. Even for experienced locals though, crossing without the footbridge was always a risk.

After school, Gordon often stopped to play soccer on his way to the dam, just for a bit so that he could still make it back before his mother got home from work. The soccer field or football pitch was located right next to Waiyaki Way and the Kangemi market on the northern edge of the neighborhood. The Kihumbuini School sports fields consisted of one actual, regulation size red-dirt soccer field with white lines that marked the center and the goal boxes. The official soccer team of the Kangemi neighborhood, Kangemi United (named after the English team, Manchester United), used this full field for their practices. Just next to this on the west side was Old Kihumbuini Primary Field, a makeshift, smaller area that the kids used as the field for their games. When they played, they could see the Kangemi team practice right next door, and they could imagine that they too were playing for the Kenyan Premier, or better yet, the English Premier league.

Various neighborhood children would gather there every day after school—everyone recognized everyone more or less and anyone could play with anyone. They started gathering around 3 p.m. at Kihumbuini, forming teams, and warming up, and they played until it got dark. They played for whichever team needed a player, whichever position, because the point was just to play. For balls, the Kangemi kids had mastered the specific skill of making a hard enough ball for soccer out of discarded plastic bags that they collected on the streets. To do this, they gathered up plastic bags from trash piles around the neighborhood (since there was no official garbage collection and everyone just dropped their trash in some discrete corner somewhere). Kids scrounged appropriately thick plastic bags from the trash and let them sun-dry until they were completely dried out. They had to be dry or else they wouldn't work. The kids then bundled them together tightly and tied them with a long string. Often boys sat in the back of the class at school and worked on their plastic-bag soccer balls. They came to school with their backpacks not full of notebooks or pencils but stuffed to the brim with plastic bags to add onto their soccer balls. Soccer-ball-making skills were a source of pride since the soccer matches were always "bring your own ball."

One day, Gordon was on his way to the dam carrying his two yellow jerry cans. He needed to get the water and get back home, since he still had homework and chores to do. He stopped for a moment when he got to Kihumbuini soccer field and watched the other kids playing. When some of his friends saw him standing on the sideline, they started calling and waving him to come play.

"Gody!" They called out.

It felt good to be known and to be wanted.

"Gody, Gody! C'mon. Come play!"

Both teams wanted him to come, and Gordon couldn't resist, so he put his jerry cans down and took off his sandals. You had to play soccer barefoot because you couldn't run very well in flip-flop sandals. The practice was to wear your sandals on your shoulders, to keep them safe. What this meant was that you slid one flip-flop up each arm, and just let them stay on your shoulders while you ran around on the field. In his excitement, Gordon forgot about this and just dropped both the jerry cans and his sandals on the sidelines.

The kids who had called him began cheering. Others began chanting his name, "GO-DY, GO-DY, GO-DY!"

More kids came to see what was happening, gathering and watching from the sidelines. In that moment, Gordon felt like he was Zinedine Zidane or better yet—*Il Fenomeno*—Ronaldo of Brazil. He ran proudly onto the field, amidst the cheering and welcome, and took up his position as a striker (he was one of the ones who put on the finishing touches and scored the goals).

They played for hours, and when the sun started to go down, it was time to call it a night. Only then, Gordon realized he had completely lost track of time. As dusk set in, he felt the cold guilt of having wasted the entire evening—he hadn't yet gotten the water or done his chores or finished any of his homework. The reality started to sink in of what his afternoon of soccer frivolity had truly cost him. Kids wondered off the field and headed home, and when Gordon got back to the sidelines, he discovered that both the jerry cans and his sandals were gone. His feet were dusty and rusty colored from all the running on the dirt, and now he didn't even have his sandals to walk home in.

As he headed home, he knew that his mom was there by now and that she would be furious with him for losing both the jerry cans and the sandals. How could he have been so stupid? He trudged back to his house, torn between the desire to walk slowly and put off the inevitable, or walk as fast as possible and not delay further. He went with the latter and walked as fast as he could. Streetlights flickered on as he wound his way toward home.

When he reached the house, he knocked on the front door since it was dark and he didn't want to frighten his mom by just barging in. There was no answer. He opened the door slowly and saw that she was cooking.

"Where are you from?" She asked without looking up.

"I had gone to play."

She turned and looked at him, and then asked, "Where are your sandals?"

"They were stolen." He didn't even try to explain more. There was no time and no point.

She let go of the wooden spoon she was stirring with, leaving it to sit in the pot. She walked over to Gordon, still standing just inside the doorway, and slapped him across his face with her open palm.

"You can't do things like this!" She yelled.

Gordon could hear people murmuring and walking by outside in the street—the iron- sheet shanty walls were thin. He knew they could hear what was going on inside the house too. They heard his mom yelling, but you always heard everyone when they yelled or fought or broke things.

His face felt hot and raw. He didn't say anything. He knew he couldn't argue and couldn't explain more. The things were gone, he had made his choice, and this was the consequence.

He knew too that when his mother was angry, he had to be punished, and it was best to just get it over with.

Sometimes she caned him with a stick instead of her sandals, always spanking him on the bottom. He knew that the point of this was to make him feel pain that was equivalent to the crime—now it was pain for having lost their precious water jugs and his sandals. It cost 70 Ksh for a pair of sandals, or the equivalent of 70 cents, which they didn't have.

There was a sort of strange strategy to being caned—Gordon knew he just had to take it, but not in a stoic way because then he would just have to endure more. That actually made it worse. Instead, he had to cry loud and fast and show that he felt the immediate pain. He faked it sometimes

Mwendo wa ngamia: the way of the camel

just to get it over with. Right from the second her sandal struck him, he'd cry like he was exploding with fire, like he'd been burned. That instant, immediate, reactionary cry was the goal. That made it seem like he was really hurt, and therefore he really felt the pain and understood the cost of what he had done.

His mother only struck him a couple times since he cried sufficiently, and it was over quickly. But they still needed the water that Gordon had failed to get. For the second part of the punishment, his mother sent him right back out to borrow the neighbors' cans and to go get the water. It was now black like the middle of the night, and after Gordon (who went barefoot) got the cans from the neighbors, he wound through the Kangemi streets back up to Waiyaki Way, angry and cursing his mother under his breath all the way to the dam and back. How could she send him out like this in the dark? He took the shorter route, of course, and darted across the highway between the headlights of oncoming cars.

When he got back home with the water, she made him go shower since he was dirty and sweaty. He took their plastic basin full of some of the newly-collected dam water and walked out to go to the public showers—they were "bring your own water." His mother kept the dinner waiting, and when it was finally time to eat, she said grace as always. After dinner it was his normal job to wash the dishes and then there was still prayer and Bible reading before bed.

Sometime later, there was a story on the news about a boy in Kangemi who had disappeared after dark. Evidently, he was abducted while walking on the street. This story troubled Gordon's mother so much that she sat him down one evening in their house and said, "If I ever ask you to go out again after dark, don't go."

Her concern made Gordon feel almost guilty for cursing her that night when he'd walked to the dam. It didn't matter anyway though, for she never asked him to go get water after dark again, even if they needed it.

*

In general, Gordon's mother didn't fear for their security in Kangemi. Although they didn't have to worry about natural threats like the hyenas of the rural country, there was a strange and specific species of "urban predator" that prowled the streets of Kangemi called *Black Maria*, or most commonly just *Maria*. Gordon's mother (who was also named Mary) feared this other Maria like the fires of Hell. She wasn't afraid for herself but for Gordon—that he would get apprehended by the Infernal Maria and be lost forever to its dark damnation.

Black Maria was, in reality, the name for the truck the police drove through the slum streets. According to popular legend, this name originated from an actual woman named Maria who lived in New England (in the US) and helped the police apprehend criminals. Now, in Kangemi, this was not "police" in any sense of a decent force meant to keep peace, prevent crimes, and arrest offenders. This was, rather, a perversion of law enforcement fueled by the desperation of poverty and greed, like so much in Kenya, that arrested people for no reason, preying on unsuspecting idlers in order to solicit bribes and fan the flames of rampant corruption.

Black Maria was a black military-style truck, with a flat-faced front cab and one large rectangular box in the back. The box functioned as the holding cell for the people that the police caught. They'd first pick up as many people as they could hold, and then, and only then, when it was full to the brim, they'd drive to a station some miles away. Once there, they'd simply ask their prisoners, "How much do you have?" If you had 100 shillings, you offered them your 100 shillings. If they accepted your offering, you were free to go. If they didn't, you still had a chance to get more from your family or friends. Somehow—before cell phones and the internet—information traveled like bush fire in the slums, so if you got arrested by Black Maria, your family or friends or someone you knew would hear about it, and they'd show up at the station to get you. If you didn't have enough, the officers would negotiate with your family and friends, and if they accepted what your family had to offer, you went free. If not, you went to jail for a made-up crime and an interminable amount of time.

The police would catch anyone in Black Maria, anytime, regardless of age. The root of Gordon's mom's fear though was that the police specifically targeted young "loiterers" and "malingerers," meaning boys who looked like thieves and drug dealers; or who could at least be accused of looking like thieves and drug dealers; or accused of intending to look like thieves and drug dealers; or accused of fraternizing with others who intended to look like thieves and drug dealers; or…well, the list goes on. They even used Black Maria to stalk unsuspecting kids outside the cinema (the neighborhood movie theater that the locals called a *video house*). In reality, this was just a shanty room with a projector, some chairs inside, and a single sheet covering the doorway to block out the light. When kids emerged from that doorway after the show, slightly dazed by the transition from the dark room to the daylight outside, the police pounced during those brief seconds of disorientation. They waited with Black Maria backed up as far as possible, almost right to the cinema's door, with the truck's back end flung open like a hungry mouth. When the kids came out, the police quickly ushered *everyone* right into the back of Black Maria, before the kids even knew what happened.

Gordon's mom made it no secret that they had no money to pay a bribe. She worried that since Gordon was tall and dark-skinned, he'd be singled out and targeted. He'd go to jail, never get out, and suffer a rotten, wasted life in some cement cell, all because they couldn't pay. She even knew someone whose son *was* caught by Black Maria and put in prison that way. That woman blamed her son for getting himself caught and for not knowing when to run.

In light of this, Gordon's mom told him, "Any time you see Maria, run as much as you can as fast as you can. JUST RUN. Run in *any* direction away from Maria!"

To drive the point home, she repeated to him a Luo saying, *Tienda gima nachamo atwoni*. This was more of a question, literally, "My legs: is there anything I have ever eaten without sharing it with you?" This was a way of reminding your legs that you had *never* denied them, and so they too should remember their debt to you in *your* moment of greatest need. Gordon's mother told him to tell his legs, "My legs: since I've always given you everything that I've eaten, now you *must* give me what I need." Any time Gordon saw Black Maria, he remembered that phrase. When he asked his legs to run, they ran, and they ran fast. They were long and quick.

He knew this wasn't a game to play or a time to tempt fate. There were some rules that he could bend and even break, but running from Black Maria was one of the aspects of Kangemi life that he didn't even think about breaking. Anytime he saw Black Maria, he ran like lightning. To be even safer, he *never* went to the cinema, not even once. Since he was going to make something of himself in life, he couldn't risk getting caught by Black Maria and throwing it all away, not for himself and not for his mother.

*

In the row of shanty houses on Gordon's street, only one person had a television. You could always pinpoint exactly where TVs were in Kangemi because those specific houses had antennas that were twice as tall as the iron-sheet structures. Those poles reached up into the sky like lightning rods, attracting all the neighboring children. When Gordon was still in elementary school, he'd huddle with a bunch of other kids inside that single room around a fourteen-inch, battery-powered black and white TV. That house, like most, used a curtain to separate the main room from the kitchen area. The kids would sit in this "living room" on the floor or even on the bed, and on Tuesdays from 8 to 9 p.m., they'd watch WWE—back when it was still WWF, the Worldwide Wrestling Federation. Gordon loved seeing those super muscular men throw each other down in the ring. The show was loud, flashy, and especially fun because he knew that his favorite players were *always* going to win. No matter what happened, Stone Cold Steve Austin and The Undertaker always came out on top. His favorite of all was The Rock. The Rock had the best catchphrase too, which was a question that needed no answer—*If you smell-la-la-la-la-la-la what the Rock is cooking!* The Rock would shout this to the cheering crowd before *BAM!* slamming some guy into the ground.

When he wasn't watching sensationalized professional wrestling, Gordon would also walk around the Kangemi streets for fun with his friend from school, Jackson Msungu. Their teacher, who was from the Kisii tribe, couldn't pronounce the *ks* or *x* sound in the name *Jackson*, so instead the teacher always said, "Jackason" with that extra *a* in the middle. The pronunciation stuck, and it became a three-syllable name. Jackason's family moved to Kangemi from western Kenya when he was in the seventh grade. They belonged to the Luhya tribe, and when Jackason started at school, the first thing that gave him away as a village boy with no experience of city life was his inability to speak Swahili.

Swahili is a Bantu language mixed with Arabic, and although it doesn't conjugate verbs like some other languages do, it still has its own share of tricky grammatical pitfalls, like noun classes and all kinds of agreement rules. Really, everything in the Swahili sentence has to agree with the noun and its class. While Swahili doesn't distinguish its nouns by gender, it instead marks them living or nonliving. To put it another way, in Swahili you have to grammatically "give life to living things." Jackason didn't know this rule about living and nonliving nouns, so he would say things like *kitabu huyu* (this book), when it should have been *kitabu hiki* (and *huyu* would only be in a phrase like *mtu huyu*, this person, since a person is living and a book is not). In this way, Jackason indiscriminately bestowed life upon everything, which might have been sort of benevolent when considered in a certain light, but in the harsh reality of the schoolyard, it was a source of ridicule. Kids didn't care about deeper, potential philosophical undertones of improper grammar; they just heard something different and marked Jackason as an outsider.

Gordon met Jackason for the first time, officially, one day at their middle school canteen, which was a little stand on the school grounds that sold various food items. Jackason was trying to buy jaggery, which was colloquially called *sukari nguru*. This was unrefined sugar made from boiled sugarcane juice that had solidified into a light brown block. The snack stand sold three different sized pieces of sukari nguru, the first for 5 Ksh (the equivalent of 5 cents), the second, even smaller, for 1 Ksh (or 1 cent), and finally the smallest option for 50 Ksh cents (too small to convert). The slang shortcut for this 50-shilling cent option, since it was both the cheapest and the most popular among the kids, was simply *sumni*. This probably derived in some part from the full Swahili phrase for 50 cents, *centi hamsini*, but the kids simply asked for sumni.

When it was his turn, Jackason stepped up to the counter to order and said, "Nataka nguru sumoni." *I want the sumoni nguru.* He overemphasized that extra *o* he'd added in *sum-o-ni* instead of *sumni*. The kids around heard and began to laugh.

"He's saying *sum-O-ni*."

Gordon was among the group gathered in front of the canteen. He saw Jack standing there, frozen as the kids laughed and jeered.

"*Sumooooni. Sumoni. Sumonisumoni!*"

Jackason had turned around to face the crowd of students and just stood there with a blank look on his face like he didn't know what to do or say next.

Gordon decided to act for him. He stepped out of the group and walked up beside Jackason.

"Guys stop laughing!" Gordon shooed the kids away with his arms.

"LET HIM BE!" He waved and pushed people away until the group dispersed and the spectacle was over.

Mwendo wa ngamia: the way of the camel

From that moment, Gordon and Jack became fast friends. Gordon even helped him correct his Swahili.

Jack began telling everyone that he was Gordon's brother even though he had lighter skin than Gordon. Since Jack's last name was Msungu, which sounded so close to *mzungu* (the Swahili word for *white person*), Jack acquired the nickname *mzungu* with the pronounced *z* sound. Mzungu actually meant *English speaker*, but the term had acquired the connotation of *white person* since the majority of Kenyans assumed based on appearance that all white people spoke English. The other kids started calling Gordon *mwafrica*, meaning a person from Africa, connoting a person with dark black skin. Together Jack and Gordon became the duo of Mzungu and Mwafrica, White and Black, the powerful combination of opposites. When they crossed the open-area school assembly ground, kids scurried out of their way.

Jack was shorter than Gordon and stockier—even as a teenager, he was already well on his way to becoming a *bobo*, a big-bodied man, one of those boss men that Gordon had always admired. This stature allowed Jack to act sort of like Gordon's bodyguard. They could get really loud when they were together, laughing and joking and not caring who heard. Jack was also a lighthearted troublemaker; he liked to push other people around and play harmless pranks for his own pleasure—but nothing seriously mean. Their teacher even once asked him, point blank, "Jackason, when will you ever mature?"

Jack responded, cheekily as always, "Not until I get married."

One of the immature things he liked to do was scare people walking on the street. As he and Gordon would be walking, Jack would stop, lean over, and whisper to Gordon, "Gody, watch this. Watch this! I'm gonna go scare that person." He'd single out someone and point at them from behind. Then he'd walk up behind the person, casually, and suddenly yell, "WAAHHH!" When the person jumped, Jack rushed away before he could be caught. He and Gordon would laugh loudly together and continue on their way.

On Sundays, Gordon and his mother went to a Catholic Church in Kangemi called "Saint Joseph the Worker," or *Mtakatifu Yusufu mfanya kazi* in Swahili. This referred to *Joseph the carpenter*, the husband of the Virgin Mary. When he sat in the pews during the service, Gordon admired the kids that got to hold the candles and stand by the priests near the altar. When he was in fifth grade, he asked his mom if he could become an altar server (also called an *acolyte*). Being shy and tentative about things like this, she wouldn't ask the priest directly. She told Gordon that he should ask the catechist teacher, who taught the class for children about the principles and rules of the faith.

One Sunday when the service had just ended and his mom had already left to go to work, Gordon was sitting alone in the pews as people chatted with each other and filed out around him. The priest, Father Michael, was still standing up in front near the altar, talking with a few other people. Gordon saw his chance. He walked out of the pew and made a beeline toward the altar. He went up to the priest and held out his hand, evidently his go-to first move. While the priest shook his hand, Gordon said confidently, "Father, I want to be an altar boy."

"What grade are you in?" Fr. Michael asked.

"Fifth."

"Come back next year when you're in sixth grade."

Gordon nodded and thanked the priest.

When his mother got home later that day, Gordon told her what had happened, saying proudly, like it was no big deal, "I asked Father Michael."

"You asked Father Michael?!" She repeated with such astonishment that you would have thought he told her he'd sprouted a third leg.

She agreed to enroll Gordon in the confirmation class, which took place from the rest of fifth through sixth grade, in the hope that after he finished, he could become an acolyte.

To complete the confirmation class, Gordon had to pass a final oral exam with the priest. On the day of this exam, the kids lined up and approached the priest one by one for their questioning. When it was Gordon's turn, Fr. Michael asked him a question about the disciples of Jesus. It wasn't some easy question that everyone knew such as, "How many disciples did Jesus have?" but instead must have been something a little more complicated, like, "Which disciple had to touch the resurrected Jesus' in order to believe?" Gordon didn't remember the answer, so he failed his first try. Fr. Michael was gracious though and said, "You need to go *revise* a little more," which meant that Gordon needed to study and then he could try again.

Gordon walked to the back of the line of kids. The catechist teacher was waiting back there to help any kids who needed reminding. Gordon repeated the question to the teacher, who gave Gordon an answer to memorize, right then and there. Gordon got back in line and repeated the answer over and over in his mind—*It was Thomas, it was Thomas, it was Thomas.*

When Gordon came up for round two of questioning, he recited the previous question he'd missed and the answer he'd memorized. He got it right, so he passed. This meant that he would be confirmed and could become an altar boy. Gordon felt such a sense of accomplishment—this was like his first job interview and he had been hired! Up to that point, this had been his dream, and it was going to become a reality.

*

Being an altar boy felt like being part of a special and secret club, like being close to celebrities and royalty. Gordon soaked up every minute of the liturgical pomp, memorizing all the ritual prayers and movements. He loved seeing the church's sacred, holy items close-up. Gordon could see and sometimes even touch the things that everyone else paid such reverence to. Above all, he got to stand close to the priest, who was the most revered and respected person of all. Everyone wanted to be close to the priests, but few really had the privilege. During the "passing of the peace" part of the Sunday service where everyone greeted those around them and shook hands, all the kids rushed to the front and formed a line to shake the priest's hand. That line somehow never got smaller as the kids moved forward but just continued to multiply (in reality, this was because once a kid had shaken the priest's hand, they ran around and got in line to do it again). Adults also wanted to shake the priest's hand, so the Peace sometimes stretched on for what seemed like hours.

During the normal Sunday morning service at their Catholic church in Kangemi, kids were supposed to sit on the uncovered cement floor in the front and leave the wooden pews for the adults. The acolytes, however, had the luxury of sitting in cushioned seats behind the altar, facing the congregation. They got to put on white robes in the special little room off to the side of the altar where the ceremonial clothing was kept—in the language of the Church, this was called *vesting* in the *sacristy*. Gordon learned and cataloged all these terms in his mind, like passwords that granted him access into this secret society. Knowledge of the Church's words, movements, and objects felt powerful.

When it was time for the Sunday service to start, one of the acolytes would ring a bell from the sacristy side door, which signaled to the adults that it was time to stand. Gordon always enjoyed this moment for its unassuming but mighty influence, each and every time when that simple, golden *ding-ding* moved the entire congregation to rise to their feet. At school, it was the other way around—all the kids were supposed to stand when the teacher entered the room, because children were always subordinate to adults and had to show their respect. But inside the church, a kid had the power to ring a bell and move all the adults. The acolytes were also the first ones to receive communion. When the time came, they knelt in front of the altar to receive *both* the little, coin-sized wafer and the sip of wine. This was not juice either, but real wine, probably some sort of port that was fragrant, syrupy, and sweet. When the members of the congregation came up for communion, they only received the wafer, since the wine was precious. But for the acolytes, the priest would dip a wafer into the wine and place it on each child's tongue.

Being an acolyte wasn't just about showing up on Sunday morning. It was also an important responsibility, which Gordon and the other kids took seriously. They treated it like their job, and they went to the church on Saturdays to prepare everything for the Sunday service. They'd first ensure all the linen cloths for the altar were washed (by hand) and then sun dried. Next, they arranged everything on the altar and made sure all the items were in place for Sunday morning. For fun, the group of acolytes practiced serving (or pantomiming) communion among themselves with empty chalices, to make sure that everyone knew when and where to move, when to kneel, and when to stand. Since the Sunday service was finely and meticulously orchestrated, everyone had to be confident in their positions and everything had to be smooth and purposeful. There seemed to Gordon a direct relationship between the quality of the liturgy and the quality (and probably also quantity) of one's faith in God. The beauty and precision of perfectly performed liturgy served to express one's deep devotion and commitment to the Church. At its very core, this was an expression of one's love for God. Simply put, the better it was performed, the stronger your faith was, and the better Catholic you were, or so it seemed at the time. Some kids would even sleep at the church overnight from Saturday to Sunday to ensure that everything stayed in place and that it was ready when the priest arrived on Sunday.

More and more, Gordon admired the priests for the incredible power they wielded and the respect they earned from everyone in every corner of society, simply for being God's appointed liaisons between the common folk and the divine. Unlike many politicians, the priests were *loved*, not feared. They didn't coerce submission and didn't take bribes. They seemed to Gordon to be the ultimate example of true, ideal benevolence. They worked for the good of the people. They enjoyed a comfortable life *because* they did good work, like a reward for being good, upright people. Above the priests, there was also the bishop (as the leader of all the churches and priests in the region). When Gordon learned more about the bishop's role, he thought to himself, *Someday I'll go all the way to the top and I will become a bishop.*

One Sunday morning when the bishop was visiting St. Joseph the Worker Catholic Church in Kangemi, in his role as acolyte, Gordon got to hold the bishop's crosier, the special silver staff curved on top like the ones held by shepherds in the Bible stories. There was a certain point in the service when the bishop would stand behind the altar and pass the staff to one of the acolytes, so that the bishop had both of his hands free to bless the bread and wine for communion. Before the service even began, one acolyte would be selected to hold the bishop's crosier in that crucial moment. On this particular occasion, Gordon was that acolyte, and he wore the special white veil that draped over his shoulders, arms, and hands. He stood beside the bishop and confidently took the tall crosier with both of his covered hands, when the moment came. Gordon knew it was just a fashioned piece of silver, and yet, even through the fabric of the white veil, it felt almost like the staff had some supernatural energy coursing through it. Gordon could feel a vibration, a pulsing, a sense of holiness physically present in this object that had been directly blessed by God himself. (Or maybe it was just the beating of Gordon's own excited heart, shaking both his body and the staff.)

On another Sunday, the bishop's assistant (also called the auxiliary bishop) came to celebrate the new *confirmands*, kids who had passed the confirmation class and were to become official members of the Church. The assistant bishop anointed each kid, including Gordon, with a little dot of holy chrism oil in the center of their forehead. Then after the service, the children lined up and took a photo together with the assistant bishop. For the group photo, Gordon got to stand directly beside the assistant bishop, and the man leaned over and asked Gordon his name. He congratulated Gordon on his confirmation and added, lightheartedly, "Now, I think you're going to become the next bishop."

Gordon smiled so hard that his whole face scrunched together. *What!? Me?* But he thought more seriously to himself. *Yes, well, why not? OH GOD YES. That can be me.*

*

On the weekends when they weren't at church, Gordon's mother sold second-hand clothes, or *mitumba*, on the street corner in Kangemi. She bought the clothes during the week after work at a bigger market in downtown Nairobi and took them back to sell in the neighborhood. Basically, everything that was sold in Kangemi was second-hand anyway and came from other places around the world.

In front of their row of iron-sheet houses, there was a row of shops, and in the midst of these shops, there was a pharmacy, called a *dispensary*. The pharmacist was a small man named Moses. Although he owned the shop, he wasn't actually a pharmacist, as he just sold whatever types of medicines he could buy over the counter in Nairobi and resold them in Kangemi, just like the process for used clothes. He was generally friendly, and he wore a pair of glasses that Gordon admired. The lenses were rectangularly-shaped with a thin black frame, and in Gordon's opinion, the glasses made Moses-the-fake-pharmacist look *smart*—with the implied double meaning, both intelligent and well dressed.

One day while Gordon's mother was out selling mitumba, Gordon went into Moses-the-fake-pharmacist's fake pharmacy. Moses was there behind the counter, and they small talked for a moment. Just "out of the blues," Gordon mentioned that he liked Moses' glasses, and Moses asked if Gordon wanted to try them on. Gordon said yes, and Moses held out the glasses for Gordon to take. Moses continued his work organizing or whatever it was he was doing behind the counter.

Gordon put the glasses on and liked the way they felt on his face. They had clear glass lenses that were just for show, meaning they didn't actually do anything to help your vision. This was fine for Gordon with his perfect, 20/20 vision, and when he looked through the glass, he felt like he now had the style factor going for him as well. He had some swag.

He turned back toward the counter to give the glasses back to Moses, but before Gordon could even take them off, the right lens popped out of the frame, for no reason at all. It fell to the floor, and with one simple *ping* on the hard cement, broke into pieces. Gordon stared down at the glass shards in disbelief and hurried to take off the glasses before anything else could break. He set them down on the counter. Moses picked up the glasses and examined the hole where the lens had been, as if he really needed to verify that it wasn't there anymore.

"What have you done?" he asked.

"I didn't do anything."

"You broke my glasses. Now you'll have to buy new ones!" Gordon had never seen Moses get angry before.

"I don't have any money."

"Then your mother will have to pay for them. Come back when you have the new glasses." He shoved the broken pair back at Gordon.

Gordon didn't know what to do. He couldn't argue or bargain with Moses. What did he have to bargain with anyway? He took the pair of glasses and walked out of the shop. He felt slightly guilty—he *had* broken the glasses, hadn't he? It was his own stupid fault. But he also felt like he hadn't done anything wrong. It just happened and was a complete accident. How would he explain this to his mom? He didn't even know how much glasses like that cost.

Gordon walked back to his house and paced a couple times back and forth in front of the door. What should he do now? Was there anything he even *could* do?

Mwendo wa ngamia: the way of the camel

He went inside and grabbed the Bible, paced a few times around the inside, and came back outside. He sat down on the single rock step between the street and their door. Gripping the Bible in his lap and still holding the glasses in one hand, he tried to reign in his sense of hopelessness. Should he pray or *what?* He opened the Bible to a random page and read some lines before flipping to another page, reading some lines, and flipping again. He sat there—awaiting judgment, trying desperately to be holy and penitent and praying that God would be merciful—until his mother came home.

When she saw him sitting outside on the step, she knew something wasn't right. She asked straightaway what was going on. He recounted the whole story, using the glasses as a prop and emphasizing that he hadn't *meant* to do anything wrong and hadn't even broken them. It had just happened, like bad luck or something. As he talked, she listened and nodded, and when he finished, she asked for the glasses and said they should go right over to the pharmacy and talk with Moses.

When they got there, she went up to Moses, gave him the broken glasses back, and told him that they wouldn't pay. Just like that. Moses tried to argue with her, saying again that it was Gordon's fault and that he had to take responsibility for his actions.

"No," she said to Moses, with a sternness that surprised Gordon. "If you give a child something, that is your choice, and it is *your* fault if something happens."

Whoa. She was authoritative in a way that Gordon had ever seen before. She again refused to pay, and she was not going to be coerced or convinced otherwise. Since she would not be moved, Moses gave in. He conceded that it had been an accident and resolved to let the matter go.

As they walked back to their house, Gordon looked at his mom with a mixture of pride and amazement. *What had gotten into her?* He realized that beneath her unassuming shyness and obedience, she concealed a strength that he had never seen before. He had never really thought about it, but he saw it now. She had believed *him*, taken his side, and fought for him. His meek mother had turned into his champion, and what's more, they had won. It was *their* victory, the two of them against the world.

2. Rural Rituals

Although Gordon's mother made sure that they assimilated into Kangemi's melting pot of cultures and languages, it was still important for her to maintain their connection to their tribe and to the Luo culture. From time to time, they would return to Migori to visit Gordon's grandma and grandpa on the Gor side of the family (not the Okumus). Together, Gordon and his mom would take the stagecoach bus from Nairobi to Migori, run by the now-defunct Kenya Bus Service. The ride up country from Nairobi to Migori on the Nairobi-Nakuru highway across Kenya's Rift Valley was approximately 230 miles long. It would take upwards of twelve hours on the paved one-lane roads (which were sometimes two-lane roads or however many lanes cars wanted to fit into them).

To come back, Gordon and his mother would leave Grandma's house in the wee hours of the morning (around 3 a.m.) and walk in the dark to the main street to wait. There was no official bus stop and no signage, so they just waited for the bus to see them and pull over. The bus only passed once going toward Nairobi and then once around 3:00 p.m. coming the other direction from Nairobi. The main road was not far from Grandma's house, but it was just a dirt road carved out of the foliage.

In order not to miss the bus, Gordon, his mother, and his grandmother would walk to the bus stop together—his mom held his hand and carried their bag, while Grandma held a kerosene lamp in one hand and a machete in the other to fend off hyenas. The hyenas were supposedly afraid of adults, but they were not afraid of little children and would not hesitate to "just eat them." Even though he could hear the hyenas' laughing howl around Grandma's property, Gordon was never scared of them while he was with Grandma. Nothing would ever happen when he was with Grandma. She was like a force of nature, larger than just a woman. Maybe it was precisely *because* she was not afraid of anything, and because she was ready to use that machete, that she never actually had to.

CROSSING WAIYAKI WAY

*

As one of Kenya's forty-five different tribes, the Luo people lived by an unwritten code of intuitions and omens, passed down and perpetuated through communal practice and collective belief. Perhaps it was all just a collection of myths and superstitions, or perhaps it was all true. No one really knew for sure because everyone believed and feared so devoutly that they never deviated from tradition. They believed that whatever happened did so precisely *because* they continued to follow the traditions. In this sense, it was a continually turning, inevitably closed circle of compulsory custom, as old as Luo culture itself.

One such belief concerned the *Nyawawa*, which were said to be spirits of the dead. They appeared during the cold, rainy season in July and August. The word Nyawawa was the specific Luo name throughout the region for spirits who had their final resting (or maybe unresting) place in the waters of Lake Victoria. They were sometimes referred to as evil spirits, but the name actually didn't imply that they were nefarious or ill-intentioned in any way. This was probably more of a misinterpretation or projected fear, for the name just referred to them as spirits—the ghosts of people who had once been among the living.

On one of their visits to the rural country during the rainy season, when Gordon and his mother had gone to visit friends in Homabay, he saw the Nyawawa. In the evening while seated inside the friends' house, they began to hear the sound that those in the region knew well. It was the banging of pots and pans, forks and spoons, mugs and cups against each other and even against the houses' iron-sheet roofs. It was the sound of anything at all that was metal and that could make noise. This banging sound came like a wave—it started softly in the distance when the first person began to bang one pot, and then others joined, and more and more, until the sound grew louder and came closer. This collective metallic ringing—*ding ding ding ding*—was what announced the arrival of the Nyawawa.

Mwendo wa ngamia: the way of the camel

When the friends heard this, they knew what to do and they acted accordingly. It was normal. It was the season. Everyone went outside (because you *had* to go outside), and they grabbed something metallic to make noise (because you *had* to make noise). The friends, like many of the families around, left certain pots and pans (often broken ones) outside specifically for this purpose. Besides, once a pot or utensil or any object had been used for the Nyawawa, it could not be brought back inside or used for anything else, *ever*. In some unknown and invisible way, when a metal object became associated with the Nyawawa, it was connected to them and always carried the future risk of invoking the spirits or calling them back.

The noise was the most important thing—it was what kept the Nyawawa away from the houses and from straying from their path. There was one main road that stretched through the town of Homabay and led right to the waters of the lake. The Nyawawa always appeared at the east end of this road, and they moved toward the lake at the west end, eventually vanishing into the water. The noise guided them on this trajectory. Some say the Nyawawa liked the noise and that they stayed on the path because they wanted to follow it; in this sense, the residents helped the Nyawawa by guiding them with sound back to the lake. If they didn't hear it, supposedly, the spirits might lose their way, scatter themselves, and disseminate among the houses and the villagers. It didn't really matter why or what *would* happen if you didn't do it though, because everyone did it. You had to make the noise, and no one—absolutely no one—stayed in their house while others banged their pots outside.

While the sound was still distant, Gordon stood outside next to his mother and their friends, holding a metallic mug and a spoon that someone had placed in his hands. He watched as his mother began beating her spoon against the pot she was holding, so he did the same—*ding ding dingding dingding*. The ringing became louder and closer as all the people at the houses around joined in. There was no talking, no asking questions.

If not for the sound of the metallic beating, the evening would have been quiet and still. Gordon concentrated on the sound of the spoon against the mug, ringing through the darkness.

As he kept up the metallic ringing, watching and waiting for something to happen in the darkness, he began to hear the sound of the Nyawawa approaching their part of the street. The sound came first, like that of a crowd of people talking in the distance—a muffled murmuring of many voices, overlapping and superimposing in a low hum without any one distinct voice rising above the rest. This was the *wawa* or *wawawawa* sound that the name Nyawawa mimicked.

After Gordon heard that low rumbling whisper, sight slowly caught up with sound. He began to see their forms moving down the street. Although there were no streetlights, there was just enough natural light from the moon to make out the movement of shadow-like figures. They appeared like a nebulous mass, moving along indistinctly as their murmuring sound followed the metallic beating down the road. They were darker than everything around, somehow, but without specific features like faces or bodies; they were just moving, murmuring shadows.

He watched and continued beating his mug along with everyone else as the Nyawawa passed by. He stood as still as possible and just moved his wrist to beat the spoon against the mug—*dingdingdingdingdingding*. They all stood still as the shadowy figures crossed in front of them on the road. The shadows kept moving, following the sound that was also moving further down the road, and soon the shadows were no longer visible. When the metallic sound had also become faint, his mother and her friends stopped the metallic clanging. It was over. It was time to leave the objects outside and go back inside.

There was no talking inside though; Gordon wanted to ask his mom about the event, but she shook her head and whispered to him that they had to go to sleep. The sight of those shadows had made him feel cold and uneasy, and he shivered as if to shake away the sight and the memory. He wondered how he would be able to sleep after that. Thankfully, his desire to not be the only person awake when there could be devils roaming around outweighed his fear, and he managed to fall asleep.

He learned that night that just as you couldn't bring objects used for the Nyawawa back in the house, you also couldn't talk about the Nyawawa afterward because even the talking might call them back or might summon a spirit that strayed from the group. If you wanted to tell your story and ask your questions, you were free to do so, as long as it was the following day, outside, in the daylight. So, Gordon obeyed, like everyone else obeyed because you had to. There was no choice.

*

Another ritual that marked rural Luo culture, but which was more annoying than supernaturally frightening (depending on who you talked to), was that of the night runners in Migori. These were living people—perhaps with some strange obsession or perhaps even some demonic possession—who derived pleasure out of disturbing others and keeping them from sleeping during the night. Night runners literally ran around in the darkness, trampling through brush, rustling through corn fields, and darting about like bolts of lightning. They ran barefoot and naked (for they were always naked), while braving the cold, rain, mosquitoes, and other wild animals lurking in the darkness. In the quiet of the night, when all should have been still and all decent diurnal folks were asleep, night runners created their disturbance by taking long sticks and banging on iron-sheet roofs, knocking on wooden windows, and kicking at doors. They beat and pounded and thumped whatever they could as much as they could to make the loudest, most absurd amount of racket possible. The habit or compulsion of night running ran in families, like a genetic predisposition or maybe a curse. If you married someone who was a night runner (male or female), it was passed to you like a virus, and you too became a night runner forever after.

Gordon first experienced the phenomenon of night runners on one of the trips when he and his mother were visiting his Gor grandparents in Migori. Grandma's compound was composed of two separate structures—one house for living and one detached hut for cooking and eating, which acted as both the kitchen and dining room. Around dusk, while Gordon, his mother, Grandma, and a multitude of other children and grandchildren were sitting in the small kitchen hut having dinner (separately from Grandpa or his sons because they received their meals in the separate, "upper house"), they were interrupted by a sudden bang on the wooden door. Gordon jumped and thought maybe someone was just knocking. The banging happened a couple more times, and he had no idea what this noise meant. Grandma knew though, and she was not disturbed.

When the banging continued, she rebuked it by name, yelling in Luo, "Odhiambo, it's still so early!"

Whoever this Odhiambo person was, Grandma knew him just by the sound he made, and when she called his name, he stopped.

Later that evening, when the real darkness of night had set in, Gordon and his mom were back in the kitchen room along with the host of other kids, this time to settle down and go to sleep. According to Luo custom, since his mother had been married, she could not sleep in her parents' house. She had to stay in the kitchen with the kids. There was one mattress where his mom lay, while the kids crowded together on mats made of coconut palm leaves on the floor. The pitch darkness expanded in the small room with an almost physical thickness, filling the air and pushing out all the light.

As Gordon was drifting off to sleep, he was shaken by that same sudden bang on the door. Then there was a knocking at the window.

BAM!

It was so loud that it sounded like an explosion or gun shot ringing through the blackness.

BAM! BANG!

Each blow seemed to reverberate for a second, before another came. They become faster and louder.

Then there was the metallic sound of a stick against the iron-sheet roof, starting from one end and being pulled over all the grooves in the corrugated sheet. The sound went back and forth on the roof's edges, capping off each run with a final blow. *Drrrrrrrrrrrrrr BANG! Drrrrrrrrrrrrrr BANG!*

Gordon couldn't see anything. He was surrounded by other squirming, murmuring kids, and by the noise of the beating and banging that sounded louder in the darkness than anything he'd ever heard. He knew though that his mother was there in that room with him, and that gave him a little consolation.

"What's happening?" he called out to her.

"It's a night runner!" She called back through the darkness. "They're here to *protect us*!" She yelled those last words especially loudly, as if to signal to the runner that she *knew* what was indeed happening and even more, to communicate to him that she did *not* fear.

She told Gordon to settle back onto his mat and go to sleep. Although he was accustomed to continuous Kangemi noise, Gordon was shaken and troubled by the night runners' specific brand of noise. It felt invasive and personal, deliberate in a way that made it seem so much louder and obnoxious than the constant background noise of general living in Kangemi. He had thought he could sleep through anything after adjusting to slum life, but that was before he experienced night runners.

Night runners certainly did not protect—as Gordon's mother had shouted—and later Gordon understood why she'd said that. The more night runners felt that they were disturbing you, the more they were motived to continue, making their noise even louder and longer. They enjoyed it when people yelled back, imploring them to stop; they wanted to scare and torment you. They wanted you to light your lamps and show that they had gotten you up; when they ruined your sleep, that was their favorite. They especially loved it when you tried to convince them with all the reasons why they *had to* stop, and then you threatened them with all the things you'll do to them if you caught them.

Even though night runners left traceable bare footprints around during their marauding misadventures (especially when the ground was wet), you couldn't just confront a night runner at their own house like that. Even if you knew full well who they were—like Grandma did (and really, the entire community knew)—it was some sort of unwritten rule that you could only catch them inside your house. If or when you caught them, you could demand payment, like restitution. Often, disputes with night runners were settled quietly and discreetly between the two parties, and there was no need to involve the Area Chief.

One of Gordon's uncles—the youngest of Grandma's sons, named Leonard—once successfully and ingeniously caught a night runner. Back when Leonard was around eighteen or nineteen years old and was still living in Grandma's house, one night he left the front door to the house unlocked and slightly unhinged but sitting in the door frame, so that it looked perfectly normal, as if it were closed. He moved everything out of the main room, spread soap on the cement floor to make it slick, and waited for the night runner to come. (Grandma had allowed him to try this plan, since she hated night runners as much as anyone else). The cement floor in the main living room was vital to the plan, since it needed to be slick, and it wouldn't have worked in Grandma's kitchen hut since it had a dirt floor. As expected, a night runner came in the dark with his usual banging and knocking. When the man tried to kick the front door, he kicked right through it, propelling himself into the empty room; his own force sent him hurtling feet first inside, and he fell flat onto the soapy floor. He slid (and was naked, of course, which only made him slide faster), all the way across the room and into the wall on the other side. Leonard was waiting, and he

Mwendo wa ngamia: the way of the camel

quickly closed the door behind the night runner, trapping the man inside the house in all his naked disgrace.

From the floor, the man pleaded, "Don't kill me!"

Leonard had never intended to kill the man. He instead insisted that they make a deal, one full grown cow for Leonard's complete silence. The night runner agreed (for he had no choice and was really in no position to bargain). Leonard then set the man free to go on his way and continue night running, just not around Leonard's house.

Since the night runners' goal was to scare and terrorize unsuspecting sleepers in their houses, the thing that *they* feared was when someone came out of their house. This was such a rare occurrence that it immediately signaled something out of the ordinary, something to be wary of; for no one chased after night runners or tried to catch them outside. Night runners were creatures of the dark, and the dense, bushy thicket between houses and towns was *their* nighttime realm. Outside, they could disappear into that brush and escape along paths only known to them.

The only *real* reason why someone would come running out of their house at night in such a way—with the superhuman force to frighten even a night runner—was if they had an overwhelming need to get to the pit latrine. In Luo, there was a phrase that beautifully encapsulated this idea: *Ikak ka ja diep*, which meant, "You're as confident as a person having diarrhea." To Gordon, this "confidence" of the diarrhea-sufferer was perhaps the greatest nighttime force available in rural Luo life. It was stronger than that of the night runners because it came from a different, purer source—an elemental, physical force that overcame all fear. Poor souls suffering from diarrhea ran with awe-inspiring speed and intuition in their moment of most dire distress. Once they had found relief at the pit latrine, they sort of woke up as if from a trance, and it was only then that the realization sank in; they were outside, in the dark, possibly surrounded by animals and night runners hiding in the bushes.

The journey back to the house was always so much harder and scarier than the one coming out.

Even though life for Gordon growing up in Kangemi had its share of difficulties and disturbances, it did not have things like Nyawawa and night runners, and it did not require the nighttime confidence of diarrhea-sufferers. With its streetlights at night that illuminated the way to the public bathrooms, Kangemi seemed to Gordon to be much more civilized and sophisticated. He never felt afraid at night in Kangemi, and he missed his home when they went to visit his grandparents, especially if they stayed for a week or more. He hated the night runners, and he felt like an outsider in that rural community. He spoke Luo and he learned about the customs, but he didn't really know the ins and outs of the rural rituals.

He was always happy when they returned to Kangemi and he could again speak English, Swahili, and *Sheng*, the cool, current slang of the slum kids—where he would say things like *Na come home* (I'm coming home) and refer to how much things cost as "50 bob" or 10 bob." The trips up country made him realize that in Kangemi, he knew how everything worked. He could navigate life with the same cleverness that rural dwellers like Grandma navigated their isolated rituals. Slum life in Kangemi was big city life for Gordon. It was exciting and cosmopolitan with its mix of people and languages from all of Kenya's tribes, and it had opportunities and possibilities.

The rural life had some simple charms, to be sure, like picking mangoes and avocados right from the trees in Grandma's front yard. For the most part though, the experiences there made Gordon feel stifled and restricted, like there was always a part of himself left back in Kangemi. People practiced the rural rituals and upheld the common beliefs because they were tradition, but Gordon began to think that tradition itself might just be another sort of trap, one of the many ways society and culture worked to keep people in line. It seemed subtle at first, for there was a certain obvious comfort in following the footsteps of one's ancestors and doing what everyone else around you did. But after years of creeping indoctrination, this mindset established itself as an unbreakable cage, condemning people to a life of impoverished servitude simply because that was the way things had always been done. When people finally realized this, it was too late. Women were already given in marriage, busy raising multiple children, and keeping a home. Husbands were busy working, looking for work, or stealing if they couldn't find work, and in the latter scenario, they were probably also drowning their idleness and wasted potential in tiny, burning glasses of homemade liquor, called *chang'aa*. Was there really nothing more?

3. Mary Auma

Gordon's mother, Mary Auma Gor, was tall with dark skin—Gordon got those traits from her—and she spoke softly and slowly—Gordon did not get those traits from her. She had a heavy Luo accent that consistently reduced the *sh* sound to a double *ss*, where her shushing turned into hissing. Something like the word *shower* under the influence of both Luo and British English pronunciation transformed into something like *sawa*, which also means *okay* in Swahili.

Mary Auma liked to sing at home, and she *did* pass this characteristic onto Gordon, but she would sing far too slowly for Gordon's fast and loud taste. One of her favorite songs was called "Dunia ina mambo." Popular culture didn't know who originally wrote this song—it was probably back in the 1950s or sometime around there—and it had since been covered by so many different bands over the years that multiple versions circulated. You could hear it everywhere. For Gordon, it seemed like it had been continuously playing since he was born.

This song was popular throughout the East African region and had Swahili lyrics, which allowed it to appeal in a general sense to a wide range of people (Swahili being the only true African language that crossed countries and cultures). The song was in the style of what was then called *Rhumba*, or Congolese music, a hybrid, multifaceted type of dance music that combined elements from folk songs with Caribbean, Latin American, and Afro-Cuban rhythms. "Dunia ina mambo" exemplified this sonic blend, where the singing sat on top of a busy, layered background—first electric keyboard chords, then drumming, then the breathy whistling of a wooden pan flute, topped off with high-pitched guitar strumming. The overall feel was what we might call *tropical*, fast-paced and feel-good. The chorus got stuck in your head and made you want to shake your body to the rhythm—that's why this style of music was also called Soukous, deriving from the French word *secouer*, to shake. This wasn't meant to encourage wild dancing but rather the style that was equally valid at both church services and political rallies in Kenya. It was restrained social dancing where you just isolated one body part and did the same small movement over and over. You just picked whatever you wanted and moved it, repeatedly and gently, to the rhythm. It didn't matter what body part you chose, as long as it stayed on the beat.

While the musical feeling of "Dunia ina mambo" was light, the deeper meaning was more melancholy. The chorus of the song went like this:

Dunia hii mama
Lukumba lukumba
Dunia ina mambo
Mwendo wa ngamia

These words expressed how the world is full of problems and how everything is always changing and moving forward, but not in a straight line. Life is messy and progress is crooked. Sometimes you cross great distances step by step with the uneven gait of a camel (*mwendo wa ngamia*), while other times you speed through tiny stretches, with the sprint of a cheetah. The key phrase in this song, *lukumba lukumba*, is, to this day, untranslatable in English, and is evidently not listed in any easily accessible dictionaries. It expresses the core theme of the song, that we move through life in crooked and uneven ways, like the lumbering movement of an elephant that steps heavily as it walks, but also the side-to-side slithering of a snake, or the light-footed leaping of a gazelle. *Lukumba lukumba*—always as a two-word phrase because there is no single *lukumba*—includes all these zig-zagging transformations and meanderings through speeds, styles, ways of moving and modes of being. It's an acknowledgment that life is always in flux, and that we are always existing in a state of constant variation, vacillation, and oscillation. Although the world is plagued with its ills, we find ways to move through them. We adjust and maneuver, side to side, back and forth, quickly and slowly, for we too are always changing. Just as these uneven ways of moving are necessary at one time or another, so the difficult journey (*mwendo wa ngarama*) of life is necessary—it comes for each of us and it cannot be avoided. Therefore, as this catchy, upbeat song teaches, the best strategy for navigating this unpredictable life is lukumba lukumba.

When Mary Auma would sing this to herself as she cooked or cleaned, she slowed it down to such a pace that Gordon found it almost unbearable. *Duun-iii-aa ii-naa mamm-booo lu-kum-baaa luu-kumm-baaa.* Her slow singing was almost a chant, repeating the words like a mantra—*this world has problems but we move through them somehow, meandering and meandering, sometimes like the camel, the elephant, the cheetah, the snake.*

Maybe partly because of her shy nature and the fact that she didn't want to draw attention to herself, she accepted the status quo and the reality that the poor have no place in society. Or rather, they do have a place, but it's at the bottom, and that's just the way it is. All she wanted was to take care of her son, provide for him, make sure he had a roof over his head, enough food, clothes, shoes, and a decent education. She wanted *him* to make something of himself, and it was her job to ensure that he could. She accepted this as her God-given lot in life. She gave money to the church and sat in the pews every Sunday with her head covered, praising God for his provision, grace, and blessings, for how he continually "filleth the hungry with good things," and "the rich he hath empty sent away." Blessed were the poor in spirit—she truly believed—for they will inherit the kingdom of God.

Mary Auma tried to balance her faith in God and his omnipotent omnipresence with her fear of society's also ever-present, invisible, and (almost as powerful) retribution for stepping out of one's place. There were real, immediate consequences for disobeying society's unwritten rules. This was not just at the macro government level but also at the micro, street level, for within the corroding, corrugated-iron lined corridors of Kangemi, vigilante justice reigned supreme. As punishment for obvious crimes like stealing someone's possessions in broad daylight, people could be beaten to near-death or set on fire by small mobs of angry slum dwellers. This sort of rough justice fueled by anger was swift and merciless.

There was, however, another sort of unseen jealousy fueled by competition that simmered below the surface and caused people to sabotage one another for no apparent reason. If others, who thought you were at the same social and economic level as them, decided that you were rising above your level, which is to say, you were succeeding in a way that they weren't or receiving something that they didn't have, they'd figure out a way to keep you down and rob you of progress. The logic behind this mentality was nebulous at best, and Gordon actually didn't understand it even though he saw it happening around him every day. It didn't seem like people benefited in any actual way from bringing others down. They didn't get anything tangible out of it, but maybe there was a spiteful satisfaction in knowing that they had thwarted someone else's success.

Gordon thought that this was stupid, frankly, because one person's failure did not give success to the other person. It seemed obvious and basic to him, so why didn't people understand? How could they not see that using a lit candle to light someone else's candle didn't extinguish their own flame. One flame could create another flame without diminishing its own light. It was a both-and principle, not an either-or. Why did this simple idea get distorted when it refracted through levels of social and economic status? Maybe it would be kinder to say Gordon concluded that this perspective was mostly a symptom of small-minded thinking, caused by scarcity and lack. Perhaps the "If I can't have it, you can't either" mentality was merely a byproduct of extreme poverty, and therefore it wasn't people's fault that they thought they way. People could only see their pressing need and could not bear it if someone had more than them. Because at least if everyone was equal, no one would have to be reminded of the injustice and near inhumane nature of their suffering.

Regardless of the exact reasoning and the real root cause, the bottom line was that this whole situation resulted in no one having anything. There was no possibility for growth or progress or innovation. For any of that to happen, someone would have to be first, and in the Kangemi logic, no one could be first because that would make everyone else last (even though everyone was already last). Everyone accepted that everyone would be last, and would stay there, so that at least they were all equal, stuck scraping the bottom of the barrel with no hope of ever getting out. Gordon later learned that this is a real psychological and social phenomenon, called the crab mentality.

Despite living in the same conditions as everyone else, Gordon was able to see past this way of living and grow up in Kangemi relatively immune, without adhering to it. Maybe this was because his mother didn't live this way either; she didn't seek to take from other people or ruin their success. She instead concentrated on what *she* alone could do, and she worked her side jobs to make her own version of success for herself and Gordon. But maybe there was something more too, something in Gordon that already knew he wanted to rise above a life of petty survival. Maybe it was also partly the influence of all that time spent in church (but everyone went to church). At church and even in school, they preached the golden-rule doctrine of "love your neighbor as yourself," but the Kangemi reality was an inversion where people often disliked and resented their neighbors. Gordon wanted people to just help each other—that was the Christian way after all—and in helping each other, they would help themselves. Then everyone could progress together.

Gordon's mother understood all of this too, but only in as much as she didn't want Gordon to invoke the wrath of societal retribution. She cautioned him to "not push too much." She believed that if you pushed against the boundaries of the box you were born into, you would break something, and you'd be punished. This would lead to repercussions, like ripples through a pool of water. She didn't want to cause any kind of waves and saw no need to stir the pot.

She used variations of this same metaphor to instill the idea into Gordon that you *must* stay in your place in society:

If you fly too high, they'll clip your wings.

If you're too loud, they'll shut you up.

She lived by these fear-filled aphorisms, and she too ascribed to the belief that you "never mention the name of the president, for the walls have ears." If it hadn't been done before, it was for good reason, and one should follow tradition. You had to obey, keep your head down, fear God, work hard, and survive.

*

One notable way that she broke with convention, however, was to teach Gordon how to cook. Maybe she allowed this because she could do it without anyone else knowing, inside the privacy of their home, even if the walls did have ears. This one deviation was radical, in its own way, especially for someone like meek Mary Auma. It was her own little seed of rebellion, a way to amend and update tradition for the better, for men did not cook in Luo culture. Usually, they weren't even allowed to set foot in the kitchen. That was the woman's domain, and if a man did go in the kitchen, it was seen as emasculating and strange. There was no reason since it was not their place.

Mary Auma decided, since it was just the two of them in their Kangemi home, that Gordon needed to learn how to cook to take care of himself. Her reasoning was, simply, "If I'm not here, you'll need to know how." Perhaps, in this sense, her decision *was* motivated by its own type of fear. She taught Gordon how to cook the essentials: *ugali*, *chapati*, and *sukuma wiki*. *Sukuma wiki* meant "to push the week" in Swahili, since this was the simple food that could fill the days and fill your belly enough to just keep going. The food behind this name was kale, sautéed with onion and tomato, then seasoned with salt. That was it. Sometimes that's all Gordon and his mom would have, and it would be enough to just keep them going. It would push them forward. It was food after all. Mary Auma never used a chopping board to prepare her kale for sukuma wiki. Instead, she'd just wrap all the leaves together and hold them tightly in her left hand, while she chopped with her right hand, and the pieces would fall right into the pot.

Compared with this common food whose value lies in it just being food, chapati is a prized specialty. It is basically the Kenyan equivalent of a tortilla, but thicker (around ¼ inch), and fried individually so that each one is perfectly soft on the inside and slightly crunchy on the outside. The dough is made from white wheat flour and water and is unsweetened and unsalted, but it does have a touch of fresh lemon zest that gives it a hint of flavor, sometimes more like a smell than a taste, but a subtle undertone nonetheless. The floury chapati flavor is not bold or flashy, and it doesn't aim to shock or amaze. It is confident and consistent, stable and dependable, like the best of comfort foods. When done just right (because you *can* make an easier, quicker, lesser-quality version), it requires a combination of precision, finesse, and a good amount of patience to achieve delicate, flaky layers on the outside of the chapati. After mixing the dough, you have to apply the right amount of oil onto each flattened chapati, then roll them up like cinnamon rolls to allow the dough to absorb the oil. Due to the time and care involved in this labor-intensive process (which everyone in Gordon's neighborhood knew about), you had to "respect the chapati" (which everyone did). Many families only had chapati for the big celebrations like Easter and Christmas.

Mary Auma knew how to make the truly good, highly desired chapati. She used to make it to sell on the street in the mornings before she went to work, to make a little extra cash. She would wake up at 6 a.m. and cook it in the house while Gordon was getting ready for school. If the timing was right, he could grab a fresh chapati to eat on his way. Even better though (and more strategic), was if he could save the chapati for trading at school. Among the kids, chapati was like gold, and if you had it, all your needs would be met. Everyone would be your friend, and everyone would be eager to help you with any unfinished assignments or get you anything you wanted.

When Gordon saved his chapati, he would cut the roughly one-foot round whole circle into one-inch squares, about the size of communion wafers at church, to get as many out of it as possible. He'd spend those 1-inch pieces like coins. All the kids knew the smell of freshly-cooked chapati—that hot, freshly-fried, still a little oily goodness. Even if Gordon put it in his backpack, it would still smell enough to distract the other kids. It was the mighty *njivaa*, as it was called on the street (emphasis on the extended *ahhhh* sound). The kids smelled it and knew right away, and whispers would start in the back of the classroom, *maboys*—hey guys—*mtu ako na Njivaa*—someone has *it*.

Gordon's mom also knew how to fry fish, which she made and sold around dinner time as a way of bookending her weekdays with street-corner side hustles. She bought raw fish from the market downtown, and brought it back to cook and sell in Kangemi. While she cooked it, Gordon sat outside under one of the streetlights to do his homework. If he didn't go outside, the mingled smells of fish and frying oil that lingered in the house settled into all his schoolbooks and papers. Fish was associated with the Luo culture (since they were predominantly fishermen) and even more with the poorest people in the slum since fish was cheaper than meat. Gordon didn't want to broadcast for the world that he was a poor boy from a Luo family, so he had to be strategic when his mom fried fish in their house. Bringing the smell of fish to school was nowhere near as advantageous as bringing the smell of chapati.

The first thing that Mary Auma taught Gordon how to cook was ugali. As this is the foundation for all Kenyan meals, it was the natural and obvious place for them to begin. Their lessons took place in their kitchen, which was just a corner space in their home, where the wall and ceiling above were blackened from the cooking smoke. They used a small, ceramic, charcoal-burning stove called a *jiko*. It was shaped like an hourglass and had a ceramic bowl in the top section that held the charcoal briquettes, surrounded by a metal casing that held it in place. This bowl had holes in the bottom to allow the ash to fall through, where it could be collected on the ground from the under section. The top section had three horizontal metal supports that held the weight of the pot. The bottom of the pan would turn black quickly from being right on top of the charcoal.

Since they didn't have electricity, Gordon and his mother used a tin kerosene lamp for light while cooking. The person who was not doing the cooking sat by the pot and held the lamp, if necessary. This was usually Gordon's job, but the day that she decided it was time for him to try the cooking, Mary Auma held the lamp and left the ugali preparation to Gordon.

"I want you to learn. You'll need to know," she said matter-of-factly. Today, you'll do it."

She never measured anything when she cooked, and there were no written recipes or instructions, but Gordon had watched her many times. She didn't give him any sort of lengthy introduction before starting and instead just told him to "do it." He knew that the necessary first step was to light the charcoal in the stove. He picked up the jiko and took it outside—you had to light it outside and let the first black smoke from the charcoal dissipate until the coals became less smoky and just smoldered. The jiko had a little flap with a hinge on the bottom section, like a door, and once he was outside, Gordon opened it and filled the bottom section with newspaper scraps. He lit the scraps with a match and closed the flap to wait for the fire inside to rise up and heat the pieces of charcoal. Once the charcoal was ready, he carried the jiko back inside.

His mother held the lamp and sat silently by while Gordon put their pot on the stove's metal supports over the charcoal and filled the pot with water. That *sufuria*, a stainless-steel pot, was their only one for ugali. It had no handle to hold but just a flattened lip around the rim. Gordon sprinkled a pinch of the ugali flour in the water to make it boil faster since that's what his mom always did. He never knew if it actually helped the water boil or not, but he did it anyway.

They waited in silence for the water to boil, listening to the simmering bubbles and the ever-growing hum of the heating water. Gordon didn't feel impatient. Although he normally never liked to wait (he liked fast things and hated slow services), he knew that this was one of those things you just can't rush. The water had to be boiling when you added the flour because if the water wasn't hot enough, the flour wouldn't cook properly. It would turn out lumpy and doughy, but also mealy and crumbly in your mouth. Ugali seemed like the simplest of things to make—it was just corn flour and water—but as Gordon watched the water start to boil, he pondered how its simplicity was deceiving. It was trying to trick him, but he would not let it outsmart him.

He waited until the boiling bubbles rose to the surface, started to pop, and became a continuous rumbling. It was time to add the flour. He grabbed a small piece of newspaper to hold onto the lip of the pan with one hand, while he added the cups of corn flour with the other hand. He stirred the flour into the boiling water with a wooden spoon or cooking stick. He stirred slowly at first, and the flour started to bubble and spurt, releasing little puffs of hot steam—*pfuuuuuuh*—and then spitting tiny bits of gooey flour up toward his face and onto his stirring hand. He stirred faster and faster, as hard as he could, until the flour and water started to coalesce into the consistency of porridge. As he kept going, it thickened into almost a dough.

One of the tricky things for Gordon while he was stirring was that the pot was slightly bigger than the top of the jiko, and as he stirred, the pot wobbled and shifted. He held on as best he could with one hand while stirring with the other—you couldn't stop stirring or else the ugali would form clumps—and he tried to keep the pot balanced on the stove supports, perfectly aligned over the charcoal. But he overestimated the density of the ugali and underestimated his own zealous stirring motion, and when he tried to flip the ugali around in the pot, he lost control. The pot slid off the jiko and landed face up on the floor with a clang.

Gordon jumped, and a trail of smoke wafted up from the uncovered fire. He looked at his mom with wide eyes—was it ruined? He didn't say anything but his silence asked, What now?

His mom didn't get up and didn't say anything either. She looked at the pot and back at him. Her silence answered his question with another question, Well, what DO you do now?

Gordon figured he had to decide for himself, and he had to act quickly if there was a chance of salvaging the ugali. He lifted the pot back onto the burner. The ugali still just sat there, half formed in a lump, seemingly unfazed by its little adventure. It looked okay. He could still do it. He resumed his stirring position with one hand holding the lid of the pot and the other trying to flip the ugali around. His mother set down the lamp and grabbed his stirring hand to help him mix it.

"Like this." They whipped the ugali around in a circle, first one way and then the other. She showed him how to flatten out all the chunks by pressing the ugali down against itself as she scraped over the top layer. Then she flipped it over and scraped it again, this time spreading out the ugali by flattening it up on the sides of the pan.

"This helps it cook."

She showed him how to reduce the heat, and once again it was time to wait. Wait a while for it to cook through on the bottom, then flip it. Wait for it to cook through on that side, then flip it again.

"You wait until it smells like burning." She instructed. That was key.

Mwendo wa ngamia: the way of the camel

Sometimes the bottom even got a little blackened, but that was fine. Gordon actually liked when the ugali got a sort of hard crust on the bottom.

After a little bit of waiting, she poked the top of the ugali. "You can touch it and see if it feels right."

Gordon poked it too with his pointer finger, making a little indent that stuck in the surface, like a crater.

He looked up at his mom. "Do you think it's ready?" he asked.

"Do *you* think it's ready?"

Gordon wasn't sure—that probably meant that it wasn't ready since she didn't just say so. He better keep stirring and waiting. He really wanted his ugali to be good, and it needed to be cooked all through. His mother had always said that whatever you cooked, you had to eat, however it turned out. There was no wasting food. So even if his ugali turned out poorly, he knew they were going to eat it, and he didn't want to endure bad ugali.

When he finally thought it was done, he grabbed the pot with both hands, one on each side, pulled it off the stove and flipped it over a plate. The ugali plopped out, landing heavily in the middle of the plate. It looked right—it was an appropriately steaming, slightly lumpy, white oval.

Gordon's mom took over and made the rest of the dinner. She prepared *omena*, tiny fish sautéed whole with onion and tomato (a Luo favorite), along with sukuma wiki.

When it came time to try the ugali, Gordon was excited but also a bit fearful. He bit into the spongy whiteness, and he tasted immediately that the middle hadn't cooked all the way. His mom told him flat out that it was "not so good." He was disappointed and they ate it, of course, but she made it his job from that day forth to cook the ugali whenever they had it so that he'd get better. Her strategy worked, and eventually he mastered the art of ugali. He knew when the water was hot enough, how much flour to add for how much water, when the texture felt right, and when it smelled enough like burning to be certain that it had cooked through. After that first attempt, his pot never slid off the stove again.

CROSSING WAIYAKI WAY

*

In 2000, Gordon heard through the Kangemi grapevine that the archbishop of the Catholic Archdiocese of Nairobi, the Most Reverend Raphael Ndingi Mwana'a Nzeki, had begun an unofficial and very hush-hush practice of hosting visitors at his residence every Saturday. Rumor had it that you could just show up for an audience with His Grace the Archbishop and ask him for whatever you needed. This had probably started with one person, who told someone else, who told someone else, and then it had snowballed. There was no advertising or publicity and no way to make an official appointment.

Even though this seemed too good to be true, Ndingi was a genuine champion of the poor and oppressed. Who knew? Maybe he did really just help random people with their random needs. Maybe he enjoyed meeting unceremoniously with Nairobi's poorest residents, those who emerged from the deepest slums within slums, the *mise-en-abyme* places like Kibera that had rules and rhythms completely unto themselves, just to ask for a simple, gift of $10 or $15. Something like that could substantially improve a life, and for someone like Ndingi, that wasn't much to give anyway. Within the Catholic Church, Ndingi was an admired and brave man who had fought for government reform (the reinstatement of a multi-party democracy), and who—allegedly—had even told the dictatorial President Moi, to his *face*, that he needed to stop "the evils of your government." Maybe Ndingi's benevolence was exaggerated, but maybe not, and in any case, Gordon thought it was worth a shot.

The archbishop's residence was not far from Kangemi to the east, and it was definitely within walking distance. When Gordon told his mom about the potential opportunity, she was unsurprisingly hesitant to agree.

"But how? How can we get there?" she asked.

"I know the way." Gordon said confidently. "Maybe there will even be food."

Surprisingly, she said that they could go.

Mwendo wa ngamia: the way of the camel

The following Saturday, they set out to see if they would be allowed to approach the archbishop's residence, maybe even go inside, and maybe they'd even get to see him. They set out in the morning and walked from Kangemi to Ewaso Ingiro Rd, only a couple of miles. From the road, they found the right address, and encountered a closed gate with tall hedges on both sides that completely blocked the grounds and the house from view. Gordon had never been this close to an electric gate before. His mom pressed the intercom button, and replied to the crackly voice that they had come to see Archbishop Ndingi. The gate opened, and they walked through onto the long driveway that led back to the house.

When they reached the entrance, there were a handful of other people waiting around, but it wasn't a crowd. They were ushered into a sitting room, and they waited for their turn. When they were eventually called, an attendant guided them back down a hallway to an office room. Gordon's mom went first and he followed. They turned into a doorway, and there, seated behind a wide desk, was the man himself, cool as a cucumber, just waiting for them. They walked in and sat down in the chairs on the other side of the desk.

Gordon felt like he was in a dream; it seemed unreal and too good to be true. He could see the surprise on his mother's face too. Maybe she hadn't thought they would really get to see the archbishop, or it hadn't been a real possibility in her mind until that very moment when they were actually there, face to face, sitting in front of him in his private office. She looked at Ndingi with wide eyes, and Gordon had never seen her so starstruck. Ndingi was the type of person you heard people talk about and whom you only saw on TV. But now they were sitting in his presence. This was the closest his mother had ever been to power, and even more specifically, power in the Catholic Church (which was God's power), and she held this in the highest esteem. She had probably never imagined that in her life she would get to sit in the presence of one of God's most holy, blessed, and truly honorable men.

Ndingi smiled and welcomed them. They had polite introductions where he asked their names and where they were from. He then got right to it and simply asked what he could do for them. Gordon realized in that second that he might have to do the talking, and he mentally scrambled to form some good sentences. Thankfully, to his surprise and relief, his mom answered right away. She smoothly stated that they needed money for Gordon's school fees. Ndingi nodded understandingly and pulled out a checkbook from one of the drawers in his desk. He asked the name of the school and then wrote them a check right then and there for $30—about one month's salary for Mary Auma.

"Take this for school." He held the check out across the desk.

Gordon's mother took it, and thanked him, smiling with a mixture of gratitude and disbelief.

Ndingi didn't stop there though. He promised to help her with her job—that was the root issue after all. He said that he didn't want to just temporarily relieve their struggles by giving them money, like a one-time band aid, if he could do something to instead address the underlying cause. Hearing this, Gordon was filled with awe—it was a strange and new sort of feeling—for here, finally, was the rare person who wanted to fix the problem instead of just covering it up. That person actually existed! Ndingi understood that Gordon's mom needed a higher-paying job, and it just so happened that Ndingi, being the archbishop, had a direct connection to the Holy Family Basilica (as that was the Cathedral Church and seat of the archbishop in downtown Nairobi). Fortuitously, the Basilica was looking for more janitorial help, and Ndingi said he'd reach out to Father Ngugi, the head priest there, and see what he could do.

As they walked home, Gordon thought about how in past years, his mother would not have agreed to something as out-of-the-ordinary and unlikely as going to visit the archbishop. Was it because they went together that she didn't seem afraid, or was she developing some of her own courage after seeing Gordon's? She had taught him everything she knew about life, so far, but perhaps he could also teach her some things too.

*

As it turned out, Ndingi was as good on his word as he seemed. He sent a letter to Father Ngugi at the Holy Family Basilica to ask about giving Mary Auma a job. By the grace of God and these fortunate connections, Fr. Ngugi agreed, and the Basilica employed her as a member of their janitorial staff. She, along with other ladies, mopped the entire sanctuary every day during the afternoon break between the four morning masses and the one evening mass. They scrubbed the tile floor by hand with towels, down on their hands and knees, until it was shiny enough to reflect the splendor of such a temple of the Lord.

The Holy Family Basilica was constructed in 1960, and although the building maintained the traditional shape of a cross, it had distinctive modernist features, like straight clean lines, cement walls with rectangular slots for windows, and a striking lack of decoration or ornamentation. It did however have four large, identical, stained-glass windows—one at the entrance, one behind the main altar, and two in the adjacent chapels. They all contained illuminated bands of zigzagging rainbow colors that stretched from floor to ceiling. The outer side of these windows that faced the lush, landscaped grounds was covered with a retro honeycomb pattern. The outer side of the entrances to the church were covered with zigzagging awnings, which further created an air of simple geometric elegance.

Gordon's mom already revered the Basilica, so she was overjoyed about this new job, both about the prospect of higher income, of course, but also about getting to spend her days serving the church in such a beautiful space. In the past, she had only taken Gordon to the Basilica for the Christmas Eve service. It had exclusively been a place for that type of special occasion, but now she got to go there every day.

Because of this blessed new job, they were able to move to a slightly bigger and better house in Kangemi. It was still a single-room, iron-sheet structure connected to others in a row, but you reached this one by first going through a gate into a patchy grass courtyard. Their front door opened onto this courtyard. Gray electric wires crisscrossed the courtyard, like streamers hung up at church for Pentecost, and below the wires, thin gray and white clothing lines stretched between the roof corners. Drying sheets and clothes wafted on the lines, and kids played in the courtyard. It felt like a wonderful place to live, their own little slice of peaceful space carved out of Kangemi's overcrowded hodgepodge. The best part of all was that inside this new house, there was one uncovered light bulb in the center of the ceiling. That single bulb, proudly illuminating their home every evening, was the shining symbol and daily reminder of their newfound prosperity. They had finally moved up in the world.

Gordon went to visit his mom at work from time to time, and he too enjoyed being in the Basilica. To him it was impressively large, fancy, and colorful; it was the only example he'd ever seen of a "great cathedral," and his only frame of reference. For him, it was *The Cathedral*. To get there, he would take a matatu downtown by himself. By now he was fourteen, dark as ever and still tall, so he could pass for older if he wanted to. He had also let his hair grow long enough to plait into cornrows, which allowed him to cast an impressively intimidating aura if he wanted to. In all, he could manage himself just fine. He and his mom would ride back on the matatu together. Once, they stayed in downtown and went out for a fast-food dinner—the first one ever in Gordon's life—where he experienced an American-style "combo meal" with fried chicken, french fries, and soda.

One of these times when he was downtown with his mom, Gordon actually saw President Moi from behind—Moi, *the* shadowy villain of legend, there in the flesh. Moi came out of some event, and a crowd of people (including Gordon and his mom) watched as Moi walked by. Gordon only saw the man from behind. Moi was wearing a fancy-

Mwendo wa ngamia: the way of the camel

looking suit, and he had a shaved, bald-looking head. His back was the regular back of any man, and seeing him in the flesh, even from a distance, made Gordon feel strangely disappointed. Moi, the man, didn't seem like anything worthy of all that awe and fear that people paid him and the hushed, frightened way people spoke (or rather tried *not to* speak) about him. He was, actually, just an old man. Because of all he'd heard, Gordon realized that he too had always (even subconsciously) imagined Moi as some sort of hyperbolic monster, who went around swinging a machete, chopping off people's hands left and right just for the fun of it.

With that glimpse of Moi's incredibly banal human form, the overblown image society had built up in Gordon's mind deflated. It was all just puffed up with air. Gordon thought about how everyone he knew—*everyone* he had ever met—feared Moi like he was the Devil incarnate. And why, really? Their fear of this Devil was as devout and fervent as their faith in God, but what did their fear ever do for them? Would their fear extend their life, bring them success, increase their income, guard them against future suffering? Everyone feared because you were supposed to fear, and the fear kept people in their place. It kept them from thinking, questioning, even dreaming. Fear maintained the status quo in Kenya more than maybe anything else—the realization hit Gordon in that moment like an epiphany.

Gordon didn't want to be ruled by fear. Fear made people small, stripped them of their hope. It reduced them to receding, withering husks of themselves. Eventually, they just crumbled into dust and mingled with all the other dust that settled on the Kangemi streets to be packed down beneath the feet of so many pedestrians and the tires of so many matatus. That was no way to go. Anyway, why should Gordon fear when he had done nothing wrong? He had no reason to be afraid of a person like Moi, who was just as much flesh and blood as he was.

Was there really nothing more?

*

Near the end of her first six months working at the Basilica, Mary Auma started to feel sick. She became weak and complained of stomach pains. Even with the higher income, she didn't have any sort of insurance and couldn't afford medical costs. Fr. Ngugi, however, decided that she should go to St. Mary's Mission Hospital near Langata Road in the south part of Nairobi. He wrote a letter to the hospital, explaining the circumstances, and the church covered her costs. She was in and out of the hospital multiple times. She would go, the church would pay, she'd be treated, and she'd come home. This became a routine because every time she came home, a few weeks later, the sickness came back too.

Then she was admitted to stay longer in the hospital. The first time it was for a full five days, and this was the first time that Gordon had ever stayed in their home by himself. When she had to stay in the hospital, he went to visit her every day after school, regardless of homework. He brought her food from home too, so she didn't have to rely on the hospital food. He even made her chapati, and she said that his chapati was good.

Despite the hospital's care, she continued to get worse. She went back and forth, and her condition deteriorated. The doctor officially diagnosed it as Typhoid, which is most commonly caught from drinking contaminated water. To make matters worse, Fr. Ngugi left for a short-term sabbatical in Rome, and the assistant priest at the Basilica assumed Ngugi's place. The assistant priest didn't send money to cover Mary Auma's medical costs, so that was the end of the Church's makeshift medical coverage.

Gordon and his mother tried to get by on their own, but since she couldn't work, they barely had money for food. When she was in the hospital, they paid the bill as best they could. They couldn't sustain this for long though, and soon she was discharged from the hospital one final time.

*

In true Catholic Kenyan fashion, they prayed for her to get well. They prayed, their extended family prayed, their friends prayed, and their church community prayed. Everyone prayed. As her condition got worse, they prayed even more. If they had nothing else, at least they had prayer.

Kenyan culture wasn't always so dependent on prayer though, and according to popular history, the indigenous people who lived in Kenya before the time of the white colonizers lived by much more tactile, traditional means. They understood all the signs and signals of nature—if they heard a frog croaking underneath the ground, it meant that the rains would come in one week. Then one week later, the rains came, just as predicted. They believed in some sort of higher power or deity, but they also believed fervently in the earth and in the rhythms of nature and the animal world, and in their connection to all of this.

When the white Englishmen arrived, they taught the indigenous people how to pray to the Christian God. The Englishmen instructed the people in the ways of the Christian faith and convinced them to supplant their traditional knowledge with the belief in one true God who rules all and orders all from on high. The people became good converts. They began to pray to a bearded, white, old-man God-the-Father figure and a blond-haired, blue-eyed Jesus-the-Son. At a certain moment, the white men told the people, "Come, let us pray together. Let us close our eyes." So, the people closed their eyes and bowed their heads, as they had become accustomed to do. While they waited with their eyes closed (so the story goes), the white men took all their land and left them only with the Bible in their hands. When the people opened their eyes, all their land was gone, and all that was left for them to have and to hold was that Bible. Since all they could do now was pray, and all they had left was faith, oh, how they prayed. They *really* prayed, and they believed that by prayer alone, God would sustain them.

While Gordon believed in the power of prayer and faith, he also believed in the power of work and making things happen. There was something in him that was unusually practical (or maybe just stubborn) and couldn't accept that the only way was to sit around and pray and wait and do nothing. He believed that God heard his prayers, but he also knew that he needed to do *something*. The first thing was to get a job and make money to buy food for him and his mom. Therefore, through a friend of a friend, he found work on the weekends as a gardener for an Indian family in the wealthy Westlands neighborhood east of Kangemi and just northwest of downtown Nairobi.

The house where Gordon worked was one of those large, fancy ones surrounded by leafy, manicured grounds, all of which required a multi-person maintenance staff. There was always conversation and gossip circulating among the "house helps," and one day Gordon heard from a coworker about "a person who can pray," like *really* pray, in the true Biblical sense where prayer directly leads to miracles and healing. The coworker told Gordon that he should go see this holy man.

The gathering for this person who can pray was in a different and not nearly as nice neighborhood further east, called Kariobangi. Really, it was another slum area, not even as well-kept as Kangemi. There are differing stories about the origin of that neighborhood's name, Kariobangi, which stem from variations of Swahili mispronunciations of English phrases. (This is common in Kenya, like the area in Homabay town called *Rodi Kopany* that had once housed a Road Company.) Regarding Kariobangi, one theory states that the name derived from the statement in English, "Carry your bags," which white settlers used to say to the native people, maybe because there was a bag factory in the area at one time. The other theory claims that the name is a misinterpretation of the phrase "Carry your *bhang*," which Swahili speakers heard white people say, in reference to *bhang* meaning marijuana. Since the contemporary Swahili word for marijuana is *bangi*, the second theory seems more plausible, if still not entirely convincing.

The coworker told Gordon that he and some friends were going to go to Kariobangi that weekend to see this holy pastor. They were going to take the bus and Gordon could come along, but for Gordon, it would take an additional matatu to get there, since there was no direct route from Kangemi and he would have to reconnect in downtown. The whole ride would cost 40 Ksh one way and take about an hour. Gordon didn't want to spend the money on bus fare, so he decided to walk, even it if took him 3 hours on foot. The event supposedly started at 7:00 a.m., so Gordon left Kangemi at 5 a.m., confident that he could comfortably arrive an hour late and no one would notice. On the way, it rained, and he arrived sweaty, hungry, and smelling like a wet dog. The whole way, he kept thinking that it would be worth it—out of this struggle and this sacrifice, his faith would heal his mother. It was the perfect combination of faith and work. God would see Gordon's effort, and he would take pity on his wretchedness. Gordon certainly had faith larger than a mustard seed, and God could do anything, after all.

The place of prayer was a sort of non-denominational, evangelical-leaning church, in a run-down part of the already run-down neighborhood. The church had a large compound, made of multiple iron-sheet buildings. To Gordon's initial surprise when he arrived, he saw that the staff were giving out porridge, tea, and bananas to all the waiting faithful who had gathered. He gratefully accepted this food offering but then realized it was supposed to keep people happy and distracted while they waited *for hours*. The holy pastor didn't arrive until three in the afternoon, and in the meantime, people just milled about, enjoyed the refreshments, and talked amongst themselves. Gordon realized later that some of the people going around must have worked for the pastor, for they were gathering information about the people there. They'd ask you for actual details about yourself, like your name, why you'd come, what you were there for, what you were hoping for, where you worked, etc. During the long wait, people continued arriving too. Gordon could not believe his eyes as people actually carried in their sick on mats, just like in the Bible stories. This made him feel like he was in one of those stories, and it reassured him that this man must truly be something.

When the man arrived, everyone ushered themselves into the sanctuary room and assembled as a standing-room only audience before a raised stage. The man proceeded to get up on the stage and pray loudly, charismatically, as if he were talking to God, *directly*. His energy was exciting and infectious. He held a microphone in one hand and raised his other hand toward heaven, repeating over and over:

Glory, glory, glory!
Holy, holy, holy!
Glory, glory, glory!

People in the audience muttered along, some repeated his words like an echo, and some even added their own praises in the gaps:

Praise God!
Jesus is Lord!
Hallelujah!
Holy holy holy!
Glory, glory, glory!
Lord God Almighty!

At one moment, the man stopped. He lowered his raised arm and extended it straight out toward the crowd to quiet the muttering. A gradual hush fell, and everyone waited, anticipating with bated breath what was going to happen next.

"Today, in our midst—" the man began, "there is a young man named Gordon."

What?! Gordon couldn't believe it.

"He's here to pray for his sick mother."

Good God in Heaven! It was as if time stopped. Gordon felt like the Holy Spirit had identified him, personally.

Mwendo wa ngamia: the way of the camel

The man then called for the young man named Gordon to come up on stage. Somehow, despite his amazement and the sense of numbness radiating through his body, Gordon found he could still move his legs, and he slowly walked through the crowd to the front. As everyone watched him, he stepped up on the stage, and the man handed him the mic.

Gordon didn't know what to do exactly or what he was supposed to say, so he basically just repeated what the man had already said. He reintroduced himself. "My name is Gordon Oduor," he said, smiling like a kid on Christmas, and added that he came, "because I heard about this holy man who could pray for miracles."

A chorus of overlapping cheers and praises erupted from the crowd:
Praise the Lord!
Glory glory!
Amen!
Hallelujah!
To God be the glory!
Holy holy is the Lord Almighty!
Gordon handed the man back the microphone and wasn't sure if he was supposed to just leave the stage or what. He stayed there, to the side, while the man called some other people up by name. He then prayed some more, shouting and stomping his feet. The man ended by raising both arms and shouting, "Receive!"

At this proclamation, women swooned, people fell to the ground, others trembled, and it seemed as though the entire gathered crowd was filled with the spirit. Then everyone cheered. Amidst more shouts of "Praise the Lord," Gordon thought it a good time to make his way off the stage.

On the walk home, he felt lighter than air. He was sure that the man's prayers would work—they had probably *already* worked—and by the time he got home, his mom would be completely cured, back to her old self. It would be just like in the Bible stories where someone comes to Jesus and asks for healing, and Jesus simply says to the person, "Go home. Your faith has made your daughter well." Or "Go. Your son will live." As Gordon walked, he could almost hear Jesus saying to him, specifically, "Go home. Your faith has made your mother well."

This wasn't a Bible story, however, and when Gordon got home, nothing had changed. His mother was still there, bedridden, and weak as she was before. Maybe the miracle just hadn't come yet, he thought. God's timing is sometimes different from our timing, anyway.

Gordon still had this hope, and he *wanted* his faith to make his mother well. After that first time, he went back five days in a row to see the holy pastor, since it was a holiday break at school. He told his mother about it too so she knew where he was, and she didn't discourage him from going. She seemed proud of his faith and of how fervently he believed that she would soon get better. She even seemed a little hopeful herself, or at least, like she *wanted* to be hopeful too.

During those three-hour walks to Kariobangi, Gordon felt like his faith was growing and burning ever brighter inside him. Bits of Bible verses and sermons and sayings he'd heard circled around in his mind as he walked:

This is going to be it. God hears our prayers, and Mom's going to get better. After this is all over, we'll tell of God's unending faithfulness and care for the little sparrow. See how God cares for the lilies of the field, so how much more he cares for us. The first will be last and the last will be first. Let not your heart be troubled. For God came to seek and save what was lost. Take heart, for he has overcome the world.

On one of the days, after all the public prayers and praises, people formed a long line down the center aisle, leading up to the pastor at the stage. Gordon hadn't seen this before and he didn't know what it was for, exactly. Maybe the pastor prayed for you personally once you got up to him, like laid his hands on you, that sort of thing. Gordon wanted to find out, so he got in line.

Mwendo wa ngamia: the way of the camel

When he reached the end of the line right at the stage, the pastor wasn't there but instead it was one of his attendants. This man offered Gordon a little bottle of oil, probably around 2 ounces. Gordon put out his hands to accept the oil, but then the attendant asked for payment. Gordon asked how much (even though he didn't have a single shilling on his person). The price was 1,000 Ksh for the bottle, they told him, the equivalent of $10. Of course, Gordon didn't have that money, and he simply said he couldn't pay. The man told him that in that case, he could wait at the back until the end, and they would see if they had any leftovers. Gordon nodded and walked to the back of the sanctuary. Something about this didn't feel very Christian to him.

He stayed and watched and thought maybe—just maybe—they *would* give him one of those bottles of oil, and maybe it really was some sort of magical, super-concentrated holy oil, blessed by Jesus himself. Soon the line of people came to an end and the men all just walked away. Gordon watched as the holy pastor came back in and said a few words to the men, then left the sanctuary again by a side door. Gordon also turned quickly and walked out the back; he wanted to see where the man was going. The man proceeded straight to a private parking space behind the church and got into a car. Then he left. Just like that. The holy pastor of God left lingering onlookers and poor hopefuls without any blessing or even a goodbye.

The next time Gordon went to the church and saw the people lined up, he did so too, this time just to try to talk to the pastor. When he got up to the front, Gordon asked specifically for the pastor and said he *needed* to speak to him. The attendant went and got him, and Gordon asked if he would be willing to come to Gordon's house to visit his mom in person and pray for her. (Gordon had again heard a rumor that the man had done this for others, and that people had been healed.)

The man said yes. He would come after the service the following day.

Gordon walked the three hours back home again feeling like he was on the cusp of the long-awaited miracle.

But the next day, the man didn't show up for the service.

The following day, Gordon waited in the line, *again,* to speak to the man. Gordon asked him when would be a good time for him to come. (All they needed to do was arrange it, just to iron out the small details, and it could be easy.)

The man answered indirectly by saying, "Just so you know, I don't eat anything when I visit homes."

Gordon was a little confused by this remark, but also relieved in a sense, because he didn't have any food at home to offer. He hadn't considered this before asking the man, but now he felt like this actually worked in his favor.

The man asked, "Where do you get money from?"

Gordon answered, "I work a little job on the weekends since Mom is sick and can't work."

"You don't have other family to contribute?"

"No, it's only the two of us."

The man nodded, and then he suggested, "How about next Sunday?"

Gordon agreed, and he again felt excited, but not quite as excited as he had been before. The questions about food and money were strange.

When Gordon came back on that Sunday, he found the pastor doing the usual service. When Gordon asked him afterward if they could *now* go see his mom, the man said that he was sorry but he needed to reschedule. Maybe they could do it a different day.

Gordon said sure, to be polite, but the man's answer caused Gordon's last shred of patience—which had by now been worn down thinly and stretched far too tightly—to snap.

Gordon felt like yelling right into the man's fake-smiling face, *To hell with you and your prayers! You CABBAGE!*

Probably, in his mind, he would have used an even more choice insult than that too, something like, *You pit latrine with a face like the bottom of a shoe!*

Gordon left that day, certain of two things—the man would never come to pray for his mom, and he would never go back to see the man again.

That final walk back to Kangemi made him feel more frustrated than ever. He had wasted so much time, thrown so much fruitless hope into the wind, spent so much stupid energy thinking that this man was the solution, and believed that this was what God wanted him to do. He began to see it all for what it was, like sun rays dispelling fog that had settled over his memories of those days and over all the things he'd seen there—the testimonies that people gave about healings and miracles were all fake, and no one ever actually got healed there. In fact, now that he really thought about it, the same people with the same sick people were there every day. Every day. Nothing ever changed, and yet the people still came. That expensive oil that they sold for the price of most people's rent was probably just olive oil, the kind that you can buy in big plastic jugs at the supermarket in downtown Nairobi. They probably just repackaged it and sold it to those poor sick people, calling it holy. What a cabbage! The cabbage of all cabbages!

When Gordon got back home, he felt like a lion that had been rained on. His anger had subsided for the most part, and now he just felt disappointed. His mom asked him how it went, and while he didn't want to disappoint her as well, he wanted to be honest. He just said, "I have a strong feeling that the guy is a liar."

"Why?"

He explained all that he had seen that day, his reflections on what had happened the other days, and how he felt, in general, about the whole thing.

She nodded and agreed that he was probably right and told him not to worry. Maybe she knew the whole time, and maybe she even felt the same way. But maybe she let him keep going to see the pastor because she just wanted Gordon to feel hopeful. She just wanted him to have something to believe in.

*

Mary Auma never stopped believing. She never once waivered in her faith in God's goodness and her conviction that everything that happened was ultimately God's will. She was not bitter or angry at God. She spoke with Gordon almost matter-of-factly about what could happen and instructed him to also never give up on his faith. He must always believe in God and believe in himself. She wanted him to keep his drive to succeed in life.

As she lay on the bed, becoming more feeble and frail with the passing of days, she told Gordon, "Don't give up. You must work hard for your dream. I want you to take care of yourself. I will leave you with enough." She pointed to their one suitcase, sitting open and full of clothes on the floor of their room. "That full suitcase there should be enough. That's what you have, and you will have enough."

She constantly repeated to Gordon, "This is the will of God." And she reassured him, "God will take care of you after I'm gone. I want you to work hard. Work, and take what is yours."

In place of any sort of written will, she just had a verbal declaration that she entrusted to Gordon, "When I die, I want to be buried in Langata Cemetery."

Gordon found out later that she had also told this to Fr. Ngugi at the Basilica. She had actually discussed it with him right when she started to get sick. She had the foresight to prepare everything in advance and plan her entire funeral, all in order to not overburden Gordon.

She told Fr. Ngugi the exact same pronouncement, "I want to be buried in Langata Cemetery."

The priest was taken aback and asked, "Mama Mary, *why?*"

Mwendo wa ngamia: the way of the camel

She explained that she didn't want to be a burden to anyone. She understood her situation, and this was the only way.

In Luo culture, it was impossible to be buried in a generic, public cemetery. It was not done. When someone died, they were buried on their family land, at their "ancestral home." No matter where they were when they died, or how, or when, their body was sent *home* for a proper, traditional burial. For a married woman, this meant that she was supposed to be buried on her husband's family's land.

Mary Auma had no husband, and in her mind, no husband's family as well. Therefore, she had no ancestral home to return to, and she was determined to choose *for herself* where she would end up. She told Fr. Ngugi, and she told Gordon.

So that there would be *no* question, she told Gordon, "Do not ask the Okumus for help. Go to the Basilica and tell Fr. Ngugi."

*

While Mary Auma was bedridden, friends came to visit now and again, and a cousin named Omondi came from Mombasa to stay with them. By this time, Gordon's mom had lost her appetite and barely ate anything. When she heard that Omondi was to come, she asked Gordon to go out and buy meat. He took this as a positive sign—maybe this would help her get better—and he excitedly went and bought a bit of meat. She was so weak though that she couldn't chew and could barely manage to swallow. The most she could do was suck the juice from the pieces of meat. That was at least something.

When Omondi was there to look after her, Mary Auma sent Gordon to school like normal. She wanted him to continue being a normal kid, to keep playing soccer and seeing his friends. Above all, she didn't want to burden him.

Gordon was in class one morning, in a sort of study hall or *free lesson* period. He was sitting near the back of the room on the side by a window, and a flickering reflection in the windowpane caught his eye. It was the image of Omondi talking to the teacher in the hallway. He was just visible through the classroom door. Gordon had the instinctive feeling that something was wrong. But he saw that the men were just talking, even laughing once, so maybe it was nothing.

"Okum." The teacher came in the classroom and called for Gordon. This teacher couldn't pronounce the "mu" sound in Okumu. He had Gordon gather his things, and sent him out into the hallway.

Omondi told Gordon that his mom had, "told me to get you." That was the only explanation, and the two of them headed back home.

When they got there, Omondi didn't come inside.

Gordon went in and found his mother still lying on the bed, same as he had left her earlier that morning. She didn't say anything and didn't move. Her eyes were open but rolling and unsettled.

Gordon stood by the bed and held her hand. His mom's hand felt small and cold. His hand was already much larger than hers. He had the feeling that she wanted to talk to him, wanted to say *something*, but she couldn't. He was sure though that she knew he was there by her side.

He thought maybe he was supposed to do something, or that his mom wanted him to do something, or that at least he was supposed to know *what* to do. He didn't know though, so he let go of his mother's hand and went to go ask the next-door neighbor. Gordon only knew her as Mama Elias, meaning the "Mother of Elias," since she was the mom of one of Gordon's friends.

Mama Elias came back to the house with Gordon, and they stood by his mother lying on the bed. He again picked up her hand, trying to absorb what it was she wanted to tell him.

Mama Elias looked at Mary Auma and then said to Gordon in Luo, *Wuoyi matin, Mama dhii*, which meant, "Young man, Mom is going."

She understood what was happening, and as Gordon looked at his

Mwendo wa ngamia: the way of the camel

mom, he understood too. In the space of a single second, right there in front of him, silently and almost imperceptibly, it happened—his mother was gone.

Mama Elias took a towel and used it to close Mary Auma's eyes.

*

Gordon acted immediately. He knew what he had to do and he was, naturally, overcome by that state of total adrenaline-fueled numbness. Mama Elias had told him to clean up the house and put everything in order because, "People will be coming." Even before he did that, he knew that the first thing was to go straight to the Basilica. Thankfully, and maybe even providentially, Fr. Ngugi had just returned to Nairobi from Rome. Gordon found him at the Basilica and told him that his mother had died. Fr. Ngugi then gave Gordon money to hire a truck and driver to pick up his mother's body and take it to the morgue.

When Gordon returned home, somehow everyone already knew, and Gordon's house *was* full of people—family, friends, church members, neighbors. Everyone came to participate in the collective mourning. The visitors held a vigil there every day for an entire week, with much crying, singing, and praying. It was a way to lessen the grief by spreading it around and sharing in it, and maybe it was a way of honoring the life that was gone. Luo culture held that no matter what, you shouldn't be alone after you lose someone. Jackason came over every day too. He was always around, like he had nothing better to do or nothing he would rather do than be there with Gordon, for whatever he needed.

In the meantime, Gordon continued to go to school and church, just as his mom had wanted. She had put her preparations in place, and by the grace of God and the work of people like Fr. Ngugi, it all happened as she wanted. For Gordon, the whole process was seamless; truly it was *easy*. His mom had died on a Tuesday, and by the following Sunday, Fr. Ngugi had organized a committee at the Holy Family Basilica to manage the funeral preparations. He also had the church take a special offering for her during the Sunday services, and the committee used those donations to choose, pay for, and arrange everything. Many people had seen "Mama Mary" working around the Basilica, and when they heard about her passing, they donated generously. In all, it was something around $1,000—an incredible outpouring—that enabled the committee to purchase a *permanent* grave for Mary Auma in Langata Cemetery, which cost around $450. The alternative was a *temporary* grave, which cost only $30. This was basically a euphemistic name for a sort of a mass grave where multiple bodies were placed on top on each other in the same hole. The first would be placed the deepest, at something like 6 feet down, then the next at 4 feet, then 3 feet, and so on until there was no more space. There were no tombstones or markers for these plots, and so another grave would be dug nearby, or possibly even overlapping an existing one. All in all, it was a very commingled and unceremonious way to be laid to rest, and Gordon was relieved that his mother would have her own, private and permanent spot.

At school, Jackason took it upon himself to collect donations from the other kids in their class for Gordon (and even other classes), and he made everyone donate something. He went around from person to person with a little sheet of paper and a pencil to write down the donations. He would hand the other kids the paper and pencil, and if they wrote 5 shillings and handed it back, he would add a 1 in front of their 5, making it 15. He would look up and stare them down, just daring them to say something. If they protested, he'd make the number even higher. In total, he raised something like 500 shillings ($5) for Gordon from the kids and classmates who literally had no money at all.

On the day of the funeral and burial, Gordon picked up his mother's body from the morgue and brought her back home in Kangemi, so family and friends there could pay their last respects. Then, along with all who wanted to come, they drove to the Basilica, since they'd assumed everything had already been planned. To their disappointment, Fr. Ngugi was busy when they arrived and something was already taking place inside the Basilica. So, they waited in the parking lot, with Gordon's mother's wooden casket sitting in the open bed of a truck. It was covered with a translucent white sheet that had flowers embroidered on it. Fr. Ngugi eventually came out and informed them that since Mary Auma hadn't been married in a Catholic Church wedding, the Basilica couldn't hold a funeral mass for her in the church. That was the rule for any woman not married according to the official procedure of the Church.

Fr. Ngugi said, in a measured and matter-of-fact way to Gordon, "I have asked my brother priests, and they have said we cannot have mass."

Ngugi said that instead they could go straight to Langata and he would hold the service there, followed by the burial. So, Gordon and the other people piled back into the trucks they'd come in, with the same driver who had taken Gordon's mom's body to the morgue. They fit as many people as they could in the beds of the trucks. Gordon sat next to his mom's casket, sandwiched amidst a bunch of other people.

At Langata Cemetery, Fr. Ngugi said the funeral mass for all the gathered family, friends, and people from the Kangemi community. He wore tiny dark sunglasses and a stole over his white robes that was red and white striped like a candy cane. Grandma had come from Migori too, wearing a white dress and white head scarf. As they stood there on the dusty orange ground, other funerals were going on that afternoon in the cemetery, and there were a lot of people milling around. The casket was lowered down with rope, and then they passed around a spade. Everyone scooped at least one shovelful of dirt to help fill the grave back in. When it was all covered, they placed a bouquet of flowers on top, and Fr. Ngugi said the final blessings. After the burial, Grandma smiled for the first time since she had heard that her daughter had died, saying to Gordon, "We have laid her to rest according to her wishes." Gordon's body felt heavy, but he also felt relieved. His mother could finally rest. She had her own grave site that was to have a cement covering and even a headstone with her name and photo on it. It would be a beautiful place, and Gordon would bring her flowers. The black pants he'd worn to the funeral now looked brown from all the dust at Langata, and his large white button-up shirt had come half untucked sometime during the day. When the sun started to set at Langata, he knew that the funeral was finally over.

The day wasn't over though because when they got back to Kangemi, there was a large dinner waiting. Some of the neighbors had stayed back to cook while the funeral was going on. They had set up huge sufurias—pots so large that Gordon could have fit inside them—over three-stone fires outside and cooked gigantic mounds of ugali. After dinner, there was still one more thing—it was the *very* last thing Gordon had to do. He had to get his hair cut. He didn't want to since he liked his cornrows, but Grandma had asked him to do it. In the Luo tradition, after any kind of loss you had to cut your hair as a manifestation or outward acknowledgment of the loss. When a woman lost her husband (such an all-encompassing loss), she was supposed to shave her whole head. It was similar to the Luo belief that if you dropped a glass or accidentally broke a plate, it meant that there had been some sort of bad luck lurking around, and the breaking of the glass also wiped away the bad luck.

Therefore, to honor Grandma's wishes and to physically mark the loss of his mother, Gordon went that evening after dinner to get his hair cut. When the actual moment came, he felt that his mom wouldn't actually want him to cut everything. She knew he liked his cornrows, and she wanted him to continue being himself, right? She hadn't wanted her death to burden him. So, he compromised by just getting a little bit trimmed off his forehead right around his hairline. Once the haircut was over, the day was finally done.

*

Weeks later, after playing soccer with his boys as usual at the field in Kangemi, Gordon lay sprawled out on his back on the orange dirt. The reality of what had happened was slowly sinking in, and he'd even begun to lose his enthusiasm for soccer. He didn't feel quite like himself, and as he lay there on the ground, he mostly just felt tired. Really, really tired, like there was a heaviness deep in his bones. He took a loud breath in and exhaled even louder, blowing the air out his open mouth.

Mom is gone. She is not coming back.

He stared up at the sky, and he felt that his mom was up there, that her soul was now keeping watch over him somewhere beyond the clouds. That thought brought him a little comfort, but he still felt like she was far away, while he was left down here, by himself.

III
Mwendo wa kobe: the way of the turtle

Atonga ma yot ema iyombo godo koth.

Translation:
A lighter basket makes it easier to run from the rain.

Paraphrase:
If your burden is light, you can navigate life's struggles with ease.

1. To Luo Land

Gordon had moved through all the hustle and bustle immediately following Mary Auma's death like he was in a dream, where none of the events had seemed truly real. He had only existed in the present, and he hadn't been allowed to think and feel beyond everyone's urgent, pressing needs from moment to moment. But, after it was all done and everyone was gone, he was finally able to stop, feel, and expand into this new reality, to understand what it actually was and what it meant for him. The first stage of this process was that when all his natural anesthesia wore off, the pain set in.

It had always just been Gordon and his mother in Kangemi, but now her absence had taken away that half of everything he knew. He felt out of balance, like a hole had opened up in the center of his life. There was no time when he didn't feel it and no place he could go to escape it. Every time he went home to the house they had shared, he felt the lack of her presence, her singing, her cooking, her smiling. The house was full of that emptiness, like an invisible smoke that Gordon breathed in and exhaled and breathed in again. He only had a single photo of his mom on the wall, and he would look at it and remember how she had been there, just a little while ago. He missed her and wished that she could come back, but then he remembered the futility of this wishing, which would only make him miss her more and feel more foolish for wishing. He went around and around with himself, caught in this self-perpetuating sad cycle of trying to reason his way out of his feelings. Most of all, he just didn't know what to feel or how to deal with it. It was a new and strange reality.

It didn't help that according to Luo tradition, when someone died, it was the responsibility and obligation of the rest of the relatives to take or repossess the deceased's things. Fr. Ngugi, although he was a Kikuyu and not a Luo, knew about this practice and had tried to nip it in the bud back at the funeral so that Gordon would still have the things he needed to live. After the funeral service, Ngugi had made a pronouncement to the group gathered there, asking that they would leave Mary Auma's property "to her child." It was a nice thought and a valiant effort, but unfortunately, one well-meaning statement can't divert an entire culture's worth of ingrained tradition.

After the flow of family members, mourners, well-wishers, and funeral-goers that had been in and out of Gordon's house finally subsided, Gordon realized that there was almost nothing left. They had taken all of Mary Auma's clothes, all the things that belonged to her, all the physical things she'd touched, used, and loved. Only bare-bones essentials had been left behind for Gordon—the single suitcase containing his clothes, the mattress for his bed, and the few things for cooking (the jiko, the sufuria pot, a few plates). As if it wasn't already hard enough to deal with the physical loss of his mother, Gordon had to be reminded in such a tangible way that his life was emptier. It was as if society didn't want him to move on; he wasn't supposed to be able to move on, but instead to sit and stew in the reminder of what he'd lost. He was supposed to feel further impoverished, undeserving of any more than essentials, and now marked by life for this bare-bones existence. The Luo tradition, which probably had ancient, well-meaning roots, just felt cruel. His culture was already punishing him for being an orphan, even if it didn't mean to.

Even though he felt like it in Kangemi, Gordon wasn't truly alone in the world, for he still had Grandma, his mother's mother. Grandpa Gor, his mother's father, had died a few years earlier, but Grandma was still out there, living in western Kenya. In Gordon's mind, she was like one of those great trees that grew in the country that had always been there and would always be there. It was battered at times by wind and rain but large, strong, and firmly rooted to the earth, unaffected by and uninterested in the vicissitudes of city life. Grandma was rooted like that to her life in Migori, keeping her farm and family as she seemingly had for centuries. (Or at least it seemed like that to Gordon. Grandma was the living embodiment of rural life. She was the exemplar in Gordon's mind, and when he thought of Migori, he thought of Grandma.

After the funeral, Grandma had returned home to Migori, and Gordon assumed that was the end of that. He hadn't made any plans for her to visit him or for him to visit her. He figured that he just needed to get on with his life in Kangemi. Then, about a month later, Grandma showed up unexpectedly at Gordon's door. He was surprised, but his initial thought was that she had come for Tero Buru, the Luo tradition of officially releasing the deceased's soul with singing and celebration. The ritual's name meant sending away the dust, and it evoked the way rustled dust dispersed and disappeared into the air like the loved one's soul as it ascended into the afterlife or faded into the beyond (however that happened, exactly). Although Gordon hadn't heard any word of preparations or plans about Tero Buru for Mary Auma, he thought that maybe Grandma wanted to hold her own personal version of the ritual. That seemed like Grandma—even if no one else was going to do it, she would do it herself, in her own time, in her own way.

Grandma didn't say much when she arrived, but Gordon knew she could sometimes be a woman of very few but carefully chosen words. That evening, she and Gordon mostly made small talk—how have you been, how are things. The next day after church, they went to visit Mary Auma's grave in Langata Cemetery. A bouquet of flowers that Gordon had placed there some time earlier had mostly been eaten, probably by stray goats that wandered the cemetery. At the grave site, which had just been covered with smooth dirt and a wooden cross, Grandma said her secret, silent prayers. Gordon figured that she asked for safe passage and blessings for her daughter's soul as it transitioned into the next stage of life. In his mind, this satisfied the Luo tradition of Tero Buru.

When they got back to Kangemi, Grandma said to Gordon, simply, "Wadhii ka NyarLuo," meaning, "We're going to Luo Land." It was a declaration, not a question. Gordon was to go with Grandma to the rural country. Gordon couldn't say no, and even if he wanted to, Luo culture made that sort of disagreement a disrespectful taboo—you couldn't say no to your elders, especially your relatives. You had to go along with it, whether or not you knew what was happening or why. And so, that was it. It had been decided before Gordon had even been given a choice.

Gordon didn't want to leave Nairobi, even temporarily, since he was just beginning to rebuild and restructure his life. It was his life after all and he felt tied to Kangemi, woven into its web of winding streets and iron-sheet structures. Grandma, on the other hand, couldn't wait to get back to Migori. Grandma never liked the city or its people, and she specifically didn't trust its food. In general, she didn't eat food that she hadn't cooked herself or at least hadn't seen cooked, and most of all, she didn't trust meat in Nairobi. She always said that beef in Nairobi was probably wildebeest, and what they called chicken was probably eagle meat. The meat just never looked the right size or shape to Grandma, and it smelled suspiciously different. For some reason that Gordon never exactly knew, she thought it was all counterfeit, second-rate meat hawked by city swindlers, and she suffered none of it. Instead, she'd bring her own food with her—enough sun-dried fish to last the entire duration of her trip, and even enough for the people she stayed with, so no one had to endure the city's fake foods.

When it came time to leave a couple days later, Gordon had the lingering thought that maybe he was just going to visit Grandma for a little while and then come back to his Kangemi life. Perhaps his mindset grew out of a refusal to believe or a simple stubbornness to accept the situation. Either way, he didn't pack much or prepare his few possessions as if he were leaving for good. Instead, he just left everything as it was in his Kangemi shanty, like he was just going out for the day. He took everything that was important to him though—his single duffel bag full of clothes and his backpack full of school materials, since even with a locked door, Kangemi shanties could easily be broken into. If passersby saw that there was a padlock on the door for even a couple of days straight, they'd know that no one was home and that the house was ripe for the picking. Knowing all this, Gordon clicked the padlock shut, and carrying his suitcase and wearing his backpack, he headed to downtown Nairobi with Grandma to catch the bus to Migori.

*

They took the familiar stagecoach bus run by the Kenya Bus Service from Nairobi to Migori. The bus was crowded that morning, so Gordon had to get on first and push his way through the packed mass of passengers to find a seat. He sat quickly, to reserve the seat and act like a placeholder for Grandma, who then got on and made her way to that seat. They switched places and Gordon stood in the aisle, along with multiple other people without seats. Gordon put his backpack down to act as a makeshift cushion and sat down in the aisle. Every time someone needed to get up or get out, everyone in the aisle would have to get up to let them pass. People were constantly moving, so it was a restless, uncomfortable journey. It took an entire, mostly miserable day to reach Migori, going north on the highway from Kangemi then west through the Rift Valley. There were no specific rest stops in the Rift Valley. When someone needed a bathroom break, they'd just yell out to the driver. The bus would pull over and people would get out and disperse themselves into the bush, men to one side and women to the other.

They arrived in Migori town around 3:00 p.m. The humid, heavy air welcomed Gordon back to the untamed, bushy fields and forests of Migori county. The name Migori referred to both a county and a town. Migori county was large enough based on population size to merit eight elected representatives in Parliament, two of those being for the Suna West and Suna East constituencies. Suna West was the poorest, most forgotten area of Migori county. Grandma's land sat in Suna East, near the border with Suna West. The word *suna* in Luo meant mosquito, since those pests were an ever-present nuisance, and Migori called to mind the act of slapping oneself to swat a mosquito. The full name Suna Migori then basically meant "the mosquito makes you slap yourself." The quick slapping sound—*pfap*—was even more pronounced out in the rural country due to everyone's sweating bodies. Moist hands against sticky skin, sweating, slapping, swatting, slapping, and swatting, all intensified the sound. It was like a continual drum beat and its reverberations, bouncing off the hills and around the town, marking the rhythm of life in Migori.

The western edge of Migori county ran into Lake Victoria and the western border of Kenya, as Lake Victoria sat on the intersection of Kenya, Uganda, and Tanzania. The bottom side of Migori county ran along the Kenya-Tanzania border. Compared to Nairobi's concrete landscape and whole neighborhoods of corrugated-iron slums, Migori was lush and natural. The majority of its still-undeveloped space was covered with a carpet of greenery that stretched across rolling hills, open fields, and individual homesteads carved right out of the foliage. There were unpaved dirt roads laden with rocks and bumps that had been worn down simply by the walking weight of many bare feet. There was an occasional creek scattered about, but rivers were rare, and individual, drilled wells were almost nonexistent. Some families had hand-dug wells to collect rainwater, where they threw down a wooden bucket on a rope and pulled up pails of brown, muddy water. Since mosquitoes were ever-present, so was the possibility of getting malaria, and consequently everyone got malaria, repeatedly. Gordon too had contracted malaria many times when he was younger.

Migori town—which was a couple hours' walk from Grandma's

house—had one main street and one central market. People would walk to the market and acquire goods and produce from other townsfolk who sold what they'd harvested that morning from their respective farms. Since everyone carried their goods in hand-woven baskets, it was important to be strategic about how much you bought per market trip. If you got too much, you might regret it when you had to carry your heavy basket all the way back home. It was even worse when it rained, for no one had umbrellas, and no one wanted to get soaked to the bone in a sudden storm. A market trip became a gamble, or more of a mathematical equation to be solved—how much you could carry multiplied by how fast you could run equaled how wet you would get. Of course, common sense taught that the lighter your basket, the faster you could run, and the less wet you'd get. When your burden was light, you could be fast and nimble if you had to run home. Market trips taught the deceptively simple art of knowing what you did and didn't really need.

*

The morning after Gordon and Grandma arrived in Migori, it was time for him to start school. There was no wasting time, no vacation, no relaxation. He was in the final quarter of his eighth-grade year, and he didn't want to fall behind and not be eligible to start high school in the fall. Thinking that the Migori school would be similar to his previous one in Kangemi, Gordon got dressed as he always did. He put on all pieces of the full required uniform, since it was the first day and he wanted to make a good impression—black shoes with knee high socks, the long shorts he'd been wearing for years, a white button-up shirt and a belt, and a v-neck sweatshirt over the top that allowed the collar of his shirt and the top of his tie to show. Above all, he wanted to look smart and not show up like some backwards boy who didn't know how to go to school.

Grandma walked Gordon from her house to St. Peter's Abwao

Primary School, about one mile down the road (primary in this case meant all grades). This was the school his mother had attended until the tenth grade. The school was at the top of a slight hill, and the buildings were set far back from the main road. When you turned off the road and went through the school's gate, you walked up a long driveway that opened onto the assembly grounds. This was a large open, grassy area in front of a small administrative building and a long rectangular building for classrooms on the left side. Off to the right, a little way behind the admin building were the teachers' living quarters. Behind the school, there was a large field and also the teachers' personal farms. All the buildings were plastered and painted a light-yellow color with green trim. Their corrugated iron-sheet roofs were rusting and fading in unequal measure, creating a patchwork effect of silver alternating with rusty oranges and reds.

Gordon and Grandma walked up the long driveway, and crossed through the assembly grounds to reach the admin building. It had a v-shaped roof, with the school's name stuck onto the front in all capital letters in a curve below the roof line. The second A in ABWAO had fallen off, along with the I in PRIMARY. Beneath the name was a small, cartoonish mural, about the size of a large window, which depicted two stick-like, light-skinned boys running a race. The boy in the front was crossing the finish line and breaking red tape that fluttered around him. He extended both his stick arms with fists-for-hands outwards in a gesture of victory, while the boy behind looked angry. Above the boys, a line of text read, "Winners abstain from sex before marriage."

Gordon glanced at this curious mural as he and Grandma walked past it into the administrative building. They went straight to the office of the deputy headteacher (who served as the vice principal). Grandma presented Gordon to the deputy headteacher, saying simply in Luo, "You have a visitor." Gordon thought it was strange that there was no more explanation than that, not even his name or where he had come from or anything.

He later realized that Grandma and the deputy headteacher belonged to the same small group at church (a Small Christian Community), so he assumed that maybe they had discussed all the details of his arrival earlier. Maybe, though, there was just no need for formality or personalized welcome, since he was just supposed to show up, blend in, and become another teachable and obedient body.

Grandma left Gordon in the office, and the deputy headteacher led him to one of the classrooms. The room had a doorway but no door (just a door-shaped opening) and a side window that was even less of a window-shaped opening. The window almost stretched all the way to the floor, as if it had become a sort of makeshift doorway. Gordon learned later that it had at one time been a true window-sized opening, but that at the end of the lessons, out of impatience and maybe also for the fun of it, kids often left the room by just jumping out that opening. Over time, the plaster and mud wall underneath had started to crumble from repeatedly getting scraped by stray feet, pressed down by hands, and battered by book bags.

When Gordon stepped into the classroom through the doorway, all the kids stared at him—and he wasn't imagining it this time. Standing there in his full school uniform, he realized in awkward shock that he was dressed fancier than even the teacher. He suddenly felt like some foreigner who had come to visit to a different country, foolishly and ignorantly expecting that all the people would be dressed the same way he was. He saw that none of the other kids were wearing shoes or socks, and many of them had tattered clothes. Holes and tears abounded willy-nilly, and none of them were patched. Some of the kids were wearing shirts and shorts that looked like they were literally hanging on by a thread, just waiting until the moment they could fall off and unceremoniously revert to being heaps of scraps. Gordon understood in an instant from surveying that room of disheveled kids that there was no dress code and no required uniform here.

At the school back in Kangemi, to accommodate the mixture

of tribes and languages, everything had been taught in English on the middle days of the week—all-English all the time on Tuesdays, Wednesdays, and Thursdays. Mondays and Fridays were the only days the students were allowed to speak Swahili. Regardless of the day, students always had to speak to the teachers in English, and they had to excuse themselves when they made any kind of request from the teachers, even if it was something simple like asking if they could go to the bathroom. Gordon had become accustomed to these simple rules of politeness and respect. Since every tribe had its own customs, it made logical sense that the school had to teach the kids generic, all-purpose, common courtesy.

With this in mind, as Gordon stood in the Abwao classroom, he thought he would make the first move, in order to show that he was knowledgeable and polite. So, he said to the teacher in English, "Excuse me, Sir, where can I sit?"

Little laughs and snickers rippled through the room of students—what was this outlandish formality? Who did this kid think he was? Was he was addressing the Prime Minister of England? Or did he think he was in the presence of His Excellency the President of Kenya?

The teacher replied simply (and rather gruffly, Gordon thought) in Luo, "Over there," as he gestured to an empty wooden desk. There were only a handful of desks in the room, and there was an empty one, even though the majority of the students sat on the floor—on the book bags or on large rocks that they'd carried in from outside. None of these seats were in rows or any apparent organization but were just scattered around the room with varying amounts of space inbetween them. Gordon nodded to the teacher and made his way through wide-eyed stares and turning heads to his seat.

*

After only a few days, Gordon stopped wearing shoes and socks to school because the other kids made fun of him for it. His knew his feet were soft by village standards, but it wasn't his fault that he wasn't accustomed to all the barefoot trips on dirt roads, gravel, and grass. He just wasn't skilled at stepping through bushes onto sticks and rocks and mud like it was no big deal. He didn't want to be the only kid at school who wore shoes though, so he told his feet that they would just have to toughen up and deal with it. He also stopped speaking to everyone in English and resigned himself to speak Luo, all the time. It was strange that everything was taught in Luo because, although it was a Luo community, all the textbooks and materials were printed in English. The national exams at the end of high school would be in English, and yet, the students at Abwao studied all subjects in Luo and through Luo. It wasn't even like there was a certain Luo period or subject. Instead, it was Math in Luo. Science in Luo. English in Luo. Writing in Luo. Everything was Luo, everyone was Luo, everywhere was Luo.

If there was a little English that had to be involved, students usually resorted to translating their Luo into English, literally, word for word, which produced Engluo statements that annoyed Gordon. This lack of linguistic separation seemed almost worse than all Luo and no English—it grated in his ears like nails on a chalkboard. He would hear the other kids and think to himself, *it doesn't have to be like this*. It shouldn't be like this. This English-filtered-through-Luo wouldn't help students succeed. It already put them at a disadvantage for the future in their own country where English and Swahili were the dual national languages, and that was without even thinking of the vast opportunities that necessitated English beyond the borders of Kenya. Despite all of this, Gordon did his best to slowly blend in out of necessity, but he missed the English-Swahili sheng of the slum with its jokes and expressions, code-switching and constant mixing with kids from other tribes. That hybrid language was the flip side of the Eng-luo coin, for it had a purpose and those who spoke it did so only because they knew both languages well enough to play with and manipulate them. It was a byproduct of knowledge and facility instead of weakness.

Although Gordon spoke Luo, his knowledge was different than that of the rural Luo kids, since he and his mom had even spoken English and Swahili to each other often. Luo was the language of his tribe and his ancestors, and he had never before been bothered by the fact that he didn't know perfect textbook Luo. The rural kids, however, knew Luo expressions that Gordon had never heard. They had a fluency in the language, a depth of vocabulary and breadth of knowledge, that he just didn't have. It was both impressive and intimidating. His trilingual capacity in English, Swahili, and Luo had always felt expansive and full of possibilities, like it could take him places and allow him entry into different circles of society. But none of that mattered in Migori. It seemed like no one cared about multilingualism or life outside of the Luo language. Far too quickly, Gordon began to feel self-conscious about his Luo. It seemed feeble and weak. He knew it was only one of his tools, but here he wasn't allowed to use his other ones.

The sudden imposition of this absolute monolingual monoculture made Gordon feel like he had been abandoned in the open ocean, taken out into deep waters so far that all traces of land had faded from his field of vision. Then he had been thrown overboard and left to tread water in the middle of this nowhere that extended endlessly on all sides, even beneath him. He was surrounded only by homogeneity, the blue of the sky and the blue of the water, where each reflected the other in itself and blended together to form one seamless all-surrounding expanse. He was just one tiny, insignificant, dark spot dropped into all that water. All he could do was work to stay afloat, keep his head up, and expend all his energy to go absolutely nowhere.

One of the worst parts of school in Migori was math class, which had always been one of his favorite subjects in Kangemi. He had even been good at it, so why was he all of a sudden so stupid? At Abwao, everything he thought was wrong, and he was always wrong. There was one way to act, to behave, to think, to be, and Gordon just didn't know it. It didn't help that the math teacher was strict, and since there was only one way to do math problems, if you didn't use that process and get the right answer on your first try, you got caned. If you got wrong answers on your homework, caned. If the teacher asked you a question in front of the class and you got it wrong, caned. If he walked by while you were working on a problem and saw you were doing it wrong, caned. Looking out the window, caned. Blinking, caned. Breathing, caned.

That's how Gordon felt anyway. The only way to not get caned was to not be in that teacher's class. Gordon dreaded going because he knew that when he entered the room, that cabbage of a teacher was going to cane him for some reason or another. At first, Gordon felt afraid of that teacher and his unavoidable punishments. This feeling then turned into resentment, which burned inside him every time he set foot in that room. It then became anger, a sort of hot hatred that pulsed through his veins and made his heart pound and his palms sweat. He wanted to learn, not be beaten for what he didn't know before he even had the chance to learn it.

Even more than the fact that everything was taught in Luo and in certain, unchallengeable ways, it bothered Gordon, on principle, that Migori school, at its essence, wasn't school at all. It simply wasn't a place of learning, or rather, the learning part felt nominal at best. Gordon decided it didn't deserve the label *school*, since that was really more of a taunting euphemism. As far as Gordon could tell, it was all just *work* under the guise of teaching and learning. Every day, the kids were put to work, meaning manual labor, which felt like being at a military camp. The rationale behind this was that physical labor was a large part of rural life, so the school felt that it was its duty to teach the students the physical skills they would need in the future—like how to keep a farm, harvest, cut grass, patch walls, and gather firewood.

Even within this reasoning, students weren't taught how to do things as much as just made to do them, over and over, until they learned (supposedly) through the repetitive, exploitative experience. Gordon almost couldn't believe that students weren't encouraged to be innovative thinkers or inventors, or to aspire for anything greater than that rural life. They didn't learn skills and knowledge to develop machines to do the labor for them. There was no learning about technology or thinking of more efficient ways to change processes and traditions. You just learned how to do it and then you did it, the way it had always been done and the way it would always be done. Students didn't learn anything that would help take them out of this place but only what would enable them to stay and make a life there. It was a self-perpetuating cycle that seemed poised to continue forever and ever, world without end.

*

In the realm of Abwao, students were supposed to serve the teachers, not the other way around. A prime example of this was how it was the students' job to park the teachers' bicycles for them when they arrived at school in the morning. No one had cars in Migori, and only some lucky wealthy people had bikes—they were a novelty. Some of the teachers who didn't live by the school had them, and when they rode to school, they'd jump off their bikes at the bottom of the hill since it was a pain to ride up the incline on the unpaved, part gravel, part clumps-of-grass path.

One morning when Gordon was walking to school by himself, he got caught in this situation. He had just crossed the school's gate, when he heard the sound of bike tires crunching gravel on the path and coming up behind him. Instinctively, he moved to the side to give way. The teacher got closer and got off the bike. He walked it up alongside Gordon and looked at him, holding onto the handlebars of the bike and walking beside

Gordon. Gordon assumed that the teacher wanted even more space to pass, so Gordon moved further to the right and stopped walking to let the teacher go by. The teacher looked at him again, expectantly, and Gordon looked back, as if to say, *I've given you more than enough space. What more can you want from me?* Gordon waited for the teacher to pass, and seeming a little frustrated, the teacher proceeded to walk his bike up the hill. Gordon resumed walking up the hill too, not giving a second thought to the teacher and his weird bike behavior. When Gordon reached the top of the hill and walked onto the school grounds, however, he found that the teacher was waiting to cane him for not taking the bike. That caning felt utterly unmerited, and it only served to fan the flames of Gordon's resentment for Abwao and its unfair ways.

As Gordon reluctantly got used to the Abwao routines, he found the schedule of the school day exhausting—class started at 7:00 a.m. He had to wake up early and use only enough water to wash his actual facial features, in a tight oval stretching from eyebrows, just around his temples, down his cheekbones, and around his chin. Since water was scarce and precious, you had to preserve it whenever you could. This meant that there would often be a line of residue on his face, from where he had washed. It didn't matter though because all the kids were unwashed in some way or another. Since Grandma didn't have electricity and there weren't any streetlights, Gordon would often try to get to school early, at 6:45, so he could do his homework there before class started. Finishing homework in the evening was a perpetual struggle, for when darkness came, it came hard, with a blackness that enveloped everything. After sunset, you were done with everything for the night.

In the morning as he was leaving for school, he'd also have to fetch whatever it was that the students were supposed to bring to school that day. There was always something, and it had been announced at the conclusion of the day before. When the bell rang in the late afternoon for the end of the school day, all the students gathered on the assembly ground. The teachers then announced to the students what it was that they needed to carry the following day. If it was ten pieces of firewood, they'd explain how each piece had to be tall enough to reach your waist when one end was touching the ground. For tall teenage boys like Gordon, this was a severe disadvantage. Or maybe the teachers needed grass to patch their roofs, for much of the labor that they put the kids through was maintenance for their own houses, crops, or fields. Alternatively, they might order the kids to each bring a handful of cow dung the next day. Dried cow dung functioned like mortar to patch up holes and cracks in school buildings and walls.

If, on a certain day, Gordon needed to take cow dung to school, he'd gather his things and go to Grandma's cowshed. The cow dung that had already dried was hard and crumbly and might be in pieces, so Gordon would have needed a sack to carry it, which he didn't have. The alternative, then, was just to go for some that was fresh, even still hot and steaming a little bit. He'd grab as much as he could with one hand, and then carry it like that, flat in his upward-facing palm as if it were a slice of bread. It didn't smell terrible since it was mostly made of grass but, of course, it didn't smell good.

When he reached the front gate of the school, someone would be there to direct Gordon along with the other arriving students, where they needed to go to put their cow dung. At least it was collected like this right on arrival. The downside though was that if you didn't have it or didn't bring it, they'd know immediately, and you'd be caned. Everyone expected this, so if you didn't want to bring it or dirty your hand, you could choose not to. Some of the bigger boys who thought they were tough just wouldn't bring the requested items and would be caned and take it like it was no big deal. They'd walk straight up to the gate and be directed over the side and told to kneel down. Gordon didn't want to be caned more than he would be anyway, if he could help it, so he brought the items, whatever they were. On cow dung days, once he'd delivered it, he then had to do something about his dirty hand. Since there was no running water at the school, he'd just find some still-dewy plants to wipe his hand on. If your hand was *visibly* clean, that was the best you could do, and you just went on with your day, touching everything and eating things with that same hand. That's what everybody did.

Before the lunch break, they'd again call all the students to the assembly ground—Gordon came to realize that every bell meant go to the assembly ground. There was always some announcement for something the kids had to do. Every day before lunch, they'd announce that the older kids, grades four–eight, (the younger kids would go home at lunch and be done for the day) had to come back with a working tool in order to perform their afternoon labor. The teachers never said a "work tool" meaning a tool designed for work but specifically a "working tool," as if the tool itself *did* the working or worked in the sense of a machine. Gordon found this little grammatical error slightly ironic—if only he really did have a mechanical tool that would do the work for him. The kids would then disperse and go home for their lunch break, to eat something if there was any food and to gather their working tool for that day—maybe a common garden hoe or a large hoe called a *jembe*, or a shovel, a machete for chopping grass, etc. You'd just grab what you could find and carry it back with you to school. It didn't matter what it was exactly because everything could be put to use. Sometimes, Gordon would get to Grandma's just as she'd finished working in her field or gardens, and he'd borrow the tool that she'd been using. It might still be warm from the grip of her hand on its handle.

When he got back to school, Gordon would take his jembe or whatever tool he brought with him back into the classroom and set it there on the floor next to him or lean it against his desk. All the kids with their hoes or shovels or machetes just sat them there until they were done with their lessons and it was time to return to the assembly ground to receive the work instructions. The teachers called the students forward by grade and assigned them jobs based on the type of tool they brought. As with everything, if you didn't obey and didn't bring a tool, you'd be told to step off to the side, and you'd be caned right there in front of everyone. Those students were *still* assigned a job (just one that didn't require a tool) like picking up and burning trash, or ferrying harvested corn from the field behind the school to the teachers' houses. Sometimes they'd be tasked with plucking the individual kernels from the heads of corn. The other students with their tools were sent to cut grass, weed the fields and farms, harvest the crops, patch the grass roofs, repair cracks in the walls, etc. Sometimes—on rare, exceptional occasions—the work might be light that day and the kids could have around thirty minutes at the end of the day to play soccer. But this was a special and sparse pleasure.

Around 5 p.m., the students were finally finished and could go home. When Gordon got back to Grandma's, however, it was time for more work. He would put his backpack down with one hand and pick up a bucket with the other to go fetch water from the river. Or he'd take dried corn to the miller to have flour made. Or take the cows to the river to drink. Or deliver bottles of milk that Grandma sold to the neighbors. Or…or…there were always, constantly, endlessly, so many things to do. It was a flowing stream of tasks and work and walking that never stopped, and sometimes he let it carry him in the current, his body going through the motions. Finally, once Grandma was done preparing dinner, it was time to eat during the last lingering bit of daylight before dark. After dinner and darkness, it was time for bed. Gordon collapsed every night onto his mat on the kitchen hut floor, feeling like he'd been run ragged at school and at home and hadn't even had time to do his homework. It was too late for that. He'd fall heavily to sleep, in the knowledge that he was just going to wake up the next morning and do it all over again.

Sometimes, Gordon had to get up extra early (around 4 a.m.) to help plow Grandma's field with a some of his cousins and the neighbor's oxen. The boys stood out in the field in the dark, walking alongside the oxen and guiding them with a stick to pull the plow in a straight line. Someone else followed behind, dropping seeds into the little plowed valley of dirt. They walked the length of the entire field around the outside, then turned around and came back, over and over, moving toward the inside each time until they had covered the entire thing. The whole process took about two hours. When they were done, Grandma had porridge made out of cassava and sorghum flour waiting and black tea with milk and *sugar from a distance*, so little that you could barely taste it. Sometimes the sugar was so faint that you couldn't even smell it, and you just had to believe Grandma when she said there was really sugar in there. It was far away, somewhere in the distance, coming from the horizon, traveling all the way from Nairobi and not yet arrived, but coming very slowly. Alternatively, Grandma made *Githeri* (called *Nyoyo* in Luo)—a slightly soupy, stew-type mixture of beans and dried-then-reconstituted corn kernels (the Kenyan version of succotash). It was hearty enough but regarded as a poor-person's food, basic and inexpensive. On mornings like this after the plowing was done, Gordon wiped his muddy feet on the dewy grass, grabbed his school bag and an open mug of githeri, and set off to school with his cousins.

Once, as they were on their way, one of his cousins made a joke about how he'd heard that in the city, kids got to eat China Bread—(or *chai na bread*), sweetened milk tea and clean, fluffy white bread, soft as a cloud—every day for breakfast. Gordon already felt so tired from the morning's work and somewhat bitter that he'd even had to do it, and he was definitely in no mood for comments about what rural kids thought life was like in the city. Just the thought that he had been one of those city kids with their (albeit occasional) china bread stung, as if he had stepped on a thorny bush. He missed that life so much that he mostly tried not to think about it. He wanted it back. It wasn't just the comfort or the relative luxury of city life that he missed either. More than anything, he wanted to regain the sense of possibility and purpose. Every day in the rural life was disappointment for him. He felt aimless and wasted.

"What do you think about that? What a life. Must be nice though?" His cousin prodded.

"Don't talk to me." Gordon snapped back.

*

Aside from the initial culture shock of school, there were other inconveniences and adjustments that Gordon hadn't even thought about, like how his immune system wasn't as robust as that of the locals. In the early days, he had an almost constant stomachache from the different foods and who-knows-what that circulated in the water fetched from rivers where people bathed and took their animals to drink. He didn't catch any serious diseases—thank goodness—and Grandma also knew how to administer all the natural cures, especially the *mwarubaini* plant. *Arubaini* was the Swahili word for the number forty (and the *mw-* prefix made it plural). Rumor had it that this plant could cure over forty ailments. Grandma would have Gordon chew the leaves, which were almost unbearably bitter, and then swallow the juice. She also boiled the bark and made it into a sort of tea, which was also almost too bitter to drink, but the bitterness somehow worked its pure, medicinal magic. It cleaned out everything and Gordon's aches would go away.

If Gordon didn't learn much actual knowledge at school, he did still learn the basic principles of how to navigate rural life, like how to recognize which plants had the good, soft leaves for grabbing when going to Grandma's pit latrine. You had to be careful *not* to grab the rough leaves that felt like sandpaper, or even worse, the ones that were sort of invisibly spiky, which would feel like scraping cactus thorns across your delicate bottom. Although he never really got used to the night runners, he did learn to tolerate them. Maybe it was just that Gordon's rural life was a constant state of exhaustion, so he found a way to sleep through the night runners' noise. There was also the ever-present possibility of being bewitched in the rural country, and Gordon learned (even more than he had already known) how to avoid this.

Witchcraft existed and happened in Nairobi, just as it happened everywhere in all dark corners of Kenya, but witch doctors were more visible and their deeds more pronounced in the rural areas. Perhaps this was yet another symptom of the extreme poverty there, and perhaps it was an unintended side effect of the rural country's monoculture. Nairobi, like any big city, was full of lights—both figuratively and literally—shining at all times, in all places, at varying degrees of brightness and dimness. When Gordon thought back to his life in Kangemi, he remembered the streetlights and the single bulb in his house—he himself had possessed electricity! Even more than these literal sources of light though, he felt like Nairobi was a place of illumination, lit by the many stars of innovation, invention, and technology. You could have bright ideas in Nairobi, and you could dream big dreams. You assumed that everyone around you also had dreams, and that you would work to achieve them, each fueled by their own internal fire.

Maybe Gordon had only been one small candle shining among thousands of others in the bright, bustling metropolis of Nairobi, but when he came to live in the rural country, he suddenly felt exposed—like he was the only candle burning in a pitch-black night. In Nairobi, everyone's light mixed and mingled and no one gave it too much thought, but in Migori, where it seemed both figuratively and literally darker, he felt conspicuous in a way he never had before. For when you're the only candle shining in the midst of a people who walk in darkness, they might not admire your light. They might not appreciate how it illuminates all that they've hidden in the shadows. They might become suspicious and jealous, and worst of all, seek to snuff you out.

The most common thing witch doctors did was to take away

someone's success. This happened not in some grand gesture of robbing you of actual opportunities or stealing physical possessions, but in a far more subtle way that led you to orchestrate your own downfall. The witch doctors would first get a hold of some physical object that you'd touched—like a piece of paper money or a coin that had crossed your hand—and then little by little, imperceptibly and untraceably, you'd become frivolous with your spending. You wouldn't even realize it, but the money you earned disappeared in unpredictable ways. It just slipped through your fingers like water, and soon, even if you still had your job and your same income, you didn't have money to buy food or send your kids to school. You weren't able to understand or plan, and some confusion or fog blocked your decisions and clouded your reasoning. Witch doctors ruined others like this by poisoning their minds.

Gordon knew to be careful whenever he had to pay for something in the rural country with paper money. He couldn't risk passing along something he'd touched to someone who wanted to harm him. Grandma spoke about this to the kids too and taught them to never drink anything from a bottle that they hadn't seen opened in front of them. If Gordon watched the bottle being opened, he also needed to hear that sound—the little *pfffsssss* of compressed air escaping from the bottle. If he didn't hear it, he couldn't be sure that the bottle hadn't already been opened and tampered with. If someone placed a bottle in front of you that fell over and spilled of its own accord, it was probably because it had been cursed, and some guardian angel or good spirit was warning you not to drink it.

Despite all this unseen danger in the rural country, life is full of irony, and although Gordon was a vulnerable outsider, he didn't have to worry too much about getting bewitched or being the target of black magic. That was at least a little backhanded gift life had given him. For he was already cursed beyond what the average witch doctor could do. Since he was now an orphan—not just half an orphan but a total orphan since he had lost both his parents—witchcraft would have been wasted on him. What possessions or success did he have that others would want? For what can you take from someone who has already lost everything?

2. Grandpa

By this time, Grandpa had passed away from some undiagnosed and untreated sickness, as was common occurrence in the rural country. What this meant was that he had fallen sick and hadn't gone to the hospital for reasons largely financial but also cultural, since it was common for people to treat themselves at home naturally. The end result, simply, was that Grandpa didn't recover, and since he was fairly old at that time, people said it must have been God's will to call him away. There had even been an owl that had perched itself in one of Grandma's jacaranda trees near the main house and wouldn't leave for something like an entire week (so the story goes). This was an undeniable omen in Luo culture, as owls were seen as the harbingers of death. The undetermined cause of Grandpa's death had been the final piece in a series of unknown and unexplainable aspects in his life. When he died, he left Grandma behind as his only widow. This was the first of two ways that he had flouted Luo culture. He had chosen to marry only one wife, or to not become a polygamous man as was common custom. Luo men bore that title proudly, always introducing themselves as, "My name is So-and-So, and I am a polygamous man."

In Luo culture, polygamy was encouraged and even desired by both men and women alike. If you had many wives, you could have many children and be prosperous. Especially for women, being married was advantageous since women needed a husband to provide them with a place to live, food to eat, and most important, an ancestral home to be buried in when they died. Besides all of that, having children and running a household was women's all-encompassing domestic duty. Often parents purposefully presented their daughters to eligible bachelors or to already married men (to try to convince them to take additional wives). Even the already married wives sometimes brought their sisters to their own husbands and tried to get them married, because then at least they would know their sisters were taken care of, and their own children would be partly parented by someone they knew (not by other second and third and fourth wives who were strangers to them).

There was even a Luo proverb, *Jadhako achiel nyawang'e otho*, meaning, "A man with one wife has a bad eye." More bluntly put, Luo common sense said that there was no good reason why a man would only want one wife. Could he not see that there were other women, right in front of him, offering themselves to him, waiting for him to take them? In spite of all this, Gordon's grandfather, Raphael Gor Onyango, only wanted one wife. Gordon never learned the reason why and no one ever spoke of it, which maybe means that it was only ever known to the man himself. Secondly, and again for reasons unknown, Grandpa Gor wanted a church wedding instead of a Luo traditional ceremony. Although he was a devout Catholic and prayed the rosary three times a day, it was extremely rare, even unheard of, for a Luo to have a Catholic-style wedding. But Grandpa did. He and Grandma were married in St. Joseph Catholic Church in Migori town. An Italian missionary performed the ceremony, and Grandma even wore a white dress.

Grandpa was a large, tall, no-nonsense man. His no meant no, and his yes was yes. Grandma and Grandpa had lived together in their two-room (one bedroom and one living room), grass-thatched roof house that Grandpa had built with his own hands, and their bedroom had two separate beds. If kids ventured back there for any reason, even if they were with Grandma, they could never sit on Grandpa's bed. They could sometimes be allowed to sit on Grandma's bed and touch her things, but not Grandpa's. No one sat in his chair in the living room either. Although Grandma might sit in it when Grandpa was gone, but even that was rare. Kids never sat in it. Instead they would sit on the floor around the empty chair.

When it was time for dinner, Grandma cooked in the separate kitchen hut, along with all the kids and grandkids and other women. Grandpa waited in the main house, sitting in his chair, listening to a small radio he held in his hand. If his sons were visiting, they could sit in the living room with Grandpa. When the food was ready, it was a production that took something like four kids to carry everything over to Grandpa. There was a basin of water for him to wash his hands in, a towel, a plate of ugali and food, and a glass of water. You could always tell which plate was for Grandpa because it had the nicest looking, perfectly cut semicircle piece of ugali. For everyone else, the ugali was just left in a mound and you could pull a piece out or pinch off as much as you wanted. This meant that there were many fingers touching and grabbing at the same ugali. Grandpa's ugali, however, was always a clean piece that had been carefully cut and placed on his plate. After the kids had taken him the food in the main house, they'd leave and come back to the kitchen. Later, they returned to retrieve his plates and any leftover food—they ate his leftovers, if there were any, before they even got back to the kitchen hut.

Even Grandpa's middle name broke with Luo custom (although this was the choice of his parents) for *Gor* didn't describe what was happening when he was born and didn't start with an O. Instead, Grandpa was proud that he had been named after the ancient Luo ancestor Gor Mahia (not to be confused with the contemporary and very successful Luo national football team, named after the same historical figure). Grandpa made sure to tell all his children and grandchildren the story of the great Gor Mahia. Gordon had heard the story many times when he and his mom had visited Migori when he was younger, and although he didn't know exactly what was truth and what was legend, he believed that Gor Mahia had been a true hero of the Luo people. Gor Mahia too had been different in many ways.

Gor Mahia was born in the late eighteenth century near the shores of Lake Victoria. His original name was Gor Obunga, and although his mother was one of multiple wives to a polygamous man, Gor was her only son. She died when Gor was still a small child, younger than five years old. One day, Gor's grandfather, named Ogalo, gathered all his grandchildren to bless them as was custom, since he could feel he was nearing the end of his life. Stories differ on the exact nature of this blessing, but they agree that after this experience, Gor began to develop magical powers.

It is said that he became supernaturally skilled with herbal cures and natural remedies, more than all of his tribes' healers. He then developed powers of prophecy and—some legends say—transfiguration, meaning he could shapeshift into the form of animals and other people. He used these abilities to walk amongst his enemies, unseen, and to help secure victory for his clan in various battles and struggles. Gor's most famous vision was that of a voracious horde of white butterflies (sometimes described as bees) who were as numerous as locusts and possessed sticks that spit fire. Gor warned his tribe's warriors about this formidable foe and cautioned them not to attempt to fight, for if they did, they would lose. The combination of all his unexplainable powers earned him the Luo nickname, *Mahia*, meaning mysterious or magical.

In a slightly less-mystical description of this man that still paints him as a hero of the Luo people, it is said that Gor became the ruler of his people and led them with characteristic foresight and wisdom through the tricky transitional period between old ways and new colonial occupation. Although Gor was Chief when the British colonizers came to Kenya, he refused to fully adopt their ways. Instead, he maintained the essence of the Luo cultural traditions, and perhaps most mystifying of all, he achieved a paradoxical and unique relationship with the white man that was neither one of complete subservience nor resistance. It is said that the colonizers respected Gor and recognized his wisdom. They too called him a wizard because they couldn't fully understand or explain his ways.

Gor understood that a political dilemma was encroaching on Kenya, and he cautioned that any leader who destroyed the past, consumed the present, and foreclosed the future should beware. In Gor's interpretation, that type of politics was just another name for destruction. He also spoke to his own people and sympathized with their suffering. They believed that their problems could not be solved, so the only option, or only possible way for relief, was to transfer their problems to others. This theory of eliminating problems was just another name for multiplying them. Gor instead taught his people to search for a solution to their suffering, one which sprang internally from their own strength, or to proceed first from what they could do for themselves instead of grasping after what others could or couldn't do for them. Through his personal and political philosophy, Gor sought to be both a model and a guide for his people. He was, perhaps, the first Luo man of the people.

Grandpa, like Gor before him, and like Gordon after him, had been the only child of his mother. Grandpa had been a successful and wealthy man in the Luo community, with many children and land and animals, and yet he did things his own way. Like Gor, there had been an air of mystery to him, for his ways were his own and his thoughts were impenetrable. Maybe in another mysterious way, some of Gor's wisdom and courage had been passed down through the ages to Grandpa, his namesake. The two men drew a straight line between them that cut through the scatterplot of their Luo lineage. Perhaps, this line extended all the way to Gordon and was still in the process of being drawn.

3. Grandma

Gordon's Grandma, named Selmina, had given birth to twelve children and had already outlived nearly half of them. She didn't know how to read or write and only spoke Luo. She was thin, basically just skin and bones, but strong from a life of working in her fields, raising children, and eating an entirely natural diet. She had dark brown, waxy skin with deep set wrinkles that looked like lines carved into clay. Her eyes and lips were both almost the same shade of brown as her skin. Most of the time, she squinted for one reason or another, and her eyes became little black almond-shaped pits of shadow. She had a disapproving way of scrunching up her face, puckering her lips, tilting her head to the side, and staring at you. If she didn't agree with you, she made you know it.

In the past, mostly during the 1990s, Grandma had engaged in the practice of making illegal, home-brewed, and incredibly potent hard liquor, called *chang'aa*. She only made it a couple of times while Gordon was staying with her as a fourteen-year-old, but he knew all about what went on. Grandpa had been totally against it back when he was alive. He didn't even drink alcohol but, for some reason, he didn't stop Grandma from making it. Grandma said that she did it to take care of her kids, to have money to send them to school and buy necessities like cooking oil. When chang'aa was done distilling, it ran clear like water, and part of the reason it was so dangerous was because it looked *clean*. It was probably closer to something like gasoline. Rumor had it that you *could* run a car with this stuff, and that if you cut a small piece of meat and dropped it into a bowl of chang'aa, the meat would cook. In light of this description—true or not—one can imagine how this liquid burned through the insides of people who drank it. Because it was so strong, people had to drink it in tiny, minuscule quantities, as fast as they could—shot style—since it was not about the taste but the effect. It was highly addictive, and since it was so quick and easy, once you had it, you knew that nothing else would ever be as strong as that little sip. That first shot of chang'aa would forever after put all other liquor to shame. Chang'aa gave you instant inebriation within seconds. It was liquid magic.

Grandma would sell her chang'aa in tiny portions, specifically in the metal caps from bottles of Treetop apple juice, at 20 shillings per bottle top. Chang'aa was of course not sold in stores, so people had to know where to go. Grandma would only sell it to friends and friends of friends, or other people she knew. Chang'aa drinkers always went to drink it at someone's house, and it had to be someone you knew because once you drank the chang'aa, most likely, you'd pass out, and then wake up eventually and stagger home. That was the process—you drink, you're drunk, you fall down, you sleep, you get up, you go to work or you go home (depending on the time of day). Then you repeat. Sometimes Grandma would let people bring their own bottles and take it away but, more often, she'd just let people just sleep outside on the grass in front of her house. Sometimes she would have to send them away, or get their wives or friends to come drag them home. If it got to that point, the chang'aa drinker was essentially a useless, deadweight of a human being.

Chang'aa had a specific smell, and all the kids and grandkids knew when Grandma was making it. She would set up her workshop far out on her property, in an area where she had planted banana trees for some cover, and near a small pond that she could draw water from to cool the tubes during the distillation process. The kids knew what she did when she was out there (it was like her office and she was at work), so they didn't bother her. Once the distillation process was started, it couldn't be interrupted or stopped. Grandma would put one lump of *sukari inguru* or jaggery (the natural, concentrated cane sugar) into her vat of millet flour and water. She'd then cover it and let it sit for about a week to ferment. One time, when Gordon was younger, together with a few other kids, they went and scooped out the jaggery. They divided it amongst themselves and ate it. After a while, they all became a little tipsy and Grandma knew what they'd done just by looking at them.

Once she'd distilled the liquor, Grandma poured it into 5-liter jerry cans, seal them tightly, and bury them in the ground, only about 1 foot down. She planted leafy green-onion plants over the top of the plot, so that the onion smell counteracted and covered the chang'aa smell. Burying the chang'aa served both the purposes of keeping it hidden and secret and letting it further ferment. Gordon could always tell where the chang'aa was buried because the plot had no weeds growing there. The plants always looked clean and well-watered. Even if someone was found out, chang'aa brewing wasn't the type of crime that sent you to jail in Migori. If the police discovered it, they might just demand a bribe for their silence, then take your money and be done. Or, on the other hand, the offending bootlegger bribed the police with their chang'aa itself, offered it to the police for free, and then the cycle continued.

Chang'aa was not a phenomenon limited only to the rural areas, and it certainly circulated in bigger cities like Nairobi. People smuggled it in because people always find a way. People probably made chang'aa in the cities too, since deep in the slums like Kibera anything was possible. Chang'aa was however still more of a practice in the rural communities. Maybe it was because there was just less to do out there; maybe the poverty seemed more oppressive and weighed more heavily; or maybe it was a self-perpetuating cycle where chang'aa was more accessible, so people drank it, so more people made more, and more people drank more.

It was widely thought that chang'aa producers mixed other things into their concoction to make it *even* more potent, lacing their homebrews with various poisons like engine oil, embalming fluid, or battery acid scrounged from garbage dumps. Supposedly these compounds could speed up the fermentation process, but it goes without saying they could also cause serious side effects. Grandma never added strange things, as her homebrew was completely natural and took as long as it needed to. She had all the time in the world to make it the right way, at least. Because of the various things that this liquor might contain, popular connotation stated that the name chang'aa meant "kill me quickly," which is what the drink definitely could do. Gordon always thought that chang'aa was the sound the drinkers made when they couldn't stand up straight anymore. The *nyaaaa* part sounded to him like the gargling moan that came from the chang'aa drunkard's gaping mouth with its telling, burnt bottom lip.

*

While Grandma's chang'aa production was occasional and eventually no longer necessary, her devotion to her faith and to the practices of the Catholic Church was unwavering and unquestionably necessary. She was as sure of God's goodness and provision as she was about the ground beneath her feet. Grandma believed in the power of prayer, and she would wake up every morning around 6 a.m. to pray for the whole world. This was not an exaggeration, as she would pray for an entire hour, using a version of a Catholic prayer that she must have heard and memorized at some point in life. It included all possible groups of people and scenarios in a list that had the rhythm and structure of a litany:

For those on a journey, that they would arrive safely.
For those without jobs, that they would find work.
For those who are hungry, that they would have food.
For those who harvest, that they would have plenty.
For those who govern, that they would lead wisely.
For those who are sick, that they would be cured.
For those who are tired, that they would have strength.
For those who are lost, that they would find their way.
For those who are suffering, that they would find relief.
For those in war, that they would have peace.

For those who mourn, that they would be comforted.
For those who have died, that they would have rest.
For those in Purgatory, that they would reach Heaven.
For those who have left the Catholic Church, that they would return.

And on and on and on, until there were no more people in need and no one left out.

This prayer, like all the ones Grandma knew by heart, had been translated into the Luo language at some point (probably from English). During that process, certain aspects had been altered in translation. Gordon later heard a different version of Grandma's morning prayer that didn't have the second piece for all the supplications. Instead, it just included the list of all the people, "For those on a journey, for those without jobs, for those who are sick..." That made sense, Gordon thought, since it wasn't our job to suggest to God *how* to help the various different types of people in need. We didn't really know what the right or proper solution was for them anyway. We only knew that they needed God's help, and the best we could do was bring that to God's attention.

There was no written prayerbook in the Luo language and, as far as Gordon understood, all the prayers that were currently spoken around in Migori were thanks to a mzungu priest (a white man) who had originally come from Italy and lived in Luo land as a missionary in the mid-twentieth century. He'd learned Luo as a foreign language. The locals referred to him simply as Father Oliech, meaning "Elephant," as a term of endearment since he was a large man. He was the one who translated the Catholic prayers into the local language, and while this was a magnanimous service, the limits of his linguistic knowledge left little traces here and there—nothing serious, no theological or doctrinal changes—but more like little cut corners and editorial adjustments. Gordon assumed that this was the reason the prayers Grandma said were slightly different from those he'd heard and learned at church in Kangemi.

A notable example of this was when Grandma would say grace before meals. Instead of the standard lines Gordon expected, *Bless us O Lord and these thy gifts we are about to receive...*, Grandma said, "Bless me O Lord and these thy gifts I am about to receive." Even when she was in a group and clearly including the entire gathering in her prayer, Grandma would always pray in the first-person, as if only for herself. At first this felt strange to Gordon, like a wrong piano key played in the middle of songs he knew so well, but he soon realized it was not just her. This was the way everyone around had learned to say the prayers, so Gordon dismissed the seeming egocentric undertone. When they were asking for God's blessing only for *me* instead of us, they were actually asking for *us*, just under the label of *me*.

Grandma also believed in the high calling of priests, as God's holy ministers, and she regarded them almost like saints. They were the most respected men in the community. Even if the priests were still young men, they were revered and respected more than the wisest of elders. Priests were shown a level of respect and honor that Gordon admired and hadn't seen anywhere else in society. Unfortunately, since Grandma's house was outside of Migori town, her area had no dedicated priest. For usual Sunday services, the catechist teacher would lead mass without communion. Once a month, however, a priest would come from Migori town for the Sacrament of Reconciliation and to serve Communion during the service. To receive any sort of blessing from this visiting priest, you had to show proof of your continued participation (meaning financial contribution) to the Church. This meant that you had to bring your tithe card, which was like a coffee shop punch card with stamps to mark your donations. If you wanted to ask the priest for anything, first you had to present your card.

The morning of the priest's visit, there would be long lines outside of the church since everyone had lined up to receive the priest's prayers and blessings. People brought water to be blessed too, in as many bottles and jars and jugs as they wanted to carry (the container didn't really matter, as long as you provided the water to be blessed). Grandma always took at least one bottle of water, and afterward she treated that full bottle like a holy relic—she used it very rarely and treasured it, as if its very presence radiated holiness. She brought out the bottle during prayers and set in on the table in the middle of a small group gathering, as if just being in the presence of something blessed by the priest was a continual source of blessing to those around it. When any of the kids were sick, she'd sprinkle some of the holy water on them.

Grandma never cut corners with her tithing to the Church, telling Gordon, "It is our responsibility to help our priest." She, like everyone around, didn't regard their giving as going to the Church, broadly, but as specifically going to help the priest, that most holy man who labored to bring God's blessings down to these lowly people. During the church service, there was a normal appointed time in the mass for the Offertory. This was standard in all Catholic services, but as Gordon experienced, Offertory in the rural community could become the longest part of the service. People took the idea of *offering* literally. You had to physically bring something to give to the priest at the altar. People brought whatever they had from their farms and harvests, as long as it was some thing or object they could carry; it couldn't be money. Flat, paper bills of money seemed like too little, like nothing even. If you wanted to just give money, you were better off using that money to buy something and bring that something in a basket, like a substantial bag of flour or cornmeal.

While the Offertory singing and music went on, everyone grabbed their things and organized themselves in front of the altar in one long line that stretched out the entrance of the sanctuary. People carried their fifty-pound bags of corn to the altar, where the priest blessed them and thanked them, then passed their gift to one of the altar servers, who placed it in a pile underneath the altar table. Next came someone with a basket full of plantains, a bundle of sugarcane tied around the middle, a bag of onions, or tomatoes. Everyone had to bring something, even little children, so parents gave them a single tomato to carry up to the altar and hold out to the priest. People even brought live chickens, goats, or cows. They'd lead their cows beside them down the aisle up to the altar or carry chickens with their wings tied and their feet tied together. When the altar server accepted the chicken and placed it with the rest of the gifts under the altar, the chicken just lay there throughout the whole rest of the service, quietly and calmly. Somehow, the offered animals were always respectful and decent, as if they knew that they were in a temple of the Lord. It was like they understood that being offered to a holy man in the name of God might actually be the highest calling a rural animal could hope for in life.

*

On Sundays, whether or not the priest was in town, Grandma would take her multitude of grandchildren to church. She always wore white on the Sabbath Day, and she didn't do any physical labor except preparing meals. She dressed all the children in white too, each with a shirt and shorts that she somehow managed to keep white. She made sure all their church clothes were ironed, and she used her charcoal-powered iron to make one crisp crease down the front of all the shorts. When they returned home after the service, the first thing was to change immediately out of the white church clothes. Grandma soaked them in water and let them sun dry, then folded and put them away until next week. No one wore those clothes except to go to church. During and after lunch, Grandma taught the kids parts of the catechism or how to recite tenets of the faith, like "I believe in God the Father…I believe in God the Son."

Sometimes on Sundays, she told Bible stories or had the kids read out loud from the Luo-language Bible. Even though she couldn't read, she had one copy of an illustrated children's Bible with drawings and depictions of the most memorable stories like Adam and Eve in the Garden of Eden, Noah's Ark, and Jesus walking on water. One time she asked Gordon to read, and the passage was the Old Testament text about Cain and Abel, the first and second sons of Adam and Eve. Gordon read how Cain killed his brother out of jealously and was punished by God. Gordon turned the book around to show the pictures to the other kids and to Grandma.

"Oh yeah, he looks really mean." Grandma said matter-of-factly.

Gordon didn't say anything, out of respect, but he laughed a little on the inside. Did Grandma not know that it was just a drawing, someone's idea of what Cain looked like? Did it really matter though?

One day, Gordon told Grandma what he thought was a catchy saying he'd heard from some other kids at Abwao. It was one of those mnemonics meant to help kids remember the order of the planets in our solar system. As these sorts of things often are, it was a nonsensical statement where the first letter of every word (in Luo) corresponded to the first letter of the planet names in English. It went like this:

Much Veronica En Much Jachien. Susana Unu Nee Polo.

Loosely translated in English:

The breath of Veronica is the breath of Satan. Susanna you'll see heaven!

When Gordon said this to Grandma in Luo, she was absolutely scandalized.

"Eh-eee! You can't say the breath of Veronica is the breath of Satan! How?"

"Grandma, it's just a funny saying. It doesn't actually mean anything."

"Veronica's breath can't be the breath of Satan," she continued, like she hadn't heard him. "How could the holy Veronica be like Satan? Oh! OH! When Veronica assisted our Lord as he carried the cross. She wiped the most holy face of our Lord Jesus Christ with her veil."

"Yeah, I know but—"

"Veronica was with the Lord, not with Satan."

"Yes, but—"

"Veronica is in heaven. Why would you say that Susanna is in heaven but not Saint Veronica as well?" She squinted and puckered her lips a little.

"Agohdee, why would you say that?"

"It's just a saying. It's not serious."

"Veronica and Satan, pffffhhhh! What a thing!" Grandma shook her head, touched the small crucifix hanging around her neck, and then made the sign of the cross over Gordon.

*

Grandma would tell all sorts of stories, not just ones from the Bible, at opportune moments when she needed to make a point, teach a lesson, or just entertain the grandchildren. The stories always had morals to teach, like the tale of *Oyundi* the lazy little bird. In the story, every time Oyundi's mother called to him, asking him to do something, Oyundi replied with a reason why he couldn't do it.

Oyundi, please go fetch firewood.

But—my leg hurts.

Oyundi, please go get water.

But—my arm is sore.

Oyundi, please go gather the chickens.

But—I'm SICK.

When Oyundi's mother told him it was time to come eat, he didn't say anything and immediately came running. The story didn't even state this but just included the sound of his little scurrying feet:

Oyundi, please come eat.

SESESESESE!

Grandma would invoke the case of Oyundi any time one of the kids didn't want to work or did so begrudgingly and lethargically. "You are Oyundi on this day," she'd tell them, because just as Oyundi's sickness was fake, so their excuses were fake. Even more, if one of the kids wore a pair of shorts that had worn holes in the underside where back pockets would be, Grandma assumed this was because of too much sitting—they'd sat so much that they'd worn through their shorts and sitting meant not working. The holes were the visible proof of too much idleness and not enough working, so Grandma would say, "Oyundi had built his nest on your bottom." None of the kids wanted to be Oyundi, and it was an embarrassment to have an "Oyundi bottom."

She also told the story of the donkey who thought it could outsmart its master. This tale began with a man who owned a donkey (as everyone did) and used it to carry water gathered from the river or whatever else the man needed. The man's main business was selling salt at the market, so he would fill up two bags of salt and put them over the back of the donkey, with one bag hanging on each side. Since he lived quite a distance from the market, the journey there was long, and the donkey tired from the weight of the heavy bags. At a certain point on the way to the market, the man and the donkey reached a river that didn't have a bridge. They had to wade through the water to cross the river, but the first time the donkey walked into the cool wetness, he let himself collapse with relief and rest for minute. While he was resting in the water, the salt in the two bags (which were now immersed in the river) started to dissolve. When the donkey stood up to continue the journey, half of the salt was gone and his burden was much lighter. It was a welcome surprise, and he finished the rest of the journey easily and quickly.

When this happened the first time, the donkey's owner thought it was just a fluke accident. But the next time they walked to the market, the donkey again sank into the water and let half of the salt dissolve. By the third time, it became a routine and the donkey thought he had figured out a way to lighten his load every time—he would never have to carry such heavy bags again! The owner realized this, however, and he was also getting frustrated about repeatedly losing his profits at the market. So, the next time he and his donkey left for the market, the owner filled the bags with dirt, not salt. The donkey didn't realize this, so when they reached the river, he collapsed into the water as usual and waited for the salt to dissolve. Since it was dirt though, it didn't dissolve but actually absorbed the water. The donkey stood up and realized—to his dismay—that the bags were heavier than before, so heavy that he felt like his back was breaking. He could barely stand up under the weight. The owner helped the donkey out of the river and made him walk the rest of the way to the market with the heavy bags weighing him down. The donkey labored as he never had before, one miserable step after another, as he struggled to reach the market.

When it came time to go to the market again, the memory of the terrible journey with the heavy weight was still fresh for the donkey, and he was so afraid that his burden would multiply like last time that he tried as hard as he could not to let the bags sink into the river. He crossed through the water as quickly as he could without resting, and he never again let the salt dissolve. When Grandma finished telling this story, she made that face as she stared down the grandchildren, as if to drive her point home—*If you think you will make your work lighter through trickery and cunning, it won't work. You can't outsmart Grandma, and if you try, it will only be worse for you.*

"Agohdee," she looked at Gordon, "Do you understand?"

"Yes."

"Don't be like the lazy donkey."

"I won't."

"You understand?"

"*Yeeeesss*, I understand."

*

Grandma always told stories during dinner while the kids ate. There was no electricity, no TV, no radio, no nothing, so Grandma was their sole source of entertainment while finishing their food. Sometimes she told stories that the kids had already heard many times and knew by heart. They still listened and whispered to each other with their mouths half full of ugali and kale. "Oh oh this is the part…" "And then it goes this way…" "That's coming next…"

One evening, as she and the grandkids sat in the kitchen hut around a big ugali and a main dish of dandelion greens cooked in milk, she told them the story of "Nyamgondho Wuod Ombare" (Nyamgondho Son of Ombare), which was a well-known piece of Luo oral mythology. There was still enough light outside for everyone to finish their dinner and enjoy the story before darkness fell. Grandma was strict about finishing dinner before it was dark because you simply couldn't eat in the darkness. She always said that in the dark, "The devil is on the other side of the plate."

Amidst the low background noise of children chewing, Grandma began. "Once there was a man named Nyamgondho Wuod Ombare, who was very poor and lived by the shores of Lake Victoria."

"Why was he very poor?" one of the kids asked.

"Let me continue and I'll tell you." Grandma replied. "He was very poor but made a living as a fisherman—"

"If he was a fisherman, he shouldn't have been poor," another interjected.

"He was a fisherman, but there weren't always fish to catch."

"Oh."

"Why didn't he do something else?" someone else asked.

"Because he was a fisherman." Grandma said sternly. "Now eat your dinner and let me tell you his story. So…where was I…oh, yes, he was a fisherman but he was also poor because sometimes he couldn't catch many fish and couldn't make enough money selling them at the market. Sometimes he would throw his net into the lake and it would just come up empty."

"He just needed to make a better net then," Gordon added.

"Agohdee—" Grandma squinted at him. "Maybe so. But—he only had this one net to use."

"Then he really wasn't a very smart fisherman if he only had one net…" Gordon muttered under his breath.

"Agohdee!"

"I'm eating, I'm eating." He stuffed a piece of ugali into his mouth.

"One day," Grandma continued, "Nyamgondho threw his only net into the lake, and when he began to pull it up, it felt much heavier than normal."

A couple of the kids looked up from their plates.

"What was it?"

"When Nyamgondho pulled the net all the way to his boat, he saw that it held a woman."

There were a few little gasps.

"This woman of the lake (Nyar Nam as Grandma called her, which meant *Daughter of the Lake*) asked Nyamgondho if he would take her to his home so she could have food and warmth, for she was very cold. He did as she asked, and, since he was still unmarried and in need of a wife—"

"Well yeah, because he was a bad fisherman," Gordon said again under his breath.

"Agohdee!"

"I said nothing!"

"So…anyway…" she looked at Gordon and paused for a second. "Anyway, Nyamgondho asked Nyar Nam to come home with him, and she said yes. After some time living together, as was the custom, she became known as his wife.

Soon, without explanation, his fortune started to grow. He became very successful and wealthy. He married other wives and acquired pieces of land and kept many animals. It was widely known that all this prosperity was due to Nyar Nam. It was said that everything she touched prospered. If she kept a chicken, it gave birth to many chicks. The same went for cows, and goats, and crops. Nyamgondho now had what he had only ever dreamed of and more, all thanks to Nyar Nam and the kindness he had showed her when he fished her out of the lake."

"That sounds like a nice happy ending to this story." Gordon interjected. He was already done with his food, as usual.

"But wait—there's more." Grandma said. "You all need to finish your food." She gestured to the other kids' and their half full plates.

"As time went on, Nyamgondho grew selfish and proud, and he lost sight of his many blessings. He began to go out drinking, and then he would come home drunk and full of anger at his wives, especially at Nyar Nam. He would insult her for no reason, saying things like *You came from nothing and you were so poor when I fished you out of the lake.*"

"Oh no!" someone said.

"Did he drink chang'aa?" someone else asked.

"I don't know." Grandma answered. "Maybe, probably. It doesn't matter what he drank, just that he did."

"Oh, okay."

"He was really stupid!" Gordon said. "What a cabbage."

"Agohdee—" Grandma stopped, but then she nodded, as if she agreed.

"One night," she resumed, "Nyamgondho came home in his usual drunkenness, but this time Nyar Nam had had enough. When Nyamgondho knocked on the door, she opened it and told him straight to his face that she was leaving.

"He cursed at her and yelled and even laughed. Then he said loudly, so that all his other wives and family on his property would hear, 'When I fished you out of the lake, you were nothing and you had nothing. I saved you, and this is how you repay me?'

"This only made Nyar Nam stronger in her resolve. She replied, 'No! All you have is *because of me*. Before me, *you* were nothing and had nothing. Without me, you will be nothing again.'

"Nyamgondho didn't take her words seriously, so he didn't do anything as she started to walk away. But then, to his surprise, *everything he had*—his wives, children, animals—all followed behind Nyar Nam and started walking away from his property. He couldn't believe his eyes.

"He ran after them, now concerned and confused, and yelled at them to come back. All his chickens, goats, cows, everything and everyone was leaving with Nyar Nam. When he glanced back toward his land, he now saw that there was nothing there anymore—even his house and wives' houses were gone. Everything had vanished, as if there had never been anything there in the first place.

"Nyar Nam continued walking, with the long procession of people and animals and possessions behind her, until she came right up to the edge of Lake Victoria. Then she stepped into the water—it reached her ankles, then her knees, then her waist, then her chest, and soon she was completely covered. As she walked further into the water, everything and everyone behind her followed. Nyamgondho could do nothing to stop them. He stood there on the shore, frozen in his horror, as one by one, step by step, animals and wives and children disappeared into the dark water.

"Then, they were all gone, and he was left standing there alone, yelling into the empty night for them to come back and pleading with Nyar Nam, begging for her forgiveness. He shouted a thousand promises into the night air, each one larger than the last, but it was all for nothing. The surface of the lake was still and flat as if it had not been even the slightest bit disturbed that night.

"Nyamgondho, now a desperate and broken man, sat down and cried so much that the spot where his tears gathered began to transform into the roots of a tree. His legs then became bark and his arms became branches. Suddenly he was fully transformed into a tree, condemned to forever stand by the lakeside and remember all that he had lost."

Grandma paused and looked across the kids' serious, sad faces. They had all stopped eating, and a few had their mouths hanging open and their brows furrowed.

"People say, to this day," Grandma added, "that if you go to the exact spot where Nyar Nam walked into Lake Victoria, there is a rock that bears the footprints of humans along with all kinds of animals, as proof that this story is true."

"But is it *really* true?" someone asked.

"People also say that there is a tree near the same spot that looks very much like the sad, crying face of an old man, with his eyes shut and his chin resting on his hand.

They say that if you cut the bark of this tree, the juice runs red, for it is actually the blood of Nyamgondho."

As Grandma stood up and started gathering the plates, she drove the moral of the story home. "So, let this be a lesson to never take anything that you have been given for granted, for just as it has been given, it can be taken away. And when you remember Nyamgondho, remember how he squandered his great many blessings and happiness and prosperity, and how he suffered."

The story was over, and Gordon felt troubled. Nyamgondho had seemed like a such a simple, foolish man in the beginning of the story, and while he had squandered his life and taken Nyar Nam for granted, getting turned into a bleeding tree seemed like such a harsh punishment! Gordon didn't want to side with Nyamgondho…but still…he almost felt for him, just a little, because the poor man didn't get a second chance. He didn't get to learn a lesson and change and become better.

As a secondary thought, Gordon wondered if Nyar Nam, this Daughter of the Lake, was one of the Nyawawa, or maybe she was the first Nyawawa. Maybe all the other people who came with her also became Nyawawa, maybe even the animals (if there are animal Nyawawa)…but she had come from the lake in the first place, so maybe she was Nyawawa even before she married Nyamgondho? Maybe she was actually a spirit instead of a real person…maybe…or maybe…Gordon made a mental note to ask Grandma about these connections with the Nyawawa, some other time.

*

The sad story of Nyamgondho (for Gordon decided it was still a sad story, even if the man got what he deserved), stuck in Gordon's mind, for he too didn't want to be ungrateful for all he had been given and for all he had. Grandma had taken him in and had made room for him in her life. She had given him a place to sleep and food to eat. She cared about him and he knew this, but he also knew he wasn't happy in Migori.

He knew that she thought bringing him to Migori was lightening his load or emptying the basket that he would've had to carry by himself in Kangemi. Grandma wanted to protect him from the rains and storms and keep him close. He recognized this as her freely offered, good faith charity, and he tried to be grateful for it—he *really* tried—he thanked God for it and asked God to help him *continue* to be thankful for it. But he felt torn inside, and his mind wouldn't settle. It was ever restless, pacing back and forth inside his head, walking around and around in circles trying to find the best solution.

He decided one day that he needed to tell Grandma, not to complain but to make his thoughts plain, to bring them out into the light of day and explain himself. So, he told her, simply, that he was contemplating going back to Kangemi.

"What will you do there?" That was her first question, as if she thought there was nothing there for him.

"I want to go back to my old school." He replied. School was the aspect of life there that loomed large in Gordon's mind. He longed for his friends, the familiar routines, and the languages he knew.

He didn't hide from Grandma how much life in Migori was wearing him down and dimming his light. It was both exhausting and yet nothing happened. He felt like nothing was ever going to happen or ever would happen. He didn't see any avenues of possibility or future directions for himself. All he felt was a bleak sense of enclosing, enfolding, sinking, and never coming back up. It was like the waters were pressing in around him and he didn't know how much longer he could keep treading water.

Grandma didn't press him about money matters, like how he would pay for school fees and rent and food, which was good because Gordon hadn't yet thought through those matters. He wasn't worried about money though, and maybe Grandma intuitively understood that. Gordon didn't consider the idea of returning to Kangemi with any sort of *what ifs*. Instead, he figured he would find a way for everything and it would all just happen. Money had been tight before with his mom, but they had still managed to pay for school. He was used to having little food and even sometimes no food, so that was not a big concern. Maybe it was just as well that he had never been the type to imagine all possible hypothetical scenarios or fixate on all the things that could go wrong. He just knew he had this nagging feeling that he was supposed to go back, that he needed to be there, and that life was waiting for him in Kangemi. He felt like it was the right thing to do, and he wanted to trust his intuition. He hoped that it was right.

One day, he made up his mind and said to Grandma, as a statement and not a question, "If nothing changes, I'm going to go."

Grandma didn't argue. She only began to ask him from time to time, "So, has anything changed?"

Gordon's answer, over and over, was always the same, "No, nothing has changed."

It became a refrain, and the more he said it, the more he came to understand it as the very core, defining characteristic of rural Migori life—nothing changed because nothing is supposed to change. Finally, after May, June, and July in Migori, there was a one-month school break during August at the end of the term (or trimester) before the next one started in September. Gordon had turned fifteen during the summer and only had that one term left in his eighth-grade year. He saw this school break as his chance, like God parting the waters of the red sea just for him. He had to act while he could, for the waters would close up again and he wouldn't be able to cross.

Again, Grandma didn't argue or try to convince him to stay. She agreed to let him go, but the problem was that she didn't have money to spare for bus fare. She said he would have to figure out how to pay for his bus ticket. Gordon was determined, so to raise enough money to buy that precious ticket, he asked a couple of his cousins to show him how to make and sell charcoal. It was a whole process to gather the wood and burn it just right, and then when the charcoal was ready, they sold it at the market and to restaurants in Migori town. They undertook this temporary business a week before Gordon wanted to leave and, thankfully, they made enough for his bus ticket.

Gordon packed his things and prepared to return to Kangemi. He had only spent three months in Migori, but it felt like an entire lifetime. It was like he had left the old Gordon back in Kangemi and had become a different, second Gordon out there. From the outside "nothing had changed," as he had said to Grandma many times. In one sense, it was true. From all external appearances, he looked the same, walked the same, had the same hair and the same gap in his front teeth. But, in another sense, he felt like he had traveled a great distance. It had been a strange journey through interior landscapes that he hadn't known he would have to walk. He had seen who he didn't want to become, and he had thought long and hard about what he wanted and how he could reach it. If nothing else, he had truly seen his life in Kangemi from the outside and become even more grateful for all of its possibility and purpose.

When the morning to leave came, Grandma said a long prayer for Gordon and gave him a live chicken tied and prepared for the journey. Gordon then set out with his duffel bag, backpack, and chicken to walk the two hours to the bus station in town—for the cheaper bus option left from the center of town, not from the stop near Grandma's house. Two of

Gordon's cousins accompanied him, as they were excited to use their share of the charcoal proceeds to buy chapati and beans in town. Gordon didn't have enough money for chapati along with the price of the bus ticket, so he just bought beans. That would be enough to last him through the journey, and soon he would be back in Kangemi where he would make his own beans and his own chapati, in his own home.

IV
Mwendo wa chui: the way of the leopard

Mbwa wa msasi mkali ni mkali pia.

Translation:
The dog of a courageous hunter is also courageous.

Paraphrase:
You learn the ways of those who raise you.

1. Return

The bus arrived in Kangemi around eight in the evening and, even though the sun had already set, Gordon could make out the familiar buildings and the twilight bustle of daytime turning into nighttime in his neighborhood. When the bus had passed the "Welcome to Nairobi" sign above the entrance to Kangemi on Waiyaki Way, it had seemed to be hanging there just for him. It felt like the neighborhood was happy to have him back too. When he stepped off the bus, the first thing that hit him was the smell—not the fresh, natural air of the rural county but the overlapping and commingling scents wafting from roadside food sellers and streaming out of people's houses. Gordon breathed in this delicious air full of sautéing onions and tomatoes, frying fish, cooking meat, chapati, and ugali burning just a little bit in just the right way. The air surrounded and enveloped him, like an embrace from invisible arms ushering him back where he belonged. *He was home!*

The next thing that struck him was the noise. He hadn't realized how much he'd become accustomed to the rural country's quiet, punctuated only by bird songs, the crackling of dirt on the roads, and the sound of grass crunching in the mouths of grazing animals. Walking through the streets of Kangemi, Gordon felt like someone had suddenly turned the mute button of his life off. The volume was now back on. He'd re-entered the real action and excitement of living, and he was surrounded once again by the sounds of humanity—people walking on the roads, kids being caned, TVs blaring out open windows and doors, radios, music, KTN news coming from one house, KISS FM radio from another, everyone increasing their volume to drown out the others' noise. Gordon loved this piling of sound and loved being part of the noise—he was eager to add his own, to live life loud. He always felt like if you didn't make any noise, you weren't really doing anything. As he walked, he felt all the pent-up energy of the

Migori months stirring inside him. He had been caged and contained, but now he was back and he was ready. He felt like running through the streets, shouting and stirring up all the dust he could, making the loudest, wildest commotion possible to let everyone know, to let the world know—*Gordon is back!*

The streetlights shining in the twilight filled him with excitement and hope, for this was the land of electricity, paved roads, and civilization. Compared to the rural country's oppressive darkness where you couldn't see your own leg even if you were standing on it outside at night, Gordon saw people walking around the Kangemi streets after dark, and he breathed a sigh of relief that he too could now go out after dark. Grandma had been so strict—as was her custom—but all her talk about how the Devil was in the darkness instilled such fear in her children and grandchildren. As Gordon wound his way through the streets, he felt relieved that now, he didn't have to fear the Devil, or night runners, or Nyawawa. In the city, life continued after dark, so much so that it seemed almost like the Devil *only* lived in the rural country. Maybe he left all the city folk alone to just go about their business, since they ignored him anyway with their streetlights and headlights and radios and TVs. Or maybe he did roam the streets at night, but so did lots of people. Maybe no one noticed. Maybe even the Devil was just one of the many city dwellers in Nairobi.

Gordon wandered with these impressions and reflections along the streets straight to the shanty where he and his mom had lived, thinking and hoping that he could just go right back to his previous house. When he got there though, he saw that the shanty room was now occupied by someone else. He went to the property owner's house, just a couple shanties down in the same plot, and knocked on the door.

The man answered and didn't seem surprised to see Gordon. "*Kijana,*" (young man), he said casually, "How are you? Where have you been?"

Gordon explained that he had come back to stay after his few months

Mwendo wa chui: the way of the leopard

up-country, and that he wanted to move back if there was a room available. Unfortunately, the property owner didn't have an unoccupied shanty in the plot to rent to Gordon, but the man had saved all of Gordon's things in a small storage room at the end of the row. He gave Gordon the key to the storage room and said he could stay there for a few days until he found a place to rent.

The room was the size of a walk-in closet, and when Gordon opened it, a musty, dustiness greeted him. Dust had settled on all his things, but he saw that they were at least still there. His mattress, complete with the blanket still on it, had been rolled up and tied, and all his cooking materials were in a pile on the floor. Everything was there, so it was a start. Gordon put down his duffel bag and his backpack, unrolled the mattress, and had his first night sleep back in Kangemi, complete with the chicken Grandma had given him lying quietly on the floor as his companion in that little storage room.

The next day, Gordon went to the Holy Family Basilica to find Father Ngugi. The priest was busy, as always, so Gordon waited in the foyer along with other people and enjoyed the tea they served to the people waiting. Fr. Ngugi's secretary knew Gordon, and when she saw him, she pulled him over and let him skip the line to see the priest. She had him follow her to the priest's office, ushered him in, and announced simply, "Kijana wa Mary is here," (Mary's kid is here). Fr. Ngugi was happy to see Gordon and asked him the same questions that Grandma had, about how he was going to pay for school and rent. Gordon said again that he would figure it out and that we wasn't worried. He would take it one thing at a time, rationally and practically, and he knew that the first thing he needed was a new place to live. Fr. Ngugi gave Gordon some money to help with the housing search, and told him that if he ever needed anything, he should come back.

Gordon then went to find Jackason. He first tried Jack's house, but

Jack's mom said he was out, probably playing soccer. Gordon knew what that meant and exactly where Jack would be, so he headed over to check the field. Even from a distance, as he walked over, he could make out Jack's figure playing keeper or goalie (his usual position), loud as ever, always yelling to his teammates about one thing or another. When there was a break in the gameplay, Gordon caught his attention and waved. Jack's face lit up and he immediately started running from the goal box before Gordon even motioned him to come over.

Jack shouted as he ran across the field, as if to notify everyone within hearing distance, "GODEEEEE! Hey! Gody is here!"

Jack was just the same and it was as if no time had passed, like Gordon had just been away for a weekend. Gordon asked if Jack would help him look for a place to stay, and of course, Jack was up for it. They spent the rest of the afternoon walking from plot to plot asking anyone and everyone if they knew of available rooms to rent. Since there were no internet or paper listings in Kangemi, everything was just done by word of mouth. This might seem low tech, but it was actually quite efficient because someone always knew someone who knew of a place. People were constantly vacating and leaving and disappearing and rebuilding, so housing (at least the very minimum style) was plentiful in Kangemi. Before the end of the day, they had found a suitable place that was actually just down the street from Gordon's previous place. The rent was 1,000 Ksh ($10) per month and Gordon also had to give a security deposit. The place had no electricity, but it did have access to a water pipe that was opened once a week.

There was still enough time left in the day for Gordon and Jack to move all his things into the new place. In Kangemi, it was common practice when someone needed to move to just rent an *mkoteni* cart on the street and pile all your things onto it. This was the type of simple cart that had a flat bed with short sides balanced on two wheels, along with two horizontal poles for handles that allowed one person to pull it. Usually, people piled the contents of their entire shanty on one cart, and the pile could be as high as two grown men. The process of pulling became a little tricky because you had to carefully balance the heaping weight on the wheels as you crossed Kangemi's dirt streets full of rocks and holes. If one of those wheels hit a rock the wrong way, the cart teetered and threatened to spill. It was overall, a delicate dance with disaster.

Gordon and Jack didn't have to worry about this though because they couldn't find an mkokoteni nearby, so they decided to just carry everything. For this new plan, they needed more manpower, so they went to recruit some more of their "boys." Jack knew where everyone was, and it also helped that it was still the holiday break and all their friends were idle, just passing time playing soccer or loitering on the streets. Jack knew who to get and where to find them, saying, "Let's pass by Sanguti's place; let's get Kinyua, and Joseph Agai; oh and Idi, Evans, and Wambeté." Soon, just like magic, they'd amassed a whole team of able-bodied boys to help carry Gordon's possessions to his new place.

Gordon really didn't have much anyway, so the team of boys was able to make the move in one trip. They each took as much as they could carry and nothing was that heavy. The majority of the bulk was from the yellow jerry cans for water. Even though they were empty, they were a pain to carry because they took up a lot of space and only had one handle on the top.

Jack took Gordon's small table and turned it upside down, piled some things on the underside, and then put it on his head, holding it steady with one hand and motioning to the boys to pile on some more.

"I'm good. It's good. Add more." They lifted some other things and he readjusted.

"I'm good. Add more."

They piled on some more.

"C'mon, c'mon. Add more." He still had one hand free to gesture.

"More, more, *c'mon guys!*"

The boys brought more, until finally, it was one-item too many, and Jack almost lost his balance.

"Wait, wait. That's too much. TOO MUCH!"

The boys rushed to grab things before everything fell, and they redistributed the objects among themselves. Once everyone had what they could carry, they caravaned down the street to Gordon's new home. They set all his things down outside because they needed to sweep the inside of the empty shanty house first. The boys helped with the cleaning too, and once it was ready, they moved everything inside.

Gordon now felt like this was the true beginning of his new life. He had friends, a place of his own, and a purpose again. The relief and excitement faded a bit though as the reality started to sink in. He would need more money and he would have to figure out a way to squeak by while still attending school. It wouldn't be easy and it might require some sacrifice and struggle. He knew how to sacrifice though, and he remembered his mom, when she had first come to Kangemi with her infant baby. Mary Auma had actually done all this first, all those years ago. She'd barely known anyone and had arrived without a job or friends or church community or anything. She'd made a life for herself and her son, all on her own, out of nothing. Gordon felt proud to be her son, and he understood how she'd been *truly* brave. He held onto that thought and packed it away carefully in the back of his mind. He knew that he would succeed because *she* had first succeeded. It was now his turn to prove himself as courageous as Mary Auma. *I can do it, and I will do it,* he promised himself. *With God's help and with mom watching from above.*

*

On that first night in his new home, Gordon didn't yet have any real food, so Jack generously invited Gordon to have dinner with his family. The next morning, Gordon went to buy the essentials—a 5-liter jerry can of kerosene for the cooking stove, some cans of dry corn to be milled into flour for ugali, cooking oil, salt, a bag of onions, and a big cabbage. In the two weeks before school was set to start, he ate ugali and cabbage every day for dinner, which was his only meal of the day. He would cut a slice out of the cabbage like a pie, and leave the rest to retain its moisture. He budgeted for that one meal per day, played soccer with his boys, and felt *good*.

The Sunday before the start of the school term, Gordon went back to Fr. Ngugi at the Basilica to ask about money for the school fees. Fr. Ngugi agreed to pay the fees for the term and sent the payment behind the scenes (since the money had to come from an adult). Gordon didn't know if Ngugi had sent someone or taken a check himself to Kihumbuini Primary School, to cover the remaining term of eighth grade. Gordon just knew that it was taken care of, so on Monday morning, he put on the full school uniform, complete with his black shoes. When he walked through the school grounds, he recognized students and heads turned when his classmates recognized him. He was like a celebrity. When he passed by, kids looked at him and whispered to each other, "Gody is back!"

Gordon was especially relieved and excited to be in class with Mr. Ruterré, the math and science teacher from the Meru tribe. Mr. Ruterré spoke English the whole time during his lessons—thank God, no more math in Luo!—and he repeated things in English until you got them. He never even resorted to Swahili. He had students come to the front of the class and do a math problem on the board, and then he would ask them to explain how they reached their answer. This always made Gordon feel like he had invented something new, like he had figured out a new way to get the correct answer. The most wonderful thing about Mr. Ruterré's math classes was that he instilled in his students the belief that there was more than one right way to do a math problem. There were in fact many ways, and they could *all* learn from each other. Mr. Ruterré's class quickly became Gordon's favorite.

Since this was the final three-month quarter of eighth grade, the school devoted most of its time to preparing students for the national exams so that they could earn the KCPE, Kenya Certificate of Primary Education. To encourage the students to work and study even harder, it was customary for family and friends to send *success cards* to the school for the students. These were notes of encouragement and congratulation for approaching such a momentous milestone. At the daily morning assembly, the teachers would stand in front of the gathered student body (nearly 1,000 children), and they'd call each student by name who had received a success card to come forward and retrieve it.

Gordon's friends and classmates started receiving success cards, but there were none for him since he didn't have any family to send them. He envied the students' excitement at the assemblies when they'd hear their names and jump up to walk proudly to the front of the student crowd. He too wanted his name to be read; he wanted to be seen and admired by other students, especially the younger students who could look up to these eighth graders and all they had accomplished and were about to accomplish. Most of all, he didn't want to be singled out as the only student who didn't receive *any* success cards.

To remedy this situation, Gordon and Jackason devised a plan. They bought a pack of four cards, and Jack wrote them all as success cards for Gordon. They needed an ingenious way to get them to the school though, and since they couldn't just deliver the cards themselves, Jack decided to entrust them to a younger girl—a fourth-grade student named Patricia. Jack instructed her to give the cards specifically to Mr. Ruterré and say that they were for Gordon. The plan was simple, should be effective, and seemed foolproof.

On the morning when Patricia was supposed to drop the cards off with Mr. Ruterré, Gordon and Jack sat in their desks in Mr. Ruterré's classroom, waiting for the morning assembly bell to ring. Gordon was brimming with excitement—today was the day! Finally, he was going to get to walk in front of the entire school. He kept looking nervously over at Jack, who nodded and winked back nervously, as if to say, *this is it, it's really going to happen!*

While they were waiting and other kids were shuffling into the classroom, Patricia walked in too. *What was she doing here?* She walked straight to Gordon's desk, pulled out the cards, and held them out for Gordon.

"Here, these are for you."

Gordon didn't know what to do. He glanced over at Jack, who was already starting to fume smoke out his ears and shoot daggers out his eyes. Other kids were watching and could see the cards, so now the entire thing was ruined. Patricia had blown their whole plan. There was no way to salvage this, so Gordon just took the cards, and tried not make a big deal or a scene. He told Patricia to just leave and shooed her away. He knew that Jack would have some choice words for her later in the day, but Gordon didn't feel particularly angry at that moment, just empty and low, like a deflated balloon.

After their failed attempt, they tried one more time—Jack was determined to make it work—and it was the same basic plan as before but just with a different student as the middleman. For some unknown reason, on the morning when they were again expecting Gordon's success cards to arrive, the school didn't call a full, all-student assembly. Instead Mr. Ruterré had the students come to the front of the class to pick up their cards. When he called Gordon's name, it was a little thrill, but it also wasn't as grand as Gordon had wanted. Everyone in his home room already knew him so, while Gordon and Jack had managed to outsmart the success card system, it had still partly thwarted their efforts.

After all the anticipation and studying and success cards, the time for the national exams finally arrived. The school held a prayer service on the morning of exam day, and it must have worked because Gordon, Jack, and his classmates passed just fine. As a reward for finishing exams (it felt like a reward anyway), they had a 2-month break during December and January before they would transition to high school.

2. Ananda Marga

For high school, Gordon had been accepted into the Queen of Apostles Minor Seminary, a fancy Catholic boarding school for boys who were planning to join the priesthood, but it was far too expensive for Gordon's budget. He also got accepted at Kangemi High School (a natural choice for students after Kihumbuini Primary), but it too was more than he could afford. Since he needed to go *somewhere* for school, he settled on Ananda Marga Secondary School, which was just down the street from his house in Kangemi. Ananda Marga Secondary was an offshoot of the Ananda Marga Mission in Nairobi, an Indian organization that fed the homeless and also ran a primary school. Before starting, Gordon went to talk to the Secondary school principal, a Filipino man who grew up in India, named Dada Vrata Dhiirananda. He always wore a turban and had a beard. To Gordon's surprise and relief, the principal accepted Gordon for admission without any long-term financial commitment. He said they would simply "figure it out." This had basically become Gordon's life motto, so he felt capable that he could figure out a way to "figure it out." Jackason was also going to attend Ananda Marga, which was a distinct plus.

Gordon still went to see Fr. Ngugi at the Basilica from time to time, and while he was grateful for that semblance of a safety net—even if it was a loosely woven net with some pretty big holes—Gordon didn't want to be or even seem wholly dependent on Ngugi for money and school fees. He didn't want to come off as entitled or lazy, like he was unwilling to work or earn his own way. At least with Ananda Marga, Gordon could pay his way partially, periodically, and still ask Fr. Ngugi for help if absolutely necessary. Gordon explained this, flat out, and Fr. Ngugi seemed pleased with the arrangement and even proud of Gordon for trying to make his own way. He said he was glad that Gordon was going to attend high school, which made Gordon feel like Ngugi had doubted that he would.

The Ananda Marga Secondary School property was shaped like a big square, where one side ran along the road and had a short, solid fence demarcating the property. The other three sides of the square were filled with buildings that bordered an internal assembly ground, like an open piazza. The school had one metal gate at the main entrance from the street, which opened right into the assembly ground of flat, burnt-orange brick that perfectly matched both the dirt streets and the shanty roofs. All the buildings were two stories tall, and one building had three stories on only the internal side, where the property descended to include a basement level of sorts, where the bathroom stalls (pit latrines) were tucked away in the bottom corner. The buildings were painted white with blue trim, and each classroom had a window. There was an open, covered hallway that faced the assembly ground, which made the entire school look like a white and blue motel. There was also a long thin balcony on the three-sided building that looked out onto the surrounding shanty roofs. Gordon and his boys liked to hang out here, as it was rare to get to look over the tops of other houses and trees. Everything was so densely packed in Kangemi that this partial view off the side of Ananda Marga could almost be called scenic. It gave Gordon the sensation of space, of being able to exhale and inhale fresh air that sat above the dirt, rusting roofs, trash piles, and exposed sewers running throughout Kangemi.

Ananda Marga's school uniform for boys required maroon pants and a white button-up shirt with a maroon and white striped tie. They could also wear a maroon sweater or a blazer over the shirt. Gordon couldn't find the exact color of maroon for the pants, but the school was lenient in that it allowed students to wear approximate colors. The closest Gordon could get was a pair of slightly reddish-brown pants and a pair of bright red pants that he wore often. His white shirts were characteristically huge on his tall, bony frame, and his ties were all a little too long, hanging down past his belt. He always rolled his shirt sleeves up to his elbow, to show that he was a serious guy, and now his cornrows had given way to a fuzzy black afro, that he kept about an inch thick. He still had a pair of glasses with thin silver frames—purely decorative—that he wore every day too.

*

To help pay for his school fees and still have a little left over for rent and food, Gordon took a weekend job working for an Indian family in the Westlands area east of Kangemi. One of his neighbors, a Luo woman who had been a friend of his mom, worked there as a *house help* or maid. She knew Gordon needed some work, so she had asked the family if she could bring her son (named Zacchaeus or Zakayo for short) and his friend to help with yardwork and the more demanding physical tasks. The family agreed, and Gordon and Zakayo worked there from about 8 to 5 every Saturday and Sunday. The family had a large plot of land, almost 1.5 acres, with a lawn that always needed weeding. The boys pulled up dandelions, one by one and helped with lifting and moving furniture in the house.

When it was time for the son to go back up-country, Gordon stayed on in the job. He washed the family's cars and did basically whatever they needed. The Indian family had three adult children who all got married while Gordon was working there. This meant that he got to help with the receptions that the family held on the property, which in turn meant larger income and overtime. The family even allowed Gordon to stay at their SQ (servant's quarters) if the reception fell during school holidays. The SQ was an old, single-room stone house on the property, slightly bigger than Gordon's Kangemi house. During those reception weekends, Gordon partly felt like he was on vacation since he received free lodging and food in addition to his normal wages.

At the beginning of eleventh grade, Gordon heard from the Indian family's *askari*, or night watchman, that the company that man worked for was hiring. He assured Gordon that he could secure for him a position as an askari at a different property in Loresho, north of Kangemi, which was owned by a Kenyan family. They agreed on a date and time, and Gordon met the askari at the property in Loresho. It was large, and this family was wealthy, but not just like all the families that lived in Loresho. They were one of the super-rich families that Gordon *never* associated with. The parents had one daughter and two sons. The daughter was Gordon's age, but she attended a fancy private school, so she and Gordon had never crossed paths before.

Gordon began working the night shift for this family while he attended school during the day. He'd go to school until about 4 p.m. on the weekdays, then go home from 4 to 5 and have dinner, shower, and prepare for work. It was a thirty-minute walk from his house in Kangemi over to the Loresho estate, and he would leave with enough time to give himself a little buffer. He'd take the Kangemi flyover to cross Waiyaki Way and then wind up through Loresho to the "Loresho Crescent" street where the family lived. He'd work from 6 p.m. until 6 a.m., a twelve-hour shift. After he finished the shift, he'd walk the half hour and cross Waiyaki Way again back to Kangemi, get his school materials, and head straight to Ananda Marga so he could do his homework before classes started at 8. Every time he crossed Waiyaki Way, it meant income and progress, and he was glad that he could make ends meet for the moment, but it also meant discipline and sacrifice since he had no time for soccer or friends. His time was stretched as tightly as possible, but he managed to make it work.

The family had a gate at the entrance to their property with a little guard box right beside it. The job of the askari was to stand in this box—standing not sitting, since there wasn't even room for a chair in there—and monitor cars that came in and out of the property. If a car arrived, Gordon had to remove the padlock from the gate and push it open, then stand on the driver side (the right side) of the car, hold the gate open, and salute the driver while the car passed. The guard box also held one huge coat for the askari to wear, along with a flashlight and the record book for the license plate numbers.

The father of this rich family would come home around midnight. Gordon had no idea what he did for work or why he was always out so late, but his schedule was consistent and predictable. When he approached the property in his car, he just flashed his headlights to signal Gordon that it was him. Gordon then opened the gate and locked it once the man had pulled through. After the man came home, Gordon knew that no one else was supposed to come during the night, and therefore, there was no more activity at the guard box and front gate. Gordon relaxed during those quiet, early morning hours where everyone was asleep and nothing ever happened. He would leave the guard box and take some time to walk around the property with his flashlight and look like he was doing something.

The property was something like five acres in total, and it had a slight hill off to the side with a chicken coop and a creek at the bottom. There was also an SQ for the family's permanent employees. The family didn't have a Kenyan-style guard dog, the type of some imposing breed like a German shepherd that would be kept in a kennel during the day and only let out at night to patrol the property. Kenyan guard dogs were supposed to be mean, and they would bark and bite anyone they didn't recognize. Many families had these types of dogs as their sole means of protection, but Gordon figured that since this rich family had opted for an American-style, domestic pet dog, he (as the askari) was supposed to fill the place of a real guard dog. He carried his flashlight conspicuously as he walked around the property, waving it across foliage and shining it into dark corners, figuring that if anyone saw the flickers of light, they'd recognize it and know that he was earning his wage, patrolling their property and keeping them safe.

Early on, after he made the rounds of the property, Gordon tried to sleep standing up in the guard box. He literally just closed his eyes and dozed on his feet, but it was difficult even for him in that uncomfortable space. He realized that since no one came home after the head of the family, he didn't *really* need to be in the guard box, and only needed to be present there in the morning when it was time for the shift change at 6 a.m. No one left earlier than that anyway. Gordon took up the habit of concluding his rounds of the property at the bottom of the little hill near the chicken coop, where there was a small hut with no door and just a roof that covered a sawdust pile. Gordon unceremoniously threw himself on that pile, still wearing the far-too-large coat that functioned like extra padding, and fell right to sleep—it was actually a comfy spot. The sawdust was cushy and warm. He slept there for about four hours each night, from 1 to 5 a.m., and then he'd wake up and head back to the askari box. He was thankful that he'd always had the sort of internal alarm clock where he could set his mind and tell himself to wake up at a certain time, and he would, as simple as that. It seemed like a win-win, for it was like one of those sayings, if a tree falls in a forest…or if an askari sleeps while everyone is sleeping, does anyone *really* know?

One day however, the father didn't come home around midnight like he always did. Gordon thought this meant that maybe he was out of town or up-country. Gordon waited and waited and still no one came, so he left the guard box, made his normal rounds, and decided that it was safe to go take his normal nightly nap. He went, he slept, and all seemed well. But, in the morning, when he headed back to the guard box, he saw that the man's car was back in the driveway. This meant that he had returned really late sometime during the night while the guard box had been abandoned. Just seeing the car made Gordon's face hot and he started to sweat in that oversized coat that suddenly felt so heavy, like a weighed blanket pushing him toward the ground. Troubling images started to fill Gordon's mind of the man coming to look for him on the property and finding him sprawled out on the sawdust pile. Oh God, maybe he had even been snoring, with his mouth open or his tongue hanging out. What if he had been drooling his poor-person's saliva on this fancy rich-man's sawdust? The disgrace of it all! Gordon wanted to curl up in a tiny little ball and just disappear. How could he even look that man in the face again? He was going to be fired. He just knew it. He was sure that such a family as this would not tolerate him slacking his duty. They didn't have to. They owed him nothing, and they could hire another askari in seconds. They surely didn't need him, but they didn't know how much he needed this job.

Gordon trudged back to work the next evening, feeling like his whole body was made of lead and embarrassed that he had to return to the scene of his shame. He didn't know what else to do. He had no cell phone and the family had no way of contacting him. If they were going to fire him, they had to do it in person, to tell it to his face. He figured it was at least the decent, dignified thing to do to show up in person to receive his official termination. Maybe it was foolishness to even think about dignity at this point, but he had to at least try.

While Gordon stood in the guard box, dreading the moment when the owner of the house returned home, Gordon saw the car pull up and the lights flicker uncharacteristically early, around 7:30 p.m. Gordon's shift had only just started and he was going to get it, right to his face, right now. *Here it comes,* he thought, *better just get it over with.*

The man pulled up in his car. Gordon went around, unlocked the gate, then stood on the right side of the driveway to hold the gate open, as always. The man pulled forward slowly and stopped when he reached Gordon. He rolled down the driver side window.

Gordon braced himself. *Be* strong. He told himself that he could withstand any amount of criticism and judgment. They were just words, and he deserved it after all. He had to face the consequences of his actions.

"How are you, *kijana?*" The man asked calmly.

"I'm fine sir, thank you." Gordon tried to meet the same level of calm, cool delivery.

"What happened last night?"

So he knew! Of course he knew. Just be cool. Be cool!

Gordon replied slowly. "I was so tired, sir. I accidentally feel asleep." *That was the truth right?*

"What else do you do?" The man asked, still much more calmly than Gordon had expected. The calm was more eerie than reassuring.

"I go to school during the day."

"Ah," the man nodded. "Okay."

Then he rolled up his window and pulled forward, leaving Gordon standing there with the open gate, feeling a confusing mixture of relief and disbelief. The man hadn't done anything or asked for any more details. Gordon told himself to just accept this unmerited grace and not overthink it. He didn't want to jinx it. Maybe the man was still going to talk to the security firm behind the scenes, maybe he would make it so that Gordon couldn't be hired anywhere else. There was really no way to know what would happen.

In the end, the man did none of those things though, as far as Gordon knew. The man never spoke about it again, and it never happened again. Gordon still napped on the sawdust pile when he could because he needed to get at least a little sleep sometimes, but he did this *only* after the man came home and Gordon saw him park his car and go inside. Gordon would always stay awake until the man came home, and he would never leave the guard box before that.

*

While Gordon was still in eleventh grade, a new student arrived at Ananda Marga Secondary school, a boy named Ben Ambani. Ben was from the Luhya tribe, like Jackason, and seemed like a cool enough guy because he played soccer with the rest of the boys and got good grades. At first Gordon didn't know Ben very well, but when Gordon learned that Ben was also an orphan, Gordon became more curious. It turned out that Ben had been living with his grandmother up-country, as he had lost both of his parents, just like Gordon. Ben had moved to Kangemi to stay with his older sister, but his sister's husband saw Ben as a financial burden. The husband didn't like that he had to spend his money to send Ben to high school, even if Ananda Marga was cheap and flexible with payment.

Since Gordon was also feeling the strain of working his overnight job and he wanted to reduce his expenses so he wouldn't *need* to work that job, he suggested to Ben that they become roommates and split the cost of the rent. Ben agreed and, after Gordon helped convince Ben's sister of the validity of the arrangement, the two boys were able to move to a slightly bigger shanty in the same plot, and they split the rent. They shared all of Gordon's things, and Ben only brought one 20-liter jerry can for water and one iron-sheet suitcase. Their new shanty house had electricity—the type with a single-bulb in the middle of the ceiling, but it was always flickering on and off. If they needed the electricity for something else, they would just unscrew the lightbulb and connect the wires from whatever else they wanted to use—like a single-coil electric burner to use as a stove. This makeshift electricity worked, and the boys felt proud that they were innovators, doing things their own way and figuring out how to make things work in unconventional ways. They knew there were risks involved, of course, but they always weighed the risks against the outcome. It was a constant balancing act of how much they were willing to risk for how much payoff. The payoff almost always seemed worth it too.

One time when they came home after being out during the day, they discovered that someone had broken into their shanty and stolen a small car radio. Even though it wasn't much (and things were always being stolen in Kangemi), it still felt like a violation and the boys decided that they needed to beef up their security. Ben suggested that they make an electric fence, and to do this, they connected a piece of metal wire to the wires in the ceiling and placed it directly against their iron-sheet walls. This had the effect of running the electric current through their entire four-wall shanty, and basically making the entire structure a live electric fence. The boys thought this was ingenious. It certainly did increase their security, and they felt like their things were very safe. They would leave it like this when they went to school during the day—four iron-sheet walls of hot, seething electric current.

During the night, they sometimes heard people passing by outside, on their way to the public latrines or wherever, who accidentally brushed the shanty structure and were instantly, ever-so-slightly electrocuted. The boys recognized this by the familiar, *bzzzzz* sound followed by some sort of quick, shaking *ahhhh* sound, before the person hurried on their way. Even worse was when the boys themselves accidentally touched the wall, if they rolled over in their sleep too close to the wall, only to be shaken awake by the *drrrrrrrr* of the current running through their bodies. They'd lie there in the dark vibrating for a minute, trying to calm themselves down from the little shock, before falling back asleep. This all seemed like a small price to pay for their protection, until one evening when they came home to find some smoke coming from their roof. They went right to the owner of shanty block and asked him to disconnect all the electricity for the plot, so that they could disconnect everything inside their shanty. They conceded that this was the end of their electrified-shanty-fence situation.

They were crazily confident teenage boys, always willing to try everything in the hope of discovering the next best thing or a different and exciting new style of doing things. They wanted to experiment and thought they could outsmart the way things had always been done. Thank goodness they didn't electrocute themselves too badly in the process. Although the two boys were never the closest of friends or confidants, they lived just fine as roommates. They were like successful business partners, both invested in making their joint endeavor flourish and prosper. Thanks to Ben's contribution, Gordon was able to quit his night job after one year there and go back to playing soccer in the evenings with Jackason and the rest of his friends.

3. Come and See

On one of the occasions when Gordon went back to the Basilica, Fr. Ngugi inquired about Gordon's future beyond high school. "So, now that you're about to complete school, what do you plan to do?"

Gordon wasn't entirely certain, but he did have an answer waiting. "I don't know for sure, but I would love to become a priest."

Gordon thought Fr. Ngugi would be happy, maybe even overjoyed at this bit of news, but instead he seemed ambivalent, unmoved. He simply asked, "Why?"

Again, Gordon *had* thought about this and he had another ready answer. "I've wanted to be a priest ever since I was young and would sit in church with my mom and watch the priests during the service. I have gone through so much and it's been hard, but I want to celebrate mass in church as a way of giving thanks to God for bringing me through all the struggles in my life. I've seen the life of priests, and I admire to have that life."

"Even priests have difficulties," Fr. Ngugi replied seriously.

Gordon nodded. He didn't mean to sound like he just wanted a cushy life. He knew that priests worked too, that they had devote their lives to serving others. It was common in Kenya for boys from poor families to become priests just so that they'd have food and shelter and a stable life. Most of all, it was a way of assuring that their families wouldn't worry about them. Unfortunately, many of those who joined the religious life didn't care deeply for the spiritual side but were more concerned with the practical benefits. Gordon, by contrast, was truly interested in the spiritual side, as he'd always been fascinated by the priests' role as God's holy minister and liaison. At the same time, he could never wipe the images from his memory of the priests receiving gifts from generous parishioners, all the sumptuous banquets prepared specifically in their honor, the reverence and respect, the way people said

Mwendo wa chui: the way of the leopard

their names with a certain gravity and awe...was it wrong to want all of that? Even just a little bit?

Ngugi continued, "Well, take your time to decide."

"I will, but I don't know much about the different orders." Gordon admitted.

Ngugi proceeded to give Gordon a brief overview of the basics: there were the more well-known orders like the Dominicans, Franciscans, Benedictines, Jesuits, and others; some orders focused mostly on preaching, or prayer, or education; some concentrated on missionary work abroad or serving the local community; some priests committed to serve and stay in a certain area, while others could travel and serve any location in the world where their order operated. It all seemed much more complicated than Gordon had anticipated. He tried to absorb all this info and file it away in his mind. He didn't know there were so many factors to consider besides just being the man who performed the mass at church.

"You should study the different orders before you make your decision."

"So...how do I find them?" Gordon asked.

"I have a booklet here," Ngugi turned to the bookshelf behind his desk, looked over the shelves, and pulled out a small book that was more like a thick pamphlet. "They sell it in the bookshop too, if you'd like to get your own copy." He held it out over his desk to Gordon, and Gordon took it slowly, purposefully, trying to conceal his eagerness and excitement at receiving something from Ngugi that would help him navigate his future.

The small book was called *Religious Men and Women Working in Kenya*. Gordon flipped through the pages and saw that it was like a directory. It listed the congregations and their contact info, addresses, and the names of their vocations directors. Even though the book didn't look like anything flashy, Gordon held it in his hands with reverence, like a treasure map. This book was his key. It was going to help him find his way, lead him to the perfect X that would mark the spot where he'd find future gold. He thanked Fr. Ngugi and then went on his way with renewed hope. There were many orders and groups listed in this book—surely one of them would be the one he wanted. Surely, one would want *him*.

*

Gordon took Ngugi's exhortation seriously, and he studied that directory book, making notes along the way of the orders that sounded interesting and worth investigating. Since he still didn't have a cell phone or computer and couldn't use the internet for email or social media or anything like that, he proceeded with his search in the only way available to him, both the lowest-tech option and the most immediately effective option. He would write down the information of the respective religious order to visit and then simply show up at their door in person. When he arrived, he would ask to speak with Fr. So-and-So, the vocations director. If the person was not available that day or was otherwise occupied, Gordon would come back another day.

With the easing of his financial burden from rooming with Ben and with some money from Fr. Ngugi to help with his vocational search, Gordon was able to take every weekend and go religious order shopping. This meant that he spent his Saturdays and Sundays mostly in Nairobi's Karen neighborhood, named after the Danish author Karen Blixen (largely known in English-speaking countries under her pen name, Isak Dinesen and from her memoir, *Out of Africa*). The Nairobi neighborhood named Karen was once the site of her coffee plantations but had since been developed and was now by far the wealthiest of all Nairobi neighborhoods. It was where wealthy politicians had their palatial houses, and it was home to the headquarters for almost all the Catholic religious orders. Going there was like stepping into the Vatican City of Kenya. Gordon would go from gate to gate, walking the clean, paved streets that were rimmed with trees and tall green hedges. The plots of land here were private and protected, which made them all the more alluring, and Gordon always imagined what grand palaces must be concealed behind those thick hedges.

The first place he visited was the vocation office of the Archdiocese of Nairobi to inquire about possibly becoming a diocesan priest, the type of priest that was geographically bound and served primarily to perform mass and tend to the needs of the congregation under their pastoral care. The first thing the vocations director told Gordon was, "This journey is not easy." The journey to priesthood there was a long one, typically six or seven years, sometimes as long as ten, or even longer depending on the circumstances. Gordon tried to keep an open mind about this prospect, since this was his dream after all, and if it was worth wanting, it was worth investing all of that time.

He came back regularly to visit with the vocations director and to get a feel for the community, but Gordon soon realized it was not what he wanted. He got a certain vibe from the diocesan priests he talked to that was some nebulous feeling of discontent and uncertainty, mixed with tiny traces of mistreatment. There was also an air of holiness at the Archdiocese that made Gordon feel wary. He had always thought, deep down, that priests were just people too, and that they were actually better as priests when they continued to be regular people. For all that he admired priests and the respect they received, he knew it was even better when they remained humble and human. In light of all this, he decided not to pursue the diocesan route.

Next, Gordon considered joining the religious order called the "Salesians of Don Bosco." This order was started by an Italian priest, John (or Giovanni) Bosco, in the latter half of the nineteenth century in Turin. Officially named "The Society of Saint Francis of Sales," the Salesians, as they were commonly called, became an order focused on rehabilitating abandoned and homeless street children. The Salesians in Kenya upheld this mission, taking in many street kids and padding the ranks of their priesthood from the ample supply of young boys in need of secure employment and housing. These poor kids were often all too eager to commit their life to the service of God and Don Bosco's mission, if it meant that they'd be assured of a roof over their heads and a reliable meal every day.

When Gordon visited the Salesians' home in the Kuwinda neighborhood just north of Karen, his initial impression was one of awe—the size of their land was incredible, and the grandeur was unparalleled. It was the fanciest place he had visited yet, with sprawling green, impeccably manicured lawns that looked like a golf course. He had never seen such lawns before. The walk from the main gate on the road to the front door must have been something like a quarter of a mile. This opulence suggested to Gordon that this order was rich and comfortable. They must treat their priests well, and their priests must be proud to be Salesians.

The Salesians had an age limit for entering the priesthood—the cutoff was twenty-six—but Gordon, at eighteen, was right in the sweet spot, not too young and not too old. He'd seen some things after all and lived some life but was not pushing their limit. When Gordon spoke with their vocations director—an Indian man with a heavy accent—Gordon felt excited that the man was immediately interested. The man even said that the Salesians would help pay for the rest of Gordon's high school fees, on the condition that he got good grades. All he had to do was bring his report card at the end of the term, and they would reimburse and reward his good work with a check. It was as easy as that.

At the end of eleventh grade, Gordon went for a retreat at the Salesians' center for prospective priests and candidates, an event generally called a *come-and-see* weekend. The retreat location called itself the "Bosco Boys Center." "Bosco Boys" were the kids that that Salesians pulled off the street and housed at their center, providing them with vocational training and counseling. Gordon arrived at the come-and-see weekend at the retreat center on the east side of Karen, along with about twenty other boys. Probably around a hundred boys total resided at the center.

Gordon's initial impression left him feeling judgmental and maybe even a bit un-Christian—but he couldn't help himself. The Bosco Boys were not at all the type of boys he expected. They didn't match the image he'd created in his mind after visiting the administrative and vocations office of the Salesians' other golf-course style headquarters in Kuwinda, with all its polish and luxury. The Bosco Boys, by contrast, seemed like they had literally *just* been pulled off the street and dumped at the center. They were dirty and unruly, wearing tattered clothes with unkempt hair, no shoes and no socks. Some were even tucked away in corners still sniffing cobbler's glue—a habit that was unfortunately common on the street. Cobbler's glue was easy to acquire and gave off a disgusting, plastic odor that could cause a hallucinating sort of high when inhaled, at the expense of brain cells and who knows what else. Lots of street kids sniffed glue so that they could forget their hardship and pass out, as if they were black-out drunk. Sometimes they'd just die there, lying on the side of the road. It was a sickening addiction, and Gordon knew that the benevolent mission of the Salesians was to take in these sorts of kids as they were and help them, with no judgment. He appreciated that, but he didn't want to be associated with this these boys. He didn't want people to think *he* was that type of boy.

After Gordon's mom passed away, acquaintances and various people had warned him not to become a street kid. Certain family members had even said that he *would* become a street kid and some had already concluded that this was his fate. It was like they had already written him off because it was simply inevitable, with no regard to his character and whether or not *he* cared for himself and his future. All of that felt to Gordon like they had no faith in him, no trust in him, no belief that he would succeed. Their words were burned into Gordon's mind, and remembering them brought back all the mixed feelings of hurt and a sort of righteous anger. He had always been determined to prove them—and everyone—wrong.

He *would not* become a homeless street kid, and so far, he felt like he was doing a pretty good job of avoiding it. He had, up to that point, (he reminded himself) *not* become a delinquent, or a glue-sniffing street boy, or a chang'aa-bumming-alcoholic. He worked hard, got good grades, went to church, and had friends. Seeing the Bosco Boys at the Salesians' retreat center made him feel like he was now stepping into his appointed place as an orphan. As he looked around, he again felt terribly judgmental, and he asked God to forgive him for these thoughts, but he knew that he didn't want to and would never be like these boys. Joining the Salesians would only prove all the doubters and naysayers right.

Gordon felt uncomfortable in that company from the get-go, and the rest of the weekend only reinforced his feelings that the Salesians weren't the order for him. The schedule of activities for the weekend was strict. The boys had to do what they were supposed to do when they were supposed to and there was no wiggle room. They also had to play cricket instead of soccer. Gordon didn't know how to play cricket (who actually played cricket anyway?). He wasn't sure how to hold the mallet or where to stand or when to run, and the whole ordeal was an embarrassment. Why couldn't they just play soccer? Everyone loved soccer and everyone knew soccer. The boys slept in wooden bunk beds that were creaky and uncomfortable, and for dinner they had white bread and cooked green beans. Again, Gordon felt like maybe he was being judgmental—he asked God for even more forgiveness—but this food offering was a disappointment. Gordon might as well be back at home with his ugali and cabbage. Who ate white bread and beans, anyway? The Psalmist in the Bible said, "Taste and See that the Lord is good," but that meager meal did not cause Gordon to taste or see God's goodness. It seemed to say, "Taste and See that the Lord is bland." After the weekend, he went home feeling like the event had fulfilled its purpose, for he had come and seen and decided that it was not for him.

*

Mwendo wa chui: the way of the leopard

At the beginning of twelfth grade, Gordon met a Jesuit novice or priest-in-training named Brother (Br. for short) Mboya, who was recently out of university and stationed in Kangemi as part of his training. He helped run the young adult service at the Catholic church Gordon attended. They became friends, and Br. Mboya advised Gordon on which Catholic religious orders to consider. Br. Mboya was a member of the Jesuits, the order officially named the *Society of Jesus*, and he whole-heartedly recommended it to Gordon, saying, "Jesuits are the best." He offered to send his personal recommendation for Gordon to the regional headquarters of the East African Province of the Society of Jesus in southwest Nairobi.

The Jesuits had three different properties in Karen, and the headquarters was called Loyola House, named after the founder of the Jesuit order, St. Ignatius of Loyola. Br. Mboya set up a meeting for Gordon with the vocations director at Loyola, Father Terry. When Gordon arrived at the property, Fr. Terry was standing at the entry gate next to the askari booth. Gordon was surprised to see that Terry was a mzungu (a white man), and that he seemed older than Gordon had expected. In reality, Terry was only in his sixties, but there was something frail about him. Perhaps it was more of a gentleness that was purposeful and unhurried. He was bald, with some white hair in the back and a thin white beard and mustache. He had squinting eyes that tilted down at the outer corners and a thin mouth that also tilted down ever so slightly when he smiled.

"Are you Gordon?" he asked, with a recognizable American accent.

Gordon nodded.

"Welcome." He motioned Gordon to follow him through the gate. They walked on a cobblestone path through the courtyard, which had a green grass lawn, peppered with trees and bushes. Everything looked clean, trimmed, and well kept. Fr. Terry was almost the same height as Gordon, wearing loose, swishing pants and socks in Velcro sandals. He led Gordon into the main building and directly to a dining room. There were other people around, but Gordon couldn't tell who were priests and who weren't—no one was wearing the white Roman collar, not even Fr. Terry.

As Gordon took a seat at their large dining table and marveled at how fancy and clean the place felt, Fr. Terry asked, "Do you drink tea with milk?"

"Yes." Gordon nodded, thinking to himself that he'd drink anything these people would place in front of him.

"Would you like something to eat?"

What a question! Of course he'd like something to eat. He could always eat. Why would he ever turn down free food?

"Sure, thank you. Anything." Gordon didn't want to seem too desperate.

Terry went to the kitchen and brought back a cup of milk tea mixed with Milo (Kenyan powdered hot chocolate), along with a bowl of peanuts.

Terry told Gordon more about the Jesuits and the process of becoming a Jesuit priest. He gave Gordon a book about St. Ignatius of Loyola, along with a promotional pamphlet about the Jesuits of East Africa. He also gave Gordon a book called *The Fifth Week,* about the process of discerning a call to the Jesuit priesthood. He explained that the process was long—Gordon would have to consider at least twelve years of study and formation before getting ordained. Jesuits are "the most learned Catholic priests," he said proudly, and they highly value education. Every priest-to-be earns the equivalent of a bachelor's and a master's degree, sometimes even a doctorate. They had the freedom to choose what they wanted to study for a master's degree, but it was important to know that they were not the final decider about what best to do with their education.

"The destiny is not shared." Terry explained.

Gordon found this a little confusing, because weren't they all Jesuits, all part of the same formation and religious calling?

"Many will be chosen, but the journey is different for each one." Terry continued.

Mwendo wa chui: the way of the leopard

This part intrigued Gordon. It seemed to him that the Jesuits didn't want to make their young candidates into cookie-cutter priests, but rather they wanted to nurture and use each boy's individual strengths and passions. This sounded ideal since he could still be Gordon but *also* become a priest.

Throughout their meeting, Gordon felt comfortable in a way he hadn't at any of the other vocations offices. There were no airs here, and Fr. Terry allowed Gordon to ask as many questions as he wanted. It was a real conversation that made Gordon feel encouraged and respected, like his opinions and desires already mattered to Fr. Terry and the Jesuits. The Jesuit emphasis on education peaked Gordon's interest, along with the intellectual and contemplative rigor of Ignatian spirituality and its unique aspects of prayer. Gordon was intrigued and wanted to learn more about the Spiritual Exercises of St. Ignatius and the "Daily Examen," a specific, prayerful way of reflecting on one's day in order to discern God's presence and direction.

When they concluded their conversation, Fr. Terry offered to give Gordon money for the bus fare back to Kangemi. Gordon gratefully accepted and watched as Fr. Terry took out an envelope of cash and pulled out fresh-looking, never-before-touched bills. He handed Gordon enough for something like fifty bus trips. Gordon left that first meeting basically already settled on the Jesuits, but he was eager to learn even more. He began visiting Loyola House about once a month. Fr. Terry had after all given him enough money to take the bus every time, and what a luxury that he didn't have to make the trek there on foot and arrive sweaty, dusty, and hungry. He could arrive in style, fresh and clean (or at least somewhat fresh and clean after being sandwiched into a crowded matatu).

Gordon soon became a familiar face at Loyola House. He made friends, met everyone, and was invited to all their events and even to the ordinations. The more time he spent there and the more people he met, the more he was amazed at how they already treated him like an equal. At Loyola, you couldn't tell who was a priest, or a deacon, or a novice, or just a visitor. You couldn't tell from the way people acted and treated each other who was in charge and who wasn't, and that was entirely the point. It seemed like an experience of true Christian community where everyone was welcomed and regarded with dignity. They had chefs working in the kitchen too, so there was always ample food. Tea was available twenty-four/seven, along with peanuts and bread. Gordon always helped himself to their free food and drink offerings, but not so much as to be obvious about it. He marveled at seeing the priests walk around in sandals without collars, no pomp or haughtiness or expectations for anything from anyone. They would sit at the dining table, just like real people, next to Gordon and across from Gordon, eating guava with the boys. This was thrilling for Gordon, it felt like meeting his heroes in the flesh and discovering that they were, in fact, kind, regular people just like him.

It seemed like every progressive experience Gordon had with the Jesuits further demonstrated their worthiness and continually affirmed that this was the place for him. The Jesuits had their own Come and See event near the end of Gordon's twelfth grade year. This took place at a retreat center in the Ngong Hills on the southwestern edge of Karen. Twenty-five boys went, including Gordon. All the others were from outside Nairobi, and Gordon felt proud to be the only local, especially the only one from Kangemi. He knew that Fr. Terry liked him as well, since Gordon wasn't a sheltered village boy but a street-smart city kid who had been through some stuff and had known true poverty and loss. Gordon also spoke the cleanest English of all the prospective boys. Because of all these factors, Terry tasked Gordon with helping to orient the out-of-town boys. Gordon felt like he was already one of the Jesuits, one of the privileged inner circle.

At the Come and See retreat, each boy was granted his own room with a key. It was like they got to stay at a hotel, with all the privacy and personal space they wanted. The boys arrived at the center around 2 p.m. and attended a 6 p.m. mass. Gordon was struck, once again, by the Jesuits' embarrassment of riches, for there were six priests at that mass. Why in the world would they need so many priests, except to show that they had them? They were flaunting their wealth, he thought during the service, but he didn't mind. He was going to be one of those priests, maybe one day up there in front of prospective candidates.

When Fr. Terry spoke to the Jesuit hopefuls gathered at the retreat, he talked mostly about their professional development, reiterating the value that Jesuits placed on education and their pride in being scholars and thinkers in addition to priests. He said that their number one vocation is prayer, and number two is education. The only condition for all the boys was that they had to pass their high school exams and graduate before they could be admitted to the Society of Jesus.

*

Gordon successfully passed his high school exams and graduated, no problem, and his sights were now firmly set on the Jesuits. This was his future. He could see it beginning to take shape before him. God had led him to the Jesuits and was now leading him toward the priesthood, and maybe even toward becoming the bishop someday, like he had dreamed about all those years ago as an altar boy. With a connection from Fr. Terry, Gordon secured a job after graduation teaching the English class at St. Martin's Secondary School. This was an all-girls boarding school located on the northeast side of the Loresho neighborhood, with students ranging in age from thirteen to eighteen. Gordon crossed Waiyaki Way every day to report to his job at the school, but since he was only nineteen and barely older than some of the girls he was teaching, this position was difficult. He'd had no pedagogical training or preparation for this. They just threw him into the job. He tried to do his best, but he learned quickly that teaching was neither his calling nor strength. He didn't have the patience when the students couldn't understand, the enthusiasm for explaining material in new or different ways, and most of all, he didn't know how to keep order and discipline in the classroom. Overall, he was relieved when Fr. Terry and the Jesuits suggested moving him to a different position.

Gordon then started working with the Jesuits at AJAN, short for African Jesuit AIDS Network, which had a facility in Kangemi, just west of where Gordon had lived with Ben. The Jesuits already had a strong presence in Kangemi, and along with AJAN, they ran a technical school and the only Jesuit parish (a district consisting of a church and a priest) in Kenya. AJAN worked specifically with people affected by HIV and AIDS, especially youth and at-risk populations, to promote education, management, and prevention. The property was like a small campus with three staff members living there, a kitchen with a cooking crew, other staff that came in and out and people who came for services. The buildings were like those that Gordon had seen in Karen, with red ceramic tile on the roofs instead of iron sheets. After graduation, Ben had also secured a teaching job nearby and had moved out, so when Gordon started working with AJAN, he left his shanty home and moved into one of the rooms at the facility. Gordon viewed his move there as further preparation to join the Jesuit novitiate; really it was like he was already a part of the order, already privy to their inner circle. In his opinion, the Jesuits operated with the "mzungu mindset of the future," investing in and looking toward what was to come and *could* come instead of only focusing on the immediate, pressing need of the present. They were training and forming him to become one of their priests, and maybe even to come back and run AJAN house one day.

Even though Gordon acted like he was already a member of the Jesuits and everyone treated him that way, he still had to officially be admitted (even if it was completely a formality). While he was working at AJAN, he received the invitation to come for his admittance interview with Father Shirima, the provincial, or the head priest who managed the entire region. Fr. Shirima had the final word on all decisions relating to the region, and his word, once spoken, was immutable. Gordon was almost twenty, the youngest of the sixteen candidates that had been selected to proceed in the process after the Come and See weekend, and even though he told himself that this interview would be a breeze, he couldn't help feeling nervous. Fr. Shirima was rumored to be mean and had the reputation of being a "great disappointer." When least expected, he could change his mind and dissolve all your hopes and plans with a single word. He allegedly cut every list in half, meaning that if sixteen boys applied for admission to the novitiate, it was possible that he would accept only eight. You could never be sure with Fr. Shirima, and people tiptoed around him like they walked on the most fragile of eggshells. One wrong step, one wrong sound, one wrong piece out of place could ruin everything. Gordon had even heard Fr. Terry curse Fr. Shirima's stubborn coldness, with choice words on more than one occasion. Gordon had never met or even seen this highly feared man, and that actually made it worse. Gordon did see a photo, but he didn't even want to look at the image of the man's face, because maybe that would jinx his chances.

When the day came, Gordon arrived at Loyola House and waited to be called up to Fr. Shirima's office on the second floor. Fr. Terry was there and told Gordon to just relax. There was also a recently ordained priest named Fr. Nzyoki who tried to comfort Gordon. Since they weren't far apart in age, Gordon trusted Nzyioki and kept telling himself that Nzyoki had not too long ago been through this same process and had survived just fine. Nzyoki kept telling Gordon, "You'll be fine. Don't be scared." But the more he repeated "Don't be scared," the more scared Gordon became. The longer he sat there waiting, the more his palms sweated and his thoughts milled around and around in circles. *Why is everyone saying* NOT *to be scared? What is actually going to happen in there?*

When it was finally time for Gordon's turn, around 10 a.m., he headed up to Fr. Shirima's office. The door was open, but Gordon wanted to be courteous, so he slowly walked in and waited to be told to sit down. Shirima was standing behind his desk with his back to the door and seemed to be searching for a book on his bookshelf.

"How are you, young man?" He didn't turn around.

"I'm fine Father, thank you." Gordon stood in the middle of the room, unsure about whether he should sit or wait or what.

Shirima seemed distracted, like he was busy and his mind was elsewhere.

"How old are you?"

"I'm nineteen, about to turn twenty in July."

"Say you're twenty then."

"Yes Father."

Gordon waited, still standing with his hands behind his back, holding a folder with papers that Fr. Terry had signed and said to give to Shirima. Gordon wondered what he was supposed to do with the folder—put it on the desk? Offer it to Shirima? Would Shirima ask for it? Did Gordon not know something about this procedure that he was supposed to know?

"Why do you want to be a priest?" Shirima asked, still with his back to Gordon.

You haven't yet asked me to sit down. Gordon thought. *And you want me to get right to my answer while I'm just standing? Can't I sit down? Maybe I should just sit down. Would that be rude?*

Gordon decided to stay standing where he was and answered, "I want to become a Jesuit priest because I'm excited about Ignatian formation and spirituality."

Shirima paused and Gordon held his breath. Then Shirima asked, "What do you do?" Gordon explained about working with AJAN, and he added a little bit about his past.

Shirima then asked about Gordon's parents, and Gordon answered that they were both gone. He told Shirima the story of the day his mother died, about how she had asked for Gordon to come home from school.

"I thought she wanted to tell me something." He said, like that was the conclusion of the story.

Shirima stopped what he was doing at his bookshelf and turned around. Seeing him from the front was even more intimidating, and Gordon almost wished Shirima would go back to face his bookshelf.

"What else were you waiting for?" Shirima continued.

Gordon waited too, wondering if he was supposed to answer.

"Did you think she had property to bequeath to you?"

What a weird question!

"No," Shirima added. "She did want to tell you, and she told you." He declared matter-of-factly, like it was some obvious piece of information Gordon should know. "The fact that she waited—that was the communication."

Why is he explaining Mom's last moments to me?

"She wanted to tell you that she didn't want to pass her last moments in the presence of strangers, to die in another's arms."

Okay, Gordon thought. *But what does this have to do with me becoming a Jesuit?*

Shirima squinted in Gordon's direction and said, "Have a seat."

Finally!

Gordon sat quickly in the single chair placed in front of Shirima's desk, perching himself on the edge of the chair, as stiff and straight as he could make his back.

Shirima held out his hand for the folder that Gordon had brought, and then he opened it and started to flip through the papers. Gordon felt sweaty and cold. He was almost shivering. What if one wrong response, one word that displeased Shirima could break the whole thing? What if he had *already* said something wrong?

"So—Gordon," Shirima set the papers down and looked Gordon

straight in the face for the first time.

Oh God, here it comes. Gordon tried to keep his face neutral and to breathe normally.

"What would you do tomorrow," Shirima said slowly, "if you woke up and found yourself with a woman in your bed?"

What?

Gordon waited for more explanation, but nothing came. Shirima just waited, staring from his hard, inscrutable face.

What am I supposed to say to that?

Gordon tried to formulate something intelligent to answer.

"That's interesting to think about," he started and paused to swallow, "because if I found a woman in my bed in the morning, she would have been there the previous night…and I would know who she was and why she was there. It's not like she would have just appeared during the night."

Was that enough? What was Shirima fishing for here?

Shirima paused. He leaned forward on his desk, pulled his glasses down his nose slightly, and stared at Gordon over the top of the glasses. That stare was the worst part yet. It was agonizing in its intensity. Gordon didn't know where to look. He couldn't look Shirima in the eyes, but he didn't want to avoid the gaze like he had something to hide.

Shirima sat there with his eyes fixed on Gordon for what felt like an eternity.

Then he leaned back and said, "Do not think that we are angels, young man."

What are we even talking about? Gordon felt more confused than ever. *I don't understand what is happening here.*

Gordon nodded a little—to show that he had heard Shirima—and tried to hide his confusion. Shirima's face never moved, relaxed, let alone smiled, and Gordon sweated even more. He felt like he was a thousand degrees. Was there actual steam wafting off his face?

Shirima didn't say anything more about that. He just took a pen and signed the papers and handed the folder back to Gordon.

"Take this back to Fr. Terry. Have a good day."

Shirima stood up and turned his back, seemingly to return to whatever he had been searching for on his bookshelf. Gordon stood up mechanically too, turned, and walked out of the room. He felt speechless—he couldn't even muster a "thank you Father." When he got out into the hallway, he let himself release all the pent-up tension in his body, but it only gave way to a heavy, hollowness in the pit of his stomach. He was sure that he'd blown his chance at entering the Jesuits, completely botched it. *The way Shirima had looked at him!* That must be evidence that he spectacularly bombed the interview. It was all already becoming a haze.

When Gordon got back down to the first floor, Fr. Terry was upbeat and excited for Gordon. He seemed almost jovial. He took the papers and congratulated Gordon at making it through the interview. Fr. Nzyoki, the recently ordained young priest, offered to take Gordon out to lunch that first afternoon after the interview. He bought Gordon ugali and fried fish, and he again told Gordon not to be worried or scared.

"But I'm so worried." Gordon admitted.

"Don't be stressed. Shirima is not the *owner* of the Jesuits. If it's God's will for you, it will work out."

Gordon tried to truly take these words to heart. Nzyoki was right. Gordon did believe that if it was meant to happen, it would. He just couldn't let go of the thought that he had messed up. While the awkwardness of the interview had seemed unbearable in the moment, Gordon realized that the waiting in the aftermath was even worse. The suspended state of uncertainty for the next week while Gordon waited to hear the verdict felt like torture. In case things didn't work out, he did have a sort of backup plan though—he didn't want to use it of course, but it was there. Fr. Terry had assured Gordon that if he didn't get admitted to the novitiate, Terry would help Gordon find some kind of job, like what he was doing at AJAN. *It'll be all right*, Gordon told himself. He had always landed on his feet and this would be no different.

Gordon concentrated on his work at AJAN while he waited for the result of the interview, and he tried to distract himself and stay busy. Then, one morning, he received a phone call from Fr. Terry.

"Gordon, I have some news."

Oh God!

Gordon waited, bracing himself for the worst.

"Fr. Shirima has approved your candidacy to be a Jesuit novice. Congratulations!"

Gordon cheered out loud and nearly dropped the phone.

"So," Fr. Terry continued, "what would you like for dinner? We're going to celebrate."

Gordon hadn't thought beyond the results, and he certainly hadn't let himself think about celebrations and festivities. It felt wonderfully mzungu to celebrate with food. He went shopping with one of the other priests who worked at AJAN, and that night they had *nyama choma* (roasted meat) with vegetables and ugali, and even ice cream for dessert. *Dessert!*

As part of the process of being admitted to the Jesuits, there was a required "home visit" to officially meet the candidate's family where they lived and to discuss the candidate's potential journey to priesthood. Gordon didn't really have family in Kangemi still, and he couldn't send Fr. Terry to Migori to meet Grandma or even the Okumus. Since this was required though, he arranged for Fr. Terry to come for lunch at his half-sister's house (on the Okumu side; they had the same father but different mothers). Her name was Maureen, and she had recently moved to Kangemi from up-country.

Maureen agreed, and when Gordon and Fr. Terry arrived, they sat at Maureen's table while she prepared lunch. She brought over all the food, and before Gordon could say anything, she just left. It was then just Gordon and Fr. Terry sitting there, face to face, like they had sat many other times in Terry's office. This really wasn't the purpose of the home visit and they both knew it, but what could they do? So, they ate the food and chatted, like friends. It was an enjoyable time, anyway, and Gordon felt ever-growing admiration for this mzungu man who had believed in him—an orphaned nobody from the slums—and who had championed his desire to become a Jesuit. The dream was now about to become a reality, and it was all thanks to this man. He had given Gordon money, friends, community, jobs, housing, hope, and now a future. Gordon knew he was one of Fr. Terry's favorite candidates. Gordon wanted to make the Jesuits proud and show them that they had made the right decision in accepting him, in taking him in and making him one of their own. They had always treated Gordon with respect and kindness, and he wanted to repay them a hundred times over.

*

When the time to leave Nairobi and travel to the seminary was drawing near, Gordon organized a home leaving party to officially bid farewell to his friends and community in Kangemi. It was the opposite of a homecoming, and while it seemed strange to celebrate leaving, it was more about celebrating the beginning of this next phase, of his Jesuit journey. They held the party at Maureen's house in Kangemi, and there was a huge gathering—Maureen invited most of her church and the entire choir. All of Gordon's friends came along with all the Jesuit seminarians and priests from St. Joseph the Worker Church, who were now his friends (and future colleagues). They bought a live goat for the event and lots of beer. There was even a cake decorated to look like an open Bible, where the page on the left said "Happy Noviate Life." The page on the right had the logo of the Jesuits, or the "seal" of the Society of Jesus, with the three capital letters, "IHS" representing the Latin acronym, *Iesus Hominum Salvator*, or Jesus Savior of Mankind). There was also a small cross above the H and the three nails used to crucify Jesus below, all contained within the center of a shining sun.

After the festivities, Gordon gave away almost all of his possessions in preparation to leave. He donated his cooking materials and everything he'd used to keep house. The only thing he wanted to keep was a wall clock with an image of the (very white) face of Mary, the mother of Jesus, looking humble and holy in the center of the clock face. His mom had bought the clock when Gordon was in fifth grade, and she'd paid for it in six installments of 100 Ksh per month. It was her most prized possession, and she'd loved that clock just as she'd loved the Virgin Mary. Gordon couldn't take the clock with him to the seminary (there were no electronics allowed), but he didn't want to just give it away to any random person, so he bestowed it upon AJAN house. They let him choose the spot to hang the face-of-Mary clock, and he put it on the wall opposite the main entrance door, so that it was the first thing you saw when you entered their building. Once Gordon left that one little piece of himself behind in Kangemi, there was no looking back, only moving forward.

Mwendo wa chui: the way of the leopard

V
Mwendo wa nyoka: the way of the snake

Ad Majorem Dei Gloriam

Translation:
For the Greater Glory of God

Paraphrase:
Everything we do in life, no matter how great or small, should be done to honor and give glory to God.

1. Karibu Tanzania

In preparation for the transition to the seminary, Fr. Terry gave Gordon money for personal shopping, so that he could buy some new clothes, get a nice haircut, and of course, obtain a passport. Since Gordon had never traveled outside of Kenya before, this short journey to Tanzania was his first ever trip "abroad." The journey was scheduled for July 10, 2006, and all the Jesuit candidates stayed the night before at one of the retreat centers in Karen. There were something like fifteen boys in total headed to the seminary in Arusha, Tanzania, and most of them had already come to Nairobi from the surrounding countries like Uganda, Ethiopia, and South Sudan. There were some accepted candidates from Tanzania too, but they would just meet everyone when they arrived in Arusha.

The night before the journey, the boys were excited and nervous to cross the Kenyan border and begin their new life in Tanzania. There was mass that evening at Loyola House with Fr. Shirima, as mean-seeming and intimidating as ever. He shook all the candidates' hands and stared at each one like he'd never seen them before. At least he wasn't going to accompany the boys to the seminary. The next day, they all piled into a public bus with their suitcases tied on the roof. This bus was slightly bigger than a matatu since it was meant for cross-country driving instead of just cross-city trips, and there were other, non-Jesuit people aboard as well. A pair of mzungu tourists sat near the boys, and Gordon, at that time like all the others, always assumed that all white people were Americans. One of the boys leaned over to the tourists and announced proudly, "We are the brothers of Obama." He smiled and flashed his white teeth. The mzungu couple just nodded and smiled but didn't say anything. Who knows if they were even Americans or not. Because Obama had just been elected as a senator in 2004, he was already a great source of pride for Kenyans—the world where a man of Kenyan descent could serve in the US government was a world where anything could happen. Gordon was especially proud because Obama's father was Luo and "Obama" was a Luo last name. Regardless of tribe though, all Kenyans were now proud to call themselves "Obama's brothers."

The bus ride was long and slow for the new seminarians as they traveled on the Kenyan and then Tanzanian stretches of the Cairo to Cape Town Highway, which was still under construction. This road was also called the Pan-African Highway and *the* fabled Trans-African Highway of centuries past. It had been discussed and planned and seemingly under construction since time immemorial. It was supposedly going to stretch all the way down Africa's Eastern side, through nine countries and over 6,000 miles. Each country was responsible for building and maintaining their stretch of the road, which meant that for somewhere like Kenya, this was a prime opportunity for corruption. Gigantic loans would be secured and plans would be announced and progress blatantly praised, all the while the money disappeared into thin air and the road was somehow slowly built. In the end, what was to be a great, paved example of African cooperation and modernization still remained a bumpy, rural road under construction.

When the bus reached the border crossing, everyone had to get out and go in person through customs. It was, back then, a two-stop crossing where they had to go through the Kenyan side, then walk across a no-man's land in the middle (the awkward empty space about the size of a two-lane road, which apparently didn't belong to any country), and then go through the Tanzanian side. The Tanzanian border marked itself with a large banner that read, "Karibu Tanzania" (Welcome to Tanzania). Underneath, in small print, it stated the country's unofficial motto and source of pride: "Hapa watu ni wakarimu" (Here people are kind).

At that first border crossing, Gordon didn't feel his Kenyan-ness particularly strongly. He was leaving Kenya after all and entering into a new phase of life in Tanzania. The boys lined up eagerly to receive the exit stamps on the Kenyan side, holding their stiff and empty new passports. There were already biometric services in place, and the boys had to get fingerprinted and get their picture taken by a little camera standing on the counter at each booth. When the attendant asked the boy in front of Gordon to "look into the camera" for his photo, the boy moved his face right up to the camera and put his eye against the lens. "No, NO! Move backward," the attendant clarified. Gordon smiled—at least he wasn't quite as green as some of these guys. But, he also knew there was still much to learn about life and especially about being a Jesuit. There was such a wide world outside of Kenya, and the Jesuit life would open many doors, he just knew it. It would lead to education and new knowledge, travel and exposure to new cities and customs, important work helping people in need, new cultures, and new languages. There was so much possibility ahead, and this very first stamp in his very first passport was the beginning.

For the remainder of the drive through Tanzania down to the city of Arusha, Gordon sat in the single seat opposite the driver, right behind the door. The driver was a Tanzanian man who talked a lot, which helped pass the time. Gordon had heard rumors about how proper and precise Tanzanian Swahili was, but he had never experienced it so much before. Even this bus driver's Swahili sounded nice—it made Gordon realize how broken and sloppy Kenyan Swahili really was. The driver's grammar was perfect, as though lifted right from the pages of a textbook. It sounded beautifully polite. It was like when an American hears the Queen's English and is struck with that mixture of admiration for its fastidious consonants and mystification by the ornate artificiality of it all.

When they reached Arusha, the driver took a longer, winding scenic route through the city to show the boys some of the sights and give them a feel for their new home. Everyone wanted to see the headquarters of the East African Community (which was one of the bigger tourist destinations in the city). The East African Community, sort of like the Pan-African Highway, had been an endeavor to unite East African countries, modeled after the European Union—where the region would have the same currency, greater mobility and easier border crossing, one passport for the region, and maybe even the same language. That was the original dream anyway, and there were many hopes for the EAC that never—or had just not *yet*—become a reality. Arusha was the site of the headquarters building because it was the geographic enter of the region, which comprised the countries of Kenya, Uganda, Rwanda, Burundi, and Tanzania. Nairobi had gotten the international airport, and when the EAC endeavor somewhat fizzled, guess who ended up with the better deal there.

Arusha was also the "gateway to the Serengeti" and the beginning stop on many tourist's safari trips to Mt. Kilimanjaro, which sat northwest of Arusha, close to the Kenyan border. There was also Mt. Meru, directly north of Arusha, which seemed to sit right behind the EAC building and cast its looming shadow over the city. Because of all this, Arusha felt like it was full of tourists. Gordon saw many mzungu people on the streets as the bus wound its way through downtown. The main street was small, and only made tighter by the bordering lines of shops, stands, and streams of people on both sides. Cars and pedestrians and bicycles and motorbikes shared the road, sometimes moving side by side, sometimes weaving around each other, sometimes pushing one another forward in a single-file line. When Gordon looked out the bus window, he could see the cars and motorcycles skirting by inches from the bus's side. It looked like they'd scrape the side, but they didn't. He also saw cars with that tiny passenger-side extra mirror, placed right above the front headlight on the nose of the car. The mirror was only about the size of a cellphone, but it allowed the driver to navigate and negotiate with the inches and centimeters that really mattered. People pulled big flat carts of produce for sale, selling sodas and bottled water under little umbrella stands; others bought food or clothing, carrying their goods in backpacks, plastic sacks, baskets, and big bundles balanced on their heads. Little food stands sold roasted corn on the cob covered with pepper, salt, and lemon, or the tropical oranges that were green on the outside and ripe on the inside.

After winding through downtown, the bus continued heading south through the "Njiro Korona" neighborhood, one of Arusha's wealthiest. Here the packed city center gave way to spacious estates with grassy lawns and ample trees. This area also housed many religious missions. The bus finally turned right off the main road onto a small dirt one, past a sign that proclaimed, "The Society of Jesus" in small letters at the top, followed by "St. Gonzaga Gonza Novitiate" below in larger, black capital letters. It had the colored Jesuit seal below that, the yellow sun rays radiating out in a triumphant circle announced that they had reached the seminary at last.

2. Poverty, Chastity, and Obedience

For all of the excitement and anticipation, the arrival at the seminary in Arusha was rather anticlimactic. The bus arrived around three in the afternoon, which just happened to be the seminary's mandated siesta time. The main gate was unlocked, and the bus driver pulled through, but the boys just had to wait. They waited, wondering exactly how long it was going to be or who was going to come. Finally, one of the three priests serving as the Novice Master at the seminary, another Fr. Shirima, came to welcome the new seminarians. This priest, named Amadeus Shirima, was the opposite of the other Shirima, meaning he was warm and approachable. He'd formerly worked as the Head of the School of Philosophy at Arrupe Jesuit University in Harare, Zimbabwe. This Fr. Shirima explained that from then on, the new arrivals were to be called the *primi*, and the existing seminarians were the *secondi*. To help get them acquainted, each primi was paired with a secondi as a sort of mentor, called a *malaika*, or "angel." Gordon's secondi malaika was someone he already knew from his past Come and See experience a year earlier in Nairobi, and together they walked to Gordon's room.

It was the size of Gordon's previous shanty home, and though spacious, it was predictably plain to uphold the Jesuit value of poverty. This meant nothing flashy or fancy, for there was a humble beauty in austerity and a certain dignity in needing and wanting nothing, all of which gave glory to God evidently. There was a twin-size bed with a mosquito net attached to the ceiling hanging down over the bed. There was an armoire in place of a closet, a kneeler for prayer, and a desk with a Bible sitting on top. The walls were white, and there was a single crucifix on one side, a copy of the peace prayer of St. Francis of Assisi on the other, and a window on the wall opposite the door, which opened into a backyard. The secondi malaika left Gordon to get

Mwendo wa nyoka: the way of the snake

settled in his room, saying to listen for the 5:00 p.m. bell that would signal time to have tea.

As all the other new arrivals were settling into their rooms, everyone came by everyone else's room to see if it was the same, to look out the windows, to express their relief at finally having arrived, and to revel in the excitement at each having a room to themselves. It was energy not unlike the first move-in day at an American university, with almost-tangible sense of freedom and potential, new friends, and new routines. Only here, it was excitement for the routines and rituals of seminary life, the prayerful, reverent, study and self-discipline that it would take to form and fashion themselves into faithful disciples of the Society of Jesus. No dreams of wild parties or adventures or experimentations, only dreams that looked to the vows—poverty, chastity, and obedience—made before God and all these holy men, in order to die ever more to the self and live more fully to God.

When the bell rang, Gordon followed the others to the dining hall, and they enjoyed an afternoon snack of tea with milk and bread with peanut butter. The dining hall was a square building with a large sitting area full of round tables and metal chairs, and it had a kitchen area in the back. The seminary employed a crew of chefs who cooked for the community Monday–Friday, and it was the seminarians' responsibility to prepare their own meals on the weekends. They all shared cleanup and other chores. After walking through the entryway to the dining hall, the young seminarians were greeted by a rather curious painting—really it was the first thing they saw when they entered—made specifically for the seminary by a Jesuit priest from Uganda, named Fr. Kizito Bushobozi. The painting depicted a traditional scene from rural African life, which was to be general enough that boys from various countries and cultures could all recognize and relate.

On the left side of the scene in the painting, there were two thatched-roof huts. The roof of the hut in the front had patches that were falling apart and showing holes. The part where the hut met the ground was in disrepair, with the stick foundation showing beneath mud plaster that had worn and fallen off. A child peered out the open doorway of the second hut in the back. There were some trees next to the huts and a green field off to the right, like an orchard or farm.

In the right foreground of the painting, a woman walked in profile, holding a tied bundle of sticks on her head (that she'd probably gathered for firewood), along with a basket of harvested fruits and vegetables balancing on top of the sticks. She had a sack of other goods hanging from the back of the bundle of sticks. The woman wore a yellow handkerchief tied around her head, and she also had a tiny, smiling baby strapped to her back. She wore a loose, blue sheet of fabric wrapped around her as a dress, which showed her prominent, protruding pregnant belly. She carried a hoe in her left hand, steadied the load balanced on her head with the other hand, and looked straight ahead with a fixed, serious gaze. In front of this woman, stood a man—apparently her husband—wearing tattered, rolled up green pants with holes in both knees and a red shirt that was nearly falling off his body. He had his left hand on one knee to support himself as he bent over, and with the other hand, he reached up to grab the woman's left breast. His hand held the woman's breast in a surprisingly pornographic squeeze, where his fingers curled around the top and his thumb circled around the bottom. He pressed her breast against his outstretched lips, as if he were a new-born baby suckling mother's milk.

Now, one could wonder why a Jesuit seminary (which made all these young boys pledge themselves to chastity) had such a painting in such a prominent place with such an exposed, bulbous breast on full display for everyone entered the dining hall. For the seminarians, this painting did *actually* depict a scene of generic rural life, and that man's strange squeeze was far from scandalous. The boys understood the painting's meaning in context, or at least they all acted like they did. They walked past it every day without much of a second thought. The painting was supposed to be

Mwendo wa nyoka: the way of the snake

instructive anyway, to serve as a continual reminder of all that women in traditional, rural societies sacrificed, especially for their boys. The woman in the painting had already given and was still giving *everything* for her family—she'd gathered firewood, weeded the garden, harvested the crops, bought supplies, carried, birthed, and cared for the children—while her husband did nothing and their house fell into disrepair. All he wanted was to take *more* from the woman for his own selfish pleasure.

Every time the young seminarians saw this painting, they were to remember their own mothers and how they had sacrificed to raise and care for them, to allow them to grow into the men they were becoming and to give them the comfortable life they now had at the seminary. It was a reminder to the boys that since they had been given much, they must now give back. It was also an admonition to *not* be like the greedy man in the painting. The Jesuits wanted their seminarians to become men of different character without entitlement, to be humble, selfless, and upright, always ready and willing to serve instead of be expecting to be served.

Later that evening, after having passed that painting multiple times, as he would hundreds more during the years to come, Gordon walked back to his room and thought about his mother. He looked up at the sky and he felt, as he often did, that she was looking down on him and that she must be so proud. The night was clear enough to see the stars. It was much quieter out here in Arusha than in Kangemi. There was a peacefulness and a stillness that didn't seem empty but full of the wonders of prayer and contemplation and the vastness of the interior life. Gordon breathed in the somber serenity that hung in the air—it felt fitting for this life of prayer, and he would grow into this new reality. He would encourage his soul to expand into the small, quiet hours, to hear God's voice without the city's chaotic noise getting in the way, and to breathe this living-giving passion of devotion. As he was looking up at the sky, Gordon saw a shooting star draw an illuminated arc across the night. *This must be a sign!* It was a blessing from God, a good omen for the start of his Jesuit journey. He had dreamt of this for so long, and now the dream had come true. He wished upon the shooting star that he would be the best Jesuit he could be and that he truly would fulfill God's will for his life.

*

Gordon had a hard time falling asleep that first night in the seminary, partly because he was still excited and partly because he wasn't used to the routine or the absolute silence yet. He lay in bed, still thinking about how his mom would be so proud. Even more than that, with a son who was becoming a priest, she'd receive such respect in society. That was a level of respect she had never experienced as a poor single mother. She had never been treated like that, but she had deserved to be treated that well, Gordon thought, for all that she had sacrificed for him. He wished that she was still there to really enjoy it now, to finally have things be easier. He wished that he could give that to her, to repay her for all that she had given him—just like the lesson of the painting—she had given of herself, selflessly, for so many years, right up until her dying breath all so that he could have a good life. Well, now he did have that life, and he would not let her down.

Gordon heard later that the social benefits of having a son who was a priest, even a grandson, did not go to waste, because Grandma, out in Migori, enjoyed them to the fullest. She was overwhelmingly proud, as Gordon knew she would be, and she told everyone, constantly, that her grandson was going to be a priest. She would even mention it—publicly—at the prayer time during the church service, when there would be an opening for people to add their own prayers, silently or out loud. Grandma would always come forward to the front of the church and add her prayer out loud, "For my grandson who is going to become a priest." Maybe people in the congregation tired of hearing about her grandson-who-was-going-to-become-a-priest, or maybe, in the privacy of their

Mwendo wa nyoka: the way of the snake

own hearts, they thought about what an honor and privilege it would be if *their* sons and grandsons were also going to become priests, and they were just a little bit envious.

The next morning, Gordon woke up to the 5 a.m. bell as if in a dream. He couldn't believe he was still there, in his new room. Every day from 5:15 to 5:45 was morning prayer in the chapel. All the boys shuffled in, still half asleep and sweaty from the night, for most didn't shower the night before, and of course they hadn't yet had time to shower in the morning. They didn't have specific pajamas either, so they just wore the same pair of shorts from the day before that they'd also slept in. In that sense, out of both necessity and expediency, they literally rolled out of bed and walked to the chapel. The seminary's chapel was shaped like a hexagon, with two rows of chairs on either side of the entrance and a small altar table in the middle. The boys filed in and each found a chair, then filled the air with their early-morning sweat. It was always warm and muggy in there, and it always smelled like sweat. Since it was a temple of the Lord though, perhaps in place of incense, the smell of their sweat could rise and give glory to God as a symbol of their early morning sacrifice.

The morning prayer was called the *Breviary*, and although it was brief and included various calls and responses with much sitting and standing, the boys still had a hard time staying awake. Gordon felt like every time he sat back down, he'd instantly start to fall asleep. Then every time he was supposed to stand up, he'd jolt back awake, only to sit back down again and repeat. It was a strange state of not-quite-awake, not-quite-asleep, murmuring along with the prayers, closing eyes, opening eyes, chanting, bowing, folding hands, lifting them, lowering them, trying to stand up straight and feeling like a dead weight. He'd see other boys nodding off too, and they'd give each other little nudges with their elbows or kick their feet slightly to help them stay awake. Father Kifle (pronounced Key-flee), who was the spiritual director for the seminary, usually ran morning prayer.

He was a thin Ethiopian man, with delicate features and kind eyes. He already had a short, fluffy Afro of gray hair, though he didn't seem that old. He spoke Swahili with a distinct Amharic accent, which caused him to insert rolled r's into all kinds of words where there otherwise weren't any r-sounds. When he addressed Gordon, it always sounded like he said, "Gorn-dorn."

Fr. Kifle taught the boys how to pray and meditate, as he was a true believer that you *really* could "see the Lord in everything you do." With his accent, this phrase sounded like, "Try tur seer the Lorrrd in everything yourr dorr." He repeated this so frequently that Gordon could hear it echoing in his thoughts even when Fr. Kifle wasn't around. During morning prayer, it didn't help the boys struggling to stay awake that Kifle was a very slow reader and a gentle talker in general. He had the kind of voice that could have been well suited to a relaxing yoga class. He often stopped during his readings of Bible passages, making long purposeful pauses, where he'd say, "And then the Lorrrrd saird to Moses…Now…let's think about that…"

Gordon would try to "think about it," but all he could really think in the fogginess of his mind was, *if I stop to think about it, I'm going to fall asleep. So, I can't think about it…or I can't think about how I can't think about it…I need to not think about that and think about the Bible. Is that what we're even thinking about? I don't even know anymore…*

In reality, Kifle knew that the boys struggled to stay awake, and he saw how some obviously slept, slouched forward in their chairs. When they went to kneel down to pray, some would bow their heads and just never come back up. Kifle was forgiving about this though, and he always said that, while you *should* try to be diligent with your prayers, if you fell asleep, you also shouldn't worry too much. Since you could do everything "in the Lorrrd," if you find yourself sleeping while praying, you'll still be "sleeping in the Lord." Gordon still always felt a little guilty about not being able to stay awake during morning prayer, and he expressed his feelings to Fr.

Kifle. Kifle only reiterated that "slerrrping in the Lorrrd" was indeed still praying in the Lord. If that was it…well, Gordon resigned himself to "sleeping in the Lord," since that was the best he could offer. God would understand anyway, right?

After morning prayer, from 5:45 to 6:30, everyone had to go back to their rooms for personal prayer, which was supposed to be a time of reverence and contemplation, but which sometimes meant more "sleeping in the Lord." Then 6:30–7:00 was mass in the chapel, and after mass, everyone would walk single file, in still-prayerful and contemplative silence, on the path than ran straight from the chapel to the dining hall between landscaped flower beds on either side. Breakfast was from 7 to 8, and there was no talking until the end. Everyone silently enjoyed their tea or coffee with *mandazi* (bits of slightly sweet, fried flour dough) until the priest tapped his mug with a spoon, as if he wanted to make a toast. Then he'd offer a prayer of thanksgiving for the meal, and after all the people said "AMEN," the great silence was broken and the breakfast hour was officially over. The silence would give way to murmuring, buzzing, and chatting amongst the boys, as everyone cleared their dishes.

Everyone helped with clean up from 8 to 9, and then it was time for class from 9 to 10. The new seminarians were instructed in the ways of Ignatian Spirituality and the various aspects of doctrine, along with how they applied to personal and communal life. They learned about how to mediate and pray in the silence of their hearts; how to understand the Jesuit constitution and the principles that governed their communities; how to interpret the Bible and preach sermons, etc. After morning class, there was a break from 10 to 10:30 for tea and bread (this was truly a plentiful land of tea and bread), then more personal prayer from 10:30 to 11, followed by a second round of class from 11 to 12. Midday prayer happened at noon in the chapel, and lunch at 12:30 to 1:30, with cleanup from 1:30 to 2. Then came the *siesta* or nap time from 2 to 3, where everyone was required to adjourn to their rooms. After siesta, they had mandatory recreation time from 3 to 4, where they could play soccer or basketball. During the harvesting season, the boys helped during this afternoon rec time with carrying corn in big sacks from the adjacent field back to the kitchen. There was another tea break from 4 to 4:15, followed by the evening class session from 5 to 6. They had evening prayer in the chapel from 6 to 7, and then dinner from 7 to 8. After 8 p.m., they were free to enjoy recreation time until 10, if they didn't have any other work to do. Recreation meant that they could play card games or table tennis, watch news, or listen to music in the recreation hall.

Gordon liked to listen to East African Bongo music really loud, and one time during recreation, he had the volume turned all the way up to the maximum. Fr. Shirima, the Novice Master, came into the hall, to see what all the ruckus was about, and he tried to shout over the sound, "Gordon, why is the music SO LOUD?"

Gordon shouted back, "BECAUSE I WANTED TO SEE IF IT WOULD REALLY GO THAT LOUD."

"WELL, IT DOES!" Fr. Shirima shouted back. "NOW TURN IT DOWN!"

Gordon did, and at least now he knew that it really did go that loud.

After recreation time ended at 10 p.m., it was the period of the officially named *great silence*, the period of quiet that lasted until the next morning after breakfast. Everyone had to retire to their room at 10, turn off all the lights, and get ready to go to sleep.

The work schedule was as carefully regimented as the daily schedule, and the duties shifted each week so that everyone had to do everything at one time or another. There was of course lots of cleaning, sweeping, and mopping to do in all of the communal rooms, the classrooms, the bathrooms, etc., but the least desirable jobs were feeding and washing the pigs. The seminary had a pig pen out behind the kitchen, where they kept a few adult pigs and many little piglets. They fed the pigs the daily leftovers from dinner, so whoever's turn it was that week was supposed to save and collect all the food scraps from everyone's plates after dinner. They had to run their hand through the food to feel for discarded toothpicks or fish bones or anything else that could pose a choking hazard for the pigs. Once they were sure that the food was fine, they'd take it out back to the pigs.

Washing the pigs felt like the ultimate exercise in futility to Gordon, and it was the task he despised. The pigs loved it, of course. They stood there patiently as the boys scrubbed their hard skin with brushes and sponges, washing off all the caked dirt and mud. But then, when the boys were done, sometimes even seconds after they finished, the pigs would turn around and roll into the dirt again. Gordon always felt like yelling his frustration straight at the pigs' dirty snouts, *Why God why? What is even the point of this?*! But then, he'd sigh to himself and hear Fr. Kifle's soothing voice, explaining that if you could do "everything for the greater glory of God," you could also wash pigs in the Lord. Gordon tried to believe this, oh how he tried, but part of him always wondered. Did clean pigs really give glory to God, *really?*

*

Just as they were initiated into the life of Ignatian Spirituality, so the new seminarians were initiated into the seminary's communal life of beer drinking. All the boys drank beer. It was like you had to or you were supposed to. It was one of the pleasures granted to you, so you should enjoy it, gratefully, in moderation, as everyone else did. Gordon had never been a beer drinker, but as an obedient student of all aspects of the life there, he too learned and followed. There were rules about drinking, and there were, of course, ways around those rules that the more experienced seminarians knew and had perfected. The secondis helped the primis learn these strategies. They were allowed to have one bottle of beer *per hour* at dinner each day. That was the rule. The dinner hour also only lasted one hour, so that meant only one bottle per dinner per day. The way around this was to be one of the last ones to go get your meal. While everyone else was lining up to get their plates and be served, you could take advantage of the little commotion while everyone was focused on the food to come. You could get a bottle and pour it out quickly into one of the opaque, silver metal cups while no one was watching. Then, once you had gotten your food, you could go pick up another bottle and have it on the table next to your cup. If it was your turn to feed the pigs, you could also easily sneak a bottle when everyone else had left you alone in the kitchen to feel through the leftovers before taking them out. If you got caught sneaking a bottle, as boys often did, there really wasn't much that the priests could do—they couldn't kick you out—instead, they would "humble you" with a long lecture about why it wasn't right and why you shouldn't do it. That was all.

Each month, the seminarians were given a fixed stipend for *personalia*, or for their toiletries like toothpaste and body wash (if they wanted something other than the bar soap provided by the seminary). It was 15,000 Tanzanian shillings per month, which worked out to about 800 Kenyan shillings or $8. They could use it for whatever they wanted, maybe to buy Vaseline petroleum jelly, maybe a new piece of clothing or new shoes. They didn't wear any sort of habit or specific robe at the seminary—Jesuits were not Benedictines after all and were even regarded as "far too casual" in the opinion of certain other religious orders—but even in their same old shorts and tee shirts, the boys didn't really need to buy clothes, and the seminary did all of their laundry for them. They also didn't have to pay for their food or housing, obviously, so this personal money felt like a lot. Most of the boys spent this when they went out drinking at the bars in downtown Arusha, buying beer or Guinness mixed with soda. Gordon would think about the things he wanted to buy during the month and plan for it—he became skilled at delayed gratification—but his personalia was always, already gone by the end of the first day of the month.

One time—after they had settled in at the seminary—Gordon and some of the other boys were frequenting one of the local bars in Arusha town, just hanging out and having some drinks with their personalia money during one of their weekend afternoons. Gordon didn't think anything about the way they acted—which was perfectly normal—until he realized that Tanzanians in the bar placed their drink orders with the utmost gentility and politeness. While a Kenyan would say, as a blunt demand, "I want this…," a Tanzanian would say something like, "Please, I am requesting to buy…" It seemed like unnecessary formality at first for Gordon, but he saw that the waitress who was helping his group was put out by their uncouth Kenyan-ness. It was like every time one of them said something, she got a little more offended, as if they were being *so* rude to her.

She walked away with their orders, went into one of the back rooms, and came back out with someone who Gordon assumed was her manager. She said something to the man, which Gordon couldn't hear and then the manager said, simply but loud enough that Gordon could hear, "They are Kenyans." The woman nodded and seemed to mouth, "Ohhhhh," like an acknowledgment that she now understood. That explained it all.

In one of those actual epiphany moments where it's like a lightbulb flickers on in your mind, it dawned on Gordon that *this* was exactly what the Tanzanian border crossing sign meant when it said, "Here people are kind." Tanzanians thought Kenyans were unmannered people by comparison, and Gordon felt humbled and a little embarrassed that he and this group of seminarians had not even realized it. They had only been focused on themselves, but part of being a good Jesuit was to focus on others and to put others before yourself. Although Gordon valued his Kenyan roots with his languages and cultural traditions, he enjoyed living with people from many different countries and being exposed to new thoughts and stories. He wanted to be able to blend in with different people, feel at home in different countries, and not make others see difference as something *wrong*. He already felt the stirring seeds of what was maybe his calling within the Jesuits to be a uniter and a leader. Above all, he wanted to help people, to raise them out of poverty and empower them to help themselves. To become the type of Jesuit priest he envisioned for his future self, he would have to become more aware of others' needs and more knowledgeable about contemporary situations. Maybe he needed to take himself more seriously since the seminary life was about more than just enjoying a comfortable life.

3. All that Glitters

The newness of initiation faded, and Gordon truly settled into life in Arusha. The next three years passed in the repetitive, reverent rhythm of the seminary's rules and rituals: praying in the Lord, sleeping in the Lord, washing pigs in the Lord, drinking beer in the Lord, studying in the Lord, waiting for personalia in the Lord, and progressing toward a future as an obedient Jesuit and humble priest in the Lord. There was a comfort to the discipline and a stability to the predictable schedule, to be sure, but also a real monotony inherent in that life.

In addition to the regular, rotating chore schedule, Gordon took on the role of "Computer Operations Manager," also called the "Director of Computer Operations." (The seminarians tried to create a worthy title for him since this position hadn't existed before.) Despite the big title, the work the job entailed was much humbler. Gordon was, simply, in charge of opening and closing the computer room for the seminarians when it was their scheduled time to use the computers. Gordon coordinated the boys' time on the computers (of which there were two, both connected to the internet), and he ensured that everyone was allowed their allotted time and no more. Each seminarian was granted forty-five minutes once per week on the computer with internet, to sends email or post on social media or watch YouTube videos or whatever they chose to do.

Gordon's IT skills put him at a direct advantage here, for while many of the others didn't even know how to use a computer and didn't have an email address, Gordon had been fortunate back at Ananda Marga to take computer classes. Therefore, he'd at least been exposed to and acquainted with this machine called a desktop computer. He'd also learned how to type, well enough, where he moved his hands to push one key with one pointer finger at a time. He even taught others how to type when he lived at AJAN house. During his time there, Gordon had helped other staff set up Yahoo.com email accounts and he'd taught them how to navigate the internet. He had also learned how to use Microsoft Office programs like Word and Excel. His knowledge of all these technological ins and outs, like how to start up and shut down the computer, how to login in, how to launch and close the programs, etc., qualified Gordon to be the seminary's Director of Computer Operations. All in all, he was happy to be able to use his skills to serve the community.

The computer room was about the size of a walk-in closet and was located next to Fr. Shirima's office. One person per evening got to use the computer for their 45-minute slot, from 8:15 to 9:00, and it was Gordon's job to get the key to the room, unlock it, turn on the computer and set up the internet before the person's allotted time was scheduled to start. This meant that Gordon could take little liberties *setting up* the computer to give himself an extra fifteen minutes of free internet browsing time. He could also linger an extra 10 minutes to *shut down* the computer. Fr. Shirima kept the key—a single loose key, not on any keychain—always sitting on the top of the door to his office. Sometimes during the siesta time, the boys would go, stealthily, slide that key off and go use the computer, then return they key before anyone even knew.

As the Computer Operations Manager, Gordon had more access to the internet than anyone else in the seminary, and he used this to his advantage. In 2008, he created a Facebook account, right when the social media platform was new and exciting. Gordon added his friends from Nairobi, along with people he knew from school, and really anyone he knew. It was cool to have *friends* online and even to connect with people he hadn't seen in years. It didn't really matter if he was friends with them in real life or not. He just enjoyed having them as part of his online social network.

On one of these occasions when Gordon was squeezing in some internet time, he searched Facebook for one of his previous classmates from elementary school—a guy named Jonathan Lando. *Lando* in Luo means *light skin*, and while this boy hadn't really been Gordon's friend, Gordon thought it might be good to add him to his network. The search produced a list of approximate results, and one of them was a man named Jonathan Landon. The profile picture showed a mzungu man smiling in a black shirt and white Roman collar—he was a priest! Gordon was intrigued, so he clicked on the photo. The man's profile page said that he was married, and he had a photo with children—Gordon was even more intrigued. Gordon clicked the friend request button and also sent a personal message to introduce himself, writing:

My name is Gordon, and I am a seminarian in the Society of Jesus. I see that you're a priest. Where are you from? To which congregation do you belong?

Father Landon (for this man *was* an ordained priest) accepted Gordon's request, and they entered into that strange technological relationship of being *Facebook friends*—two people who had never physically met in real life and, if not for the internet, would never have had any knowledge of each another. They'd never seen each other in the flesh, but they wrote back and forth from time to time. Fr. Landon belonged to the International Communion of the Charismatic Episcopal Church (ICCEC), which operated throughout the world and was also known under the shorter name, the Charismatic Episcopal Church (CEC). This organization was not and had never been affiliated with the Episcopal Church of America. Instead, their name used the term "Episcopal" because it described the leadership structure of the organization as it was governed by a Bishop. The CEC operated in a "unique place between the protestant and catholic formations of faith," as their own description on their website stated, and as Gordon learned more about it, the beliefs and practices seemed very similar to his Catholic upbringing.

Fr. Landon and Gordon corresponded regularly, and they talked about all sorts of things—the priesthood, religion, vocational life. Gordon was curious to hear about Fr. Landon's family (he *was* married with children), and his work as a chaplain in the US Army. Gordon also got acquainted with his children—Fr. Landon had one son and two daughters, who were around Gordon's age (the oldest was two years younger than Gordon). Gordon added them on Facebook as his friends too, and then some of their friends and members of their church added him, and so on and so forth. Before long, it all snowballed and all of a sudden, Gordon had *so many* online mzungu friends—his Facebook feed was full of white faces from America. It felt good.

At the same time, Gordon became progressively more interested in Barack Obama, especially during Obama's first presidential run in 2008. All of the other seminarians (even if they were from other countries) supported Obama too, and they believed that his presidency would help not only the US, but the entire world. It would be a victory for all of Africa. Within the turbulent world of Kenyan politics, in 2007, Raila Odinga, the highly favored, man-of-the-people Luo-candidate for president, had lost the presidential election due to corruption. Everyone knew that he had been rigged out, and consequent post-election violence fueled by tribalism and an utter loss of hope in the possibility of *ever* having a free and fair Kenyan election tore a bloody path through the country. Thousands of people died senseless, needless deaths. In light of this, Obama's campaign for President of the United States of America gave many Kenyans a sense of renewed hope and faith in democracy—if he could get elected *there*, how much more could happen in Kenya? Gordon too felt like a victory in the US for Obama would signify a much larger victory, on such a global scale that it could even redeem Raila's stolen victory in Kenya.

Gordon, along with two other seminarians, decided that they wanted to donate to Obama's presidential campaign. Obama always said in his speeches that his political aspirations had started off small, but these humble seeds had grown into a mighty dream and a powerful run for the

Mwendo wa nyoka: the way of the snake

presidency. This proved that great things could sprout up from the humblest of means. Obama had always said, "Yes we can," and Gordon loved this motto and mindset, the rhythm and simplicity of the phrase, and the way Obama punctuated almost every line in his speeches with it, like a refrain. Gordon watched all of Obama's speeches religiously, in the sense that—just like everything else he did at the seminary—he could "watch Obama *in the Lord.*" When Obama said that anything helped, every little bit mattered, and every single person who supported him mattered, Gordon believed him. This felt like a true reflection of the Bible story where Jesus told the onlookers that the woman who had given her last penny had greater faith than the pharisees who flaunted their wealth. It didn't matter how much you gave because it was all relative to what you had, and those who gave out of the little they had, still gave a great deal.

These young men who had taken a vow of poverty truly had little to give. They didn't own property or possessions and only had the personalia money that was granted to them each month. They decided, nevertheless, that they would pool their resources and send a donation to Obama's campaign. Between the three of them, they saved up 500 Ksh or the equivalent of $5 to send. Apart from the amount, the actual problem was how to send their money because you had to donate online through a website with a credit card number. Since none of them had credit cards or bank accounts, Gordon reached out to the finance account manager at AJAN House in Kangemi. When he was visiting Kangemi for a few days of *home visit*, Gordon took their $5 in cash to the account manager, who deposited it in his own account and then donated via credit card to the campaign, on behalf of Gordon and the other seminarians. It was admittedly a lot of effort for that little donation, but Gordon felt like they had accomplished something great and truly done their part.

Gordon was overjoyed when Obama won the presidential election in November 2008, and there was much rejoicing throughout the entire seminary. Gordon watched Obama's acceptance speech over and over, until he could nearly quote the entire thing, line for line, pause for pause. Obama was the best speaker Gordon had ever heard, and Gordon soaked up Obama's inspirational words a little more each time. There was no one like him. He was eloquent and confident, and he struck the perfect balance between levity and gravity. Gordon sat in the tiny seminary computer room, listening to Obama recount triumphantly in his speech, how he had never been "the likeliest candidate." When he stated, "this victory belongs to *you*," Gordon felt like Obama was speaking directly to him. That was *his* $5 that Obama mentioned and thanked him for. His $5 had helped prove that "a government of the people, by the people, and for the people has not perished from this earth." When Obama said, "This is your victory," Gordon thought, *Yes—this is MY victory too*. Obama had done the impossible. He had given an answer to anyone who longed for change but doubted that it was possible. His answer—the answer that his presidency posed to the entire world—was a resounding *Yes we can*.

In his speech, he spoke of, "the enormity of the task that lies ahead," and how the "road will be long" and the "climb will be steep." He acknowledged that there "will be setbacks and false starts." Gordon listened to these phrases and thought, *now here is a person who knows how to move in the world, lukumba lukumba. Obama does truly have the Kenyan spirit in him.* Obama had been the camel, the turtle, the cheetah, and the snake. He would now become the eagle, as was fitting, to lead the great nation of the United States of America. Gordon felt such an affinity with Obama and he listened to the speeches so much, that he soon realized he began to copy Obama's recognizable inflection. When Gordon spoke to his fellow Jesuits, gave an answer in class, or even preached a sermon, he started to sound like Obama.

The line that resonated most with Gordon from Obama's acceptance speech was the one near the end, when Obama directly addressed those "watching tonight from beyond our shores...those who are huddled around radios in the forgotten corners of our world." Obama said that though they were separated by distance, culture, and singular stories, "our destiny is shared." These words vibrated deep within Gordon like the bells of a large cathedral, ringing and overlapping and layering their sound in waves. That someone as great and illustrious as Barack Obama, president-elect of the most powerful nation on Earth, could claim—would *choose* to claim—that they shared a common destiny, was almost too much for Gordon. Obama too had been a brown boy from a Kenyan father, a kid with a head full of dreams staring down unlikely odds. He had navigated twists and turns and finally succeeded. Gordon marveled at the thought that the future of Gordon Oduor Okumu could be intertwined with that of Barack Obama. It was more than words could express.

Gordon wanted to be like Obama, do great things like Obama, and participate in some small way in shaping and fashioning the great destiny that they shared. He felt like a fire had been kindled inside him. Maybe it had always been there and had just been dormant, or maybe it had been buried under other thoughts and desires but was now given the space and oxygen it needed to grow and burn. If this was Gordon's destiny, "to answer that call," to rise to the occasion and to help his people, he wanted to seize the moment. He wanted to "restore prosperity and promote the cause of peace," and above all, stand up next to Obama and reaffirm that "where we are met with cynicism, and doubt, and those who tell us that we can't, we will respond with that timeless creed that sums up the spirit of a people, Yes, we can."

*

From then on, through listening to Obama's speeches and following his work in the American government, the fire of Gordon's interest in leadership and political ideology grew and burned ever brighter. He began seriously considering how he could manage a political career in the future with his calling to Jesuit priesthood—couldn't he do both? He didn't mind the vows of poverty and chastity, but it was obedience that began to seem like an obstacle. "Obedience" in the Society of Jesus didn't just mean following the rules and keeping the daily schedule, but, on a deeper level, it really meant that everything would be decided for you by those above you, and you had no choice but to agree. Vowing your life to serve the Society meant that even if you chose what you wanted to study at university, they would choose where to send you for your studies, and after, where to place you when you returned home.

The Jesuits also did not want to get involved in politics, but Gordon saw politics as the place where real change needed to happen. The Jesuits prayed, fervently and devotedly, for people, with people, for each other and with each other, for the health and peace of the whole world. But Gordon saw that change needed to happen *in the government*, at the level of laws and policies. Prayer never stopped corruption. Prayer couldn't give starving people food to survive for another day. Prayer couldn't reform the judicial system, hold people accountable for crimes, create unions and give representation to workers. While the Jesuits prayed for the government, the government rolled around in its corruption like pigs enjoying their mud.

What's more, Gordon realized that while the Jesuits *did* prize education and the priests and brothers were highly educated intelligent men, many of them didn't get to use their education in their actual work after university. This left them feeling wasted and undervalued. Many Jesuits obtained doctoral degrees in the advanced sciences, but then were sent to serve as parish priests for small churches in the slums. Or, they'd study anthropology and linguistics, only to be stationed at a remote village in South Sudan, ministering to a community wrecked by civil war. That was valuable work—there was no doubt—but it didn't require all that education. Even Fr. Drasiga, one of the priests working at the seminary in Arusha, had earned a doctoral degree in some specialized science like radiology, but now he was corralling sweaty seminarians each day and washing pigs and scrubbing bathroom floors. Was there really nothing more they could use him for? Gordon was thinking that he'd study journalism or political science, maybe even media studies, but where would they send him and what would he get to do with it?

The area where *poverty* and *obedience* overlapped was, of course, money. It often, unfortunately comes back to money. All Jesuits funneled their incomes into one communal pot, and even Jesuits who served as university professors, doctors, or lawyers, (which is to say, in a position that earned a substantial income), sent their salary right to the Society. They never personally saw a cent of it. It was money that you earned *for* the Society and that was distributed throughout the Society as the provincial and those in leadership saw fit. Gordon knew about all of this before he joined the Society, and it was no big secret or surprise. Still, there was something in him that couldn't reconcile his initial impression, all those years ago, of the Jesuits as an egalitarian order with the reality he saw where seasoned Jesuit priests possessed nothing of their own and had to ask even for the little money to buy shoes.

Related to this was an even stickier situation. Gordon knew that "African culture mattered," which meant that all these Jesuits from various African countries had left behind struggling parents and families. They all wanted to help their families and especially their aging parents by sending them some financial support—this was a common practice in regular society. Gordon too wanted to be able to send money to Grandma in Migori, even if it was just a little money, enough to buy an extra bag of flour or a bottle of cooking oil. For the Jesuits, this was like anything else, and you didn't have any money to send, for the money was not yours. You had to make a request, and if the Society agreed, they could send something to your family specifically. You could ask the provincial, but everyone knew that he would say no, so no one even bothered to ask. That was the sad reality.

Gordon always felt like if the Jesuits were so keen to invest in *him* as a person and a priest, why were they not willing to help his family as well? His family was an important part of him as a person, and the Jesuits couldn't ask him to sever his ties with his family. He resolved that he simply would *never* stop caring if Grandma had money to buy food or if she would go hungry; if she fell sick and couldn't pay hospital bills; or, most of all, if she needed money to buy medicine that could potentially prolong her life. Gordon had been through that experience before, back when it had been out of his control. Now that he was an adult, he was determined to never let that happen again.

Through talking with Jesuits who were further along and some who had even already been ordained to the priesthood, Gordon realized that many of them shared his feelings and that there was an immense amount of pent-up frustration simmering below the satisfied façade of poverty, chastity, and obedience. Some of them felt so constrained by having to choose between their loyalty to their families or to the Society that they were pushed into light corruption, where they'd start lying just a little bit, here and there, cutting corners and concealing bits and pieces. They had to find ways around sending their entire salary to the Jesuits, ways of keeping a little to send to their families. They didn't want to ask for it because they knew their desires would be rejected. There was, in fact, a deep running current of dissatisfaction with what many felt was misalignment between the seminarians' and priests' gifts and talents and how they were used to meet the needs of the Society. This wasn't the case for everyone, but for some, it could lead to a lifetime of frustration, an existence of having taken vows that slowly turned into resentment, and faith that slowly eroded into bitterness, souring the promised life of holy service and sweet self-sacrifice.

Mwendo wa nyoka: the way of the snake

The final straw came in 2009, when Gordon received an email sent out to *all* Jesuits in East Africa, to officially explain and address a most grievous and tragic matter: a seminarian who was two years ahead of Gordon and who had been stationed in Nairobi for what is called *regency*, a period of service and work in the community. He had been found dead in a hotel room. It was an apparent suicide, and the man had left a note. He admitted that he had "misused money," and there were various theories that circulated via hearsay about what this meant exactly. Crucially, he wrote in the letter—maybe speaking figuratively or literally—that he thought, "Fr. Shirima will kill me." That was the same Fr. Shirima that struck fear into the hearts of hopeful candidates and ruled over the Society with an iron fist, a tight grip that had evidently begun to suffocate and strangle, even unto death.

It wasn't that Gordon personally feared Fr. Shirima to that extent (he didn't at that time anyway, and he couldn't imagine that he ever would). However, he couldn't help but wonder, *What if there comes a time when I do something wrong and I need to ask for forgiveness?* Was forgiveness not possible? Gordon didn't really have family he could go back to. There was no home waiting for him and nowhere to welcome him back if he failed in the Society. What if he wanted to explain himself at some point, and there was just no possibility or chance? These unsettling thoughts made him feel existentially constipated. It was a sense of claustrophobia, like the walls of this life were slowly closing in, and he had to make a break for it before it was too late. He wanted to do great things with his life, not be forced into submission and fear. Would he have to fear for the rest of his life as Jesuit, if he ever stepped out of line? Was there truly no grace here? Was there no mercy? Where was that greatest of all the Christian virtues after the love of God: to love your neighbor as yourself?

Right away, Gordon expressed his feelings to Fr. Landon, the American priest he corresponded with on Facebook. Fr. Landon offered wise and welcome counsel, not simply trying to persuade Gordon to stay the course. He helped Gordon think through all sides of the matter, and above all, he encouraged Gordon that if this was how he truly felt and if he had offered the matter up to God in prayer, Gordon needed to withdraw from the Society of Jesus before he got further along. There was no point in continuing down a path he didn't see for himself any longer, that he had discerned was *not* God's will for his life.

Gordon had to talk with Fr. Kifle, the spiritual director, who preached to Gordon a long sermon about how he was still new in the Society and how it was always "difficult to start." *It's been years*, Gordon thought. Kifle continued, saying that Gordon was probably just overthinking and he was still adjusting. *I'm not overthinking*, Gordon said to himself. *I have thought through this thoroughly and calmly. I have been rational.* Kifle told Gordon to pray about it and ask for God's direction. *I have prayed about it and I have asked God's direction.* Kifle prayed for Gordon right there, asking that God would illuminate the way forward and uncloud Gordon's troubled mind. *My mind is not troubled. It's clear.* Gordon thought. *The way forward is already illuminated. It is done.*

Next, Gordon had to have a conversation with the Fr. Shirima, the Novice Master at the seminary, telling him simply that he'd discerned that he needed something else. It was always a bit risky to claim to know what God *wanted*, but Gordon added anyway, "This is not the place where God wants me to be."

Fr. Shirima asked what Gordon thought *he* wanted.

"I don't know. I just know what it's *not*, right now."

Shirima asked if Gordon would like more counseling to help with his decision.

Gordon politely declined.

He was thankful that ensuing conversations with the provincial (the *other* feared Fr. Shirima) took place in writing and were very formal. Then

Mwendo wa nyoka: the way of the snake

began the process of undoing much of what had been done and letting everyone know. Gordon started by sending Fr. Terry at Loyola House in Nairobi an email, and Fr. Terry was understandably shocked. Mostly though, he was disappointed. Gordon could sense it behind every word in his emails. Terry wrote that out of all the candidates he had prepared the year Gordon got admitted, Gordon had seemed the "most ready," the most suited for the Jesuit life. So, what had changed? Terry had dreamed big dreams for Gordon, just as Gordon had dreamed big dreams for himself. But much had changed.

There were other administrative procedures, papers to sign and preparations to make, and soon enough, it came time for Gordon to pack his things. The night before he was scheduled to leave, the seminary had a going away party in the dining hall, and then a bunch of the other seminarians came to Gordon's room to personally wish him farewell. Many revealed that they too were unhappy or had doubts about this or that aspect of the life, and they admired Gordon's courage for choosing to leave. It was not an easy decision, and most feared disappointing their families, friends, and all the Jesuit leaders. Gordon had always seemed fearless though and he spoke his mind, regardless of what anyone would think. His stubbornness and individuality had perhaps always been doomed to run contrary to the Jesuit life of sacrifice, and obedience "for the greater glory," or maybe it was just incredibly rare that they survived in that place where progressive indoctrination and ever greater submission were the goal.

The next day, Fr. Drasiga drove Gordon to the bus stop in Arusha. The seminary had booked him a seat on that same bus route that he had come by years ago, from Arusha to Nairobi. Drasiga took out an envelope and gave Gordon 3,000 Ksh ($30) in cash right as Gordon was about to board the bus. That money hadn't been negotiated or discussed at all, but it was far too little to really help Gordon start a life outside of the seminary. It was too late to ask for more though or to do anything about it, so Gordon accepted the money, thanked Fr. Drasiga, and got on the bus.

Once the bus left and Gordon was on his way, he first felt a little excited to *return to freedom*. A tingling sensation ran through his body, and he leaned back in his seat and relaxed. He breathed deeply, thinking about how that life was *over*. He would once again be the master of his time, money, and choices. He tried to savor the relief and the sense of open-ended possibility that awaited him back in Nairobi, but there was also a hint of apprehension creeping into his excitement, like a cloud moving in front of the sun. He wondered if he had made the right decision…or had he thrown everything away, been frivolous and stupid? He thought back to the Nyamgondho of Grandma's folktale—was he too going to suffer some terrible fate for squandering the blessings he'd been given? Would he receive some cosmic retribution for defying God's call to the priesthood? *Maybe*—and this was perhaps the biggest and most difficult question of all for it was also the most nebulous—had he misinterpreted God's will? Had he not listened, not recognized the signs and the guidance, not had eyes to see or ears to hear? How did he even know these feelings were from God?

He sighed and told himself to let these feelings pass like fallen leaves floating down a river. It didn't really matter if his decision was right or wrong—what mattered was that it was done. He had made his choice. Now he needed to turn his mind to the more pressing, practical decision—what to *do* next. The Nairobi he was returning to was an expanse laid open before him—he had no house, no possessions, nearly no money, no job, no future plans. This was one of those situations, or maybe the greatest of all the situations he had ever faced, where he would have to muster his strength and resilience and just figure it out. He told himself, once again, that he must be brave. He held onto the most affirming, hope-filled phrase he knew, and he said it over and over in his mind as the bus bumped along the dusty road back to Nairobi—*Yes we can.*

VI
Mwendo wa ngarama: the difficult way

Msafiri mbali, hupita jabali.

Translation:
The determined traveler will pass the mountain on the horizon.

Paraphrase:
If you work hard,
you can achieve even more than you intended.

1. The Bottom Again

Gordon arrived in downtown Nairobi with the money from Arusha in his pocket, his backpack over his shoulder, and the rest of his things in his suitcase. Right when he stepped off the bus, the zipper broke on his suitcase and everything spilled out onto the dusty street. *This is a bad sign,* he thought. *Or maybe this is Nairobi's way of welcoming me back to the city. Maybe it doesn't even want me back.* The disheveled mess of his dusty few possessions, sprawled out on the street, seemed like a fitting representation of his life. He was starting over, once again, and he had no plans except to get back to Kangemi. He gathered up everything and stuffed it into his suitcase. Then he held it together under his arm as he walked to go hail a taxi.

After the taxi ride to Kangemi, his money was spent. He went to his half-sister Maureen's place, and she agreed to let him stay until he could find a suitable shanty of his own. He then went to go ask for his old cellphone (that he had given to a Jesuit brother friend when he left Kangemi to go to Arusha), and he also reached out to AJAN House and Fr. Terry. The response from all these former contacts and confidants as a disheartening version of "We are not interested." Gordon hadn't anticipated this cold shoulder, but he now felt the icy breeze blowing off all these cooled friendships. He understood that since he had left the Jesuits, he was no longer *one of them*, but he had assumed—maybe naively—that friendship ran deeper than adherence to the religious order. Since he had chosen to become an outsider, to refuse all their charity and kindness, now they evidently refused to offer it back.

Although Gordon was disappointed, he knew he would have to make his own way, so the next thing to do was to go to a cybercafe and email the American priest, Fr. Landon. At least Gordon still had this one contact, this one person who had not severed the friendship. Gordon felt a little nagging doubt in the back of his mind though—how well did he really know this man? How well did the man really know Gordon? Would this relationship go cold like the others, and would this man decide he didn't want to be involved in Gordon's life? People often enjoy offering superficial help, but when they're asked to really get their hands dirty, they pull away. What if the man secretly harbored suspicion that Gordon was going to become a drunkard, or that Gordon wasn't really who he said he was. What if Gordon were actually a con man out to scam Fr. Landon of all his American money? How would Gordon prove to him that everything was genuine, and that he was exactly who he said he was? There were many open questions roaming around in Gordon's mind, like a pinball game that wouldn't stop.

A few weeks after returning to Kangemi, Gordon found a suitable shanty room, the same ten-by-ten-foot style as always. By reaching out to his past high school friends and with some help from Maureen, he acquired enough essentials to get by. Gordon had always felt that it was easy anyway not to care about what he didn't have. He could keep his desires within his means, for the moment, and he didn't mind living with the most basic, bare bones essentials.

In his continuing correspondence with Fr. Landon, Gordon decided that he could try to enroll at an American university. Fr. Landon helped him navigate the complicated world of US universities and colleges, and they identified a handful that looked good for Gordon. Gordon applied and even got accepted at a few, but the bottom-line issue was the cost. They were far too expensive, and even if Gordon could receive financial assistance and scholarships, the universities still wanted him to provide proof of available financial resources before coming. This felt a little bit unfair for him as a foreign applicant because he knew that local students didn't have to prove that they could cover the entirety of the tuition costs *before* even starting. Did foreign students from places like Europe and

Canada have to do this? Or students from China? Gordon didn't know for sure, but he had a gut feeling that it was related to him being a student from an economically disadvantaged country in Africa.

As his next course of action, he set his sights on local Kenyan universities. There was Daystar University, a private institution with a good reputation, but even though Gordon got accepted there, it also proved too expensive. He then considered public schools, like the University of Nairobi and Multimedia University. This latter school had previously been called the Kenya College of Communication and Technology (or KCCT) but had changed its name in 2010 to the Multimedia University College of Kenya. Kenyan institutions of higher learning loved to include the word Kenya in their long names—the longer the better it seemed—and this forced them to rely on acronyms. A good example of this was the Kenya Polytechnic University College of Kenya or KPUCK, which later changed its name to the Technical University of Kenya. Newly named Multimedia University used a fairly short and simple acronym, MMU, and it had two possible start date for students, either at the beginning of the Kenyan academic year in July or at the midpoint in January. MMU accepted Gordon with a start date of July 2010.

In the meantime, Gordon had started attending the Charismatic Episcopal Church (or CEC) in Nairobi, the branch of the church that Fr. Landon belonged to. Since Gordon felt alienated by the Catholic Church, he enjoyed being a part of this new community. It was admittedly very small, but at least it was welcoming. The church's entire congregation, around five or six people, met each Sunday morning at a rented room in an office building in downtown Nairobi. Gordon would then head to a cybercafé after the service to chat and message with the Landon family before they went to church (since it would still be their Sunday morning with the time difference). Gordon returned home to Kangemi later in the afternoon.

One Sunday when he arrived back in Kangemi after church, he was met with an unpleasant but all too common occurrence in the slums—there had been a fire on his block. Fires happened every day in the slums, and all it took was one spark to set ablaze the myriad hazards nestled within the tightly packed houses, with all their open cooking fires and exposed electrical wires. Since they were so common, fires usually weren't a huge cause for alarm (except for the specifically affected). The slum streets were always so crowded and the ramshackle structures so labyrinthine that fire trucks couldn't squeeze through and therefore didn't even attempt it. They simply wouldn't come, leaving the people to fend for themselves. Most lost everything, and that was normal.

Everyone knew how it worked, and since living in the slums meant constantly being at risk, you had to be vigilant not to leave anything in your shanty that you weren't prepared to lose. Slum dwellers especially knew better than to leave paper money at home. When fires started, people around would run into the shanties to salvage all the possessions as onlookers and gawkers gathered. People brought out what they could and placed it on the street, but once you set something down and turned your back to go salvage more from the house fire, it was gone. Every time you brought out more, all your possessions were already taken. People even offered to help and ran in to get things and ran out with them, only to get lost among the other people and the commotion. In this sense, fires were like free-for-alls, and some people even waited for them so they could plunder and pillage, like a lion waiting for a deer to give birth. Property owners sometimes started the fires themselves as a way to get rid of difficult tenants.

By the time Gordon reached his block, the entire area had been reduced to an open field full of rubble. People had mostly dissipated, and all of the shanty structures were gone, striped so bare that there was almost no evidence there had even been a fire. All that was left was the blackened ground, like the bones of a carcass picked clean by vultures. Really, even most of the bones were gone. Gordon had carried his small backpack with him to church that day, fortunately, so he still had that, along with his wallet, cellphone, a Bible, and the clothes on his back. That was now, literally, all he had in the world.

Gordon stayed with friends in Kangemi for a while, bouncing from place to place, sleeping on couches and extra mattresses on the floor. He was still supposed to start his university studies in a couple of months though, so he needed a place to live. Fr. Landon suggested that Gordon apply for the student dorms at Multimedia University, but Gordon thought that staying in the dorms would only delay his actual house search, since he would have to move out at the end of the term. He thought it would be more efficient and more permanent to just find another shanty home, as he had always done. Fr. Landon vetoed that idea. He was adamant that Gordon needed a *real* apartment, somewhere safe and stable. Even though this made finding an apartment slightly harder and it certainly would be more expensive, Gordon felt encouraged that someone cared so much for his well-being, even someone halfway across the world. This felt different than the way the Jesuits had treated him, for Fr. Landon wasn't getting anything out of this deal, other than the satisfaction of helping Gordon. There was no promise of Gordon giving him back anything, and Gordon understood, *now*, that this was what true grace felt like.

Gordon then set his sights on a *real* apartment like he had never lived in before, the type of place that would live up to Fr. Landon's requirements. Gordon found one that looked good in the Uthiru neighborhood west of Kangemi, but the place seemed wildly expensive. Gordon carefully broached the subject of payment with Fr. Landon, saying, "But I know Father, it's going to be very expensive." The rent was $180 per month, and Gordon couldn't get his mind to move on from the $30 per month shanty rates in Kangemi—they could save a lot by choosing something like that, and Gordon knew how to get by just fine in the slums. But Fr. Landon again insisted that the price was not a big deal. The apartment also required a security deposit, raising the total cost to move in to $360, or the equivalent of 36,000 Ksh. Gordon had never even held that much money in his hand. It seemed extravagant and maybe unnecessary, but Fr. Landon said it was fine, and they went with it.

The following Sunday, the few congregants of the CEC in Nairobi brought Gordon whatever they wanted to donate for his new apartment — cooking materials, linens, housewares, etc. Many donated clothes, and the priest even gave Gordon some pants, but the man was at least two times Gordon's size. Once again, it always seemed to happen, Gordon ended up with clothes that were too big for him. He was, of course, grateful for their charity and he gladly accepted all of their gifts.

He moved into the new apartment in May, and it was the classiest place he'd ever lived. It had one bedroom, a living room, and a kitchen. He also had his own bathroom with clean and always-available running water—no more public latrines and lining up for showers on the street. The apartment even had closets, the kind of real closets that are set back into the walls. Even if Gordon didn't have things to put in the closets, it still felt good that they were there. When Gordon first moved in and the place was still mostly empty, it felt impossibly large, like he was living in the center of a soccer stadium. Jackason even came by and teased Gordon, addressing him with an overly formal tone, "*Mr. Gordon, how can you afford this mansion?*" In truth, he was only able to afford it with the help from Fr. Landon and his church community in Atlanta, Georgia. With that support, Gordon also furnished the new luxurious-seeming apartment with secondhand pieces. He got a couch and a coffee table for the living room, a twenty-one-inch TV to watch news, a bed, and even a small refrigerator with a freezer. It felt comfy and fancy. Gordon had never had his own fridge or freezer, and the possibilities seemed endless.

Mwendo wa ngarama: the difficult way

The first thing Gordon bought to christen that small freezer was a pint-sized tub of ice cream. He brought it home and put it in the freezer, closed the door, and relished the satisfaction of just *knowing* that it was there. He could have it whenever he wanted. What decadence! After thinking for a moment, he decided that right now was when he wanted it, so he took out the pint and scooped himself some in a bowl. He sat down on *his* couch in *his* living room in *his* apartment to watch *his* TV and enjoy *his* dessert for no reason at all other than that he could have it. After he finished his bowl, he decided he could have a little bit more, because why not? He was the king of this kingdom after all. After the second helping, he went back for a third, and then another, and soon, the ice cream was all gone. Even the fact that it was gone was strangely kind of satisfying, for he thought, *If I ever want to have ice cream in my apartment again, I can just go out and buy more.* That was, perhaps, the most mzungu thing he had ever thought in his whole life. He smiled to himself, happy that he could now even *think* such things.

2. Mr. President Sir

With his secure living situation and even a home desktop computer, Gordon was ready for studies at Multimedia University when it came time to start in July 2010. He knew no one who went there, and his first impression was that the campus seemed quiet and dated. The school had started in the 1970s as an offshoot of the Kenya Telecommunications Company as a means to train their employees. By the 2000s, the school had branched out into other domains and had three departments: media, engineering, and business. The campus had a library, student dorms or *hostels*, a cafeteria (the pavilion), a recreation center with a swimming pool, a dusty soccer field, and a local students' radio station. Although the campus had some open grassy areas lined by palm trees and bushes, much like the quads of American university campuses, the classrooms were mostly in prefabricated buildings and low-roofed portables.

The campus was situated at the southern edge of Nairobi, further south than Langata Cemetery, and the edge of campus touched the border between Nairobi County and Kajiado County. Across Magadi road, the main street that marked the eastern border of campus, sat the sprawling 45-square-mile Nairobi National Park. Because of this proximity to the park, the MMU campus was home to many wandering animals, particularly warthogs and baboons. The baboons were mostly harmless, except that they were always looking for food, and they did not hesitate to snatch anything out of your hand as you walked across campus. Baboons could even climb into open dorm room windows and rummage through your things. They'd ransack your room, overturning baskets, shaking out book bags, and opening closets, but then they'd leave the way they came when they discovered there wasn't any food. The warthogs were medium-sized wild pigs with a distinctly scruffy appearance. Their snouts were long and flat all the way from their eyes to the tip of their noses. They had two sets of tusks that curved out from their snouts, and two sets of their characteristic warts on the sides of the face, which looked more like prosthetic lumps protruding from just above their tusks, next to their eyes. They had coarse brown hair and one fluffy strip of mane that ran down their spine. Although their appearance was imposing, the warthogs weren't mean. They were actually quite simple creatures.

Often, since the classroom buildings were left unlocked during the night, the first students to arrive in the morning would open the doors and have the initial shock of seeing a warthog or even a family of warthogs that had wandered in and decided to stay the night in a warm corner. Students then kicked or threw something in their direction, and the warthogs grunted or squealed and made a run for it. They had such short memories that even when students chased and shooed them away, the warthogs ran something like 10 feet, then stopped, and started chewing the grass again like nothing had happened. The students even had a saying, "you're as forgetful as a warthog." Even though the strange creatures already had short legs, the warthogs would crouch down with their forelegs bent backwards at the knee joints whenever they stopped to eat, so that their snout could reach the grass. This always made them look like they were bowing or kneeling while they were grazing. They never attacked students and weren't violent, and they just ate their grass in peace. So, for the most part, everyone shared the MMU campus and minded their own business.

*

In Gordon's incoming class for the communication studies program, there were about ninety students, divided into two groups of forty-five. The way the university schedule worked was that the students stayed in their cohort and were assigned to a single classroom where they had all their lessons. The professors would come to the students at their classroom. The university also decided the students' schedule, depending on their chosen path of study. It was basically like the university handed the students their schedule each semester, seven courses and no electives. Students could of course spend time in the library for their research and go to the labs for radio and television-specific classes.

Gordon's freshman cohort seemed kind of shy (in his opinion), but maybe it was just early, and everyone was trying to get a feel for everyone else. At the beginning of the term, one of the standard procedures was to elect a class prefect, also called a *class monitor*, which meant a student who would act as the liaison between the cohort and the professors. The class monitor helped manage the logistics involved with turning in assignments and disseminating important information and updates to the students. Surprisingly—even though MMU was an institution of communication and technology—it had no content management system and no central email system. All assignments had to be printed out on paper, collected by the class monitor, and then delivered to the professor. If class had to be canceled or rescheduled or the professor was out sick, they would simply inform the class monitor, and it was the monitor's responsibility to tell the other students. To pass back graded assignments and tests, the professor gave the stack of papers to the class monitor, who distributed them accordingly to the students (which of course meant seeing everyone else's grades, but that was an understood part of the job). When it was time for Gordon's cohort to elect their class monitor, no one volunteered. They all just sat there in that awkward silence where everyone expects someone else to do it, and everyone just waits, listening to the seconds tick loudly on the wall clock. The students waited and nothing happened. The clock ticked and the air felt thick, so Gordon raised his hand. If no one else was willing to step up, he figured that he could do the job just fine. This seemed like a small side gig anyway.

What was initially a humble entry into student leadership proved to be the first stepping stone of a much larger journey. At that time, the university had no central governing student union or council. The elder students had wanted to form one for a while, but it was still in the very formative stages. As part of the ongoing discussion, all the class monitors came together and decided to send a formal proposal to the university leadership. During that first meeting, Gordon didn't know why exactly, but he felt moved to stand up and make a speech, full of enthusiasm and confidence. He had only been at the university for about two months, but he fully supported the desire for a students' governing council. He was assertive in a way that other students weren't, even though he was an unknown, brand-new freshman. He could already feel that perhaps the students' desire was strong enough, but they were sorely in need of someone who could be their voice, someone who would stand up and take charge and turn that desire into a reality.

Gordon saw the clear and pressing need and envisioned how he could fill it. He enjoyed public speaking, and he knew how to speak clean English. He had also learned much from his time with the Jesuits—he had read widely and preached sermons after all. He had studied some philosophy and theology, and he could drop some big, impressive terms now and again. It also helped that he didn't have a heavy Luo accent, or any kind of overpowering regional accent from years of living in the rural country (like many of the students). He could speak Swahili and knew the cool, current slang, and could associate with both senior university officials and the common students. Gordon loved the idea of this entire challenge—he had nothing to lose anyway. His position at the university was not precarious and he didn't have family breathing down his neck, reminding him every day to just stay in line, keep his head down, and complete his studies quietly. For the most part, Gordon didn't do things quietly anyway, and he saw this as a real chance to make some real noise. He was in an opportune position and could take the risk—it's not like he had parents who had sacrificed the little that they had or even sold a cow to pay for him to go to college.

*

After the students drew up a proposal for their fledgling Students' Governing Council, it had to be approved by the university leadership, so both the tentative students' council and university council met for a meeting. There was one long rectangular table in the room, with the university vice president sitting at the head of the table, a row of professors on one side, and students sitting around the other two sides.

Gordon stood up to give the opening remarks, as he was the students' designated speaker. He faced the professors with all their plaques, framed degrees, and awards behind them on the wall. He did not beat around the bush, but got right to it, saying, "As I stand before you as a freshman on behalf of the students at this university, we assert that the professors are working to deter us from governing ourselves."

A cheer erupted from the students, while the professors grumbled and murmured. One of the professors stood up.

"We are not deterring you. We are trying to ensure that the style of leadership will be good."

Gordon was still standing and replied, "We are the students and you are the professors. We learn what *you* teach us. Everything we do will be a reflection of what you have taught us. Therefore, there should be nothing to worry about."

The students cheered even louder and clapped. Gordon could feel them looking at his back and thinking, *Who is this guy? Where did he come from?* Their cheers and applause only fueled his confidence. He *was* their voice, and he would be their champion.

After the discussion settled into more civil back and forth, the professors and the university dean accepted the students' proposal for their governing council. The agreement was conditional though, and the first thing the university required was a more detailed structure and a clear hierarchy for how the council and student government would be organized and conducted. The students would have to hold elections for specific positions and draft a constitution that would have to be voted on and approved by the entire student body. This all seemed like a tall order with little time to accomplish it, but the students were also fueled by the momentum of their first success. There was a current of excitement rippling through the university student population. Something new and exciting was happening, something that had never happened before. They were defining their own future, and they were going to make it happen.

The still-forming students' council drew up a constitution based on one they'd borrowed from the students at Kenyatta University. Everything had to be voted on though, and all the information about developments had to be communicated to the students. Gordon continued to be the voice and the face of the students' council now that there was more information than ever to communicate and explain. He was invited to speak almost every day on the university radio station. He spoke about the council and their constitution, explaining the policies and procedures in language that the students could understand. He told stories, anecdotes, and metaphors—the way Raila Odinga did in his political speeches—to make things relatable and even enjoyable to hear. He used soccer metaphors (because everyone understood soccer) and included Biblical references, just like all the national politicians did. The radio station even recorded Gordon's voice to use for intro and outro soundbites for their various segments. The sound of his voice became ubiquitous and synonymous with the progressive student spirit of change and progress. Students even started referring to Gordon as the "Raila of the school," the one who would fight with pure heart and humble strength for the needs of the common man. He felt like David up against Goliath—a lowly shepherd boy who, with help from God himself, overcame impossible odds and became king.

One of Gordon's teachers, named Professor Majany, became his political advisor. Majany was a true doctor, meaning he'd really earned his doctoral degree (and it wasn't the sort of the nominal one that politicians acquired through bribery and coercion). He taught classes about political science and media law and ethics. Gordon was always amazed at Majany's seemingly bottomless wealth of knowledge—the man was like a walking encyclopedia, and he talked like a brand-new radio. Majany would arrive in class for his lesson with no materials or books or anything. He'd proceed to just talk and to give a fully formed lesson, right off the top of his head. He could answer any question about the law or the new Kenyan constitution, and he encouraged the students to develop their own interpretations and become critical thinkers. Almost all students did well in his classes, as he awarded high marks for original argumentation. Even if he disagreed with you, he would still give you the grade if your argument and analysis was coherent and convincing. Gordon also continued to rely on Fr. Landon for wise counsel with navigating his new leadership endeavor. If Majany filled the role of political advisor for Gordon, Fr. Landon truly filled the role of *father*, as the caring, paternal figure that Gordon had never had.

With the support of his advisors and the momentum of the nascent students' council, Gordon ran for the position of secretary general at the university's very first student election that November. Since Gordon was still only a freshman, it was too soon for him to run for a bigger position like president. Another student (a senior) became president but served mostly as a figurehead. Gordon served as the ongoing voice of the students, and his presence provided stability and continuity. He knew, and the students knew, that with him as their champion, he would not lead them astray.

*

As the secretary of the students' council, Gordon's political efforts started to really gain momentum. He worked to help streamline the Council's new constitution, and he created contacts with other student leaders. In Kenya, most national politicians started out as student leaders anyway, and it was common practice to use university leadership as a springboard into national leadership. The younger population in Kenya was larger than the older, so national politicians also had it in their best interest to keep an eye out for the up-and-coming student leaders. The youth were the ones who could be riled up and called into mass action. They had the energy, the enthusiasm, and the sheer numbers. They were the ones who didn't care if they got tear-gassed at protests or rallies. They were a force to be reckoned with. Gordon began to think seriously about his position in student leadership and to visualize a pathway forward as part of the rising generation—he couldn't help but dream.

One of the first issues that Gordon wanted to confront (which affected him personally) was the university's lack of convenient transportation options. Most of the students at MMU were what they called "day scholars" like Gordon, who commuted to campus during the day for their classes, and returned home in the evening to neighborhoods in the north like Kangemi, and Kawangware, or the slums of Kibera and Mathare. To get to campus from his neighborhood just west of Kangemi, Gordon had to take a matatu to the train station downtown and connect to another matatu that took him to MMU. Matatu prices changed all the time, depending on various factors like the time of day and weather, and the drivers knew that they had a captive population of students that they could exploit. It was a frustrating burden on already financially overburdened students, and Gordon decided that he was going to change it.

As he waited at the bus stops, Gordon looked around at the other gathered students, and he began to talk to them and ask them what they thought about the available transportation options, to learn what would be most useful to them. He said that he'd work to change this situation, as he was one of them. He too felt the strain, and he was just like all the other commuting students. They wanted a direct bus from MMU to downtown, reserved for students, and they wanted it to be free. It would be like the university shuttle, dedicated to students with no fluctuating price.

Gordon took these desires and ran with them. He started a petition and got enough signatures to present it to the university council. He argued the students' case, detailed the cost and the benefits, and explained why the overwhelming need warranted such a solution. In the end, it passed, and just like that—Gordon had his first political success.

The students' governing council began holding baraza townhalls, basically like school board meetings where students could voice their opinions, desires, and concerns about on-campus life. One of the issues that kept coming up was the cost of food in the cafeteria. Students, of course, wanted lower prices for the same quantity (or better yet, larger quantity), and the university, of course, agreed to offer lower prices for lower quantity. There were many negotiation sessions, and Gordon found these the most fun part of all. He was in his element when he could explain and reason with others, and saw diplomacy in his future, maybe even at the international level. To remedy the cafeteria situation, he offered the university a compromise. If the university would not budge on the cafeteria price per quantity, it should allow students to prepare food in their dorm rooms. Students were currently not allowed to have even a hot plate to heat up water, but if they could have a single coil burner or something similar, they could make their own ugali and sauté their own cabbage. This would ease some of the burden of having to buy food every day.

The university leadership agreed to the compromise, but as an unanticipated side-effect, students started selling the food they cooked to other students, making little person-to-person under-the-table transactions in the hallways. It was as if, all of a sudden, all the students became hustlers. If they could earn a little extra money, they wanted to go for it. Dorm rooms transformed into shops, and you could walk down a hallway and get hard-boiled eggs in one room, ugali in another, kale in another, and so on. The university, of course, was not happy about this development, so Gordon (together with the students' council), came up with a second compromise: students could continue to sell their homecooked food, but they could only do so from approved stands in the students' center. This meant that a specific area of the students' center would be reserved for student businesses. Students could apply for a stand, pay to rent it from the university, and also pay a percentage of their sales in tax to the students' council. Both sides agreed to this compromise, and just like that—Gordon had his second political success.

*

Gordon's growing notoriety brought with it many perks, from both his fellow students and the wider university community. There were suddenly many people who wanted to be his friends and wanted to say that they knew him. He started getting word-of-mouth endorsements from students, for students talking to other students was still the best way to gain prominence. The teachers' union supported his endeavors—as he was a good student and got good grades—and he even befriended the non-teaching staff, like the janitorial and maintenance workers. Gordon figured that he needed to reach out to all areas of the university since they all shared the campus. He wanted to show all groups that he cared about their concerns and that he was willing to listen. Nothing was too small or too trivial.

The university also allowed him to eat free at the cafeteria and provided him with a dorm room, free of charge. Gordon made this room his administrative center on campus since he already had his apartment off campus. Prof. Majany advised Gordon to make his movements a little mysterious, since increased popularity inevitably meant more of both admirers and enemies. Gordon also received a small monthly salary, as did all the elected student leaders, that came out of a fee all students paid, specifically for the council. Strangely enough, this fee had always been a part of the required student university fees before there had even been an *actual* students' council. No one knew for sure where the fees had gone in the past, but general understanding was that they had disappeared into some professor's pocket.

In his second year, Gordon decided to run for president of the students' governing council. The election would be in November of 2011, and although Gordon was an obvious choice, he still had to officially get elected by the student body. In October, only one month before the election, he and his team of friends and advisors decided that they needed to have a proper campaign launch. Gordon didn't want to just put posters up and continue to speak about his campaign. Rather, he wanted to create an unforgettable and unprecedented spectacle. It needed to be big and flashy and loud. He wanted students to be so impressed and awestruck that they would be convinced right then and there to vote for him. It needed to be unlike anything that had ever happened at MMU and showcase his undeniable appeal. In the brainstorming process, his team threw around all kind of outlandish ideas. One of his friends suggested that he ride into campus on a horse, waving at his subjects like a royal prince in one of those very English processions full of pomp and flag-waving.

After more serious strategizing, they settled on an idea that was not that far from having Gordon charge in on a horse like some conquering hero, but was, actually, even bigger. The event was to start around four-thirty in the afternoon in front of the cafeteria at the center of campus. There was already a sort of stage or raised area carved out of the dirt and grass there, and Gordon's team set up big posters of Gordon on each side. They taped his campaign poster everywhere, covering entire poles and walls on campus end-to-end copies. They set up huge speakers and played music, just to attract some attention and get the noise going. Meanwhile, Gordon and the rest of his team headed south of campus, across the county border to a small town called Rongai. Many MMU students rented studios down there, and there was always a steady stream of students going back and forth to campus from that direction.

Mwendo wa ngarama: the difficult way

There was a taxi station in Rongai, about ten minutes from campus, and Gordon and his team started their procession from there. The taxi ride to campus cost about $1. Gordon's team went around the station, speaking to the drivers and explaining their plan, and they then hired *all* the available taxis. Other members of the team held Gordon's campaign poster and gathered any and all students who were at the station about to catch their own taxi back to campus, or who were just arriving from campus and didn't mind heading right back. Many students were idle or just up for the excitement, and they agreed to take part in the event. The team taped copies of Gordon's campaign poster to all the taxis—the posters just had to stay put for the short journey back to campus.

When everything was ready at the station, the procession set off. There were about thirty taxis total, each full of four or five passenger students, and they headed down the road, one right after another in a single long line. This stream of taxis branded with the face of Gordon Okumu for MMU Student Council President stretched for nearly a mile. Once the taxis got onto the main road, the drivers started honking and flashing their lights, and the passengers rolled down the windows and leaned out, waving, yelling, cheering, and generally creating as much hullabaloo as possible. People walking on both sides of the street stopped and stared. Students waiting at the bus stops turned and headed back toward campus, eager to see what this was all about. Gordon was in one of the taxis in the middle, which had a sunroof. He stood up in the back seat, stretched out of the sunroof, and waved to all the onlookers, just like the politicians always did when they drove their big cars through the slum streets. The entire scene was not unlike that day, many years ago in Migori, when the Honorable Dalmas Otieno Anyango had ridden through town on his way to the church. Only this time, Gordon wasn't the little boy who was supposed to sit quietly and watch. He was now the important man that everyone stopped to see. All of this was for him and because of him.

When the first taxi in the line reached the MMU campus, it turned left off the main road onto the divided entryway at the main entrance. The entryway had two white metal gates, flanked by tall palm trees, with a median separating the entry lane from the exit lane. When the taxi arrived at the closed gate, it stopped and a security officer came over to speak with the passenger, who was Gordon's second-in-command, named Robinson. Robinson explained what was happening to the officer, who radioed another officer on campus, saying simply, "Gordon's campaign team is here." The officers then opened both gates and let the taxis pass through.

The procession drove slowly and majestically through campus, with even more honking and cheering and light flashing. Students streamed out of the university buildings, leaving open books in the library, half-finished exams in the classrooms, and partially eaten meals in the cafeteria. They turned and followed the procession, and soon there were long streams of students walking alongside the cars. Gordon later heard from a friend that—coincidently—the power had gone out in the computer lab when someone had jumped up to see what the commotion was about and had accidentally tripped over the main cord. It seemed fitting that Gordon's procession had interrupted and halted *everything* on campus. Teachers and administrators came out of their offices too or at least opened their windows to watch. When the procession drove past the Communication Department, people cheered extra loud and professors waved. Gordon could see how proud they were that he was one of their own.

The taxis pulled up in front of the parking lot where the stage was set up and dropped off their passengers, car by car. By the time Gordon's taxi arrived, there was a swarm of students packing in around the taxi. Members of his team ushered people backwards and made way for Gordon. He stepped out and walked up to the stage through a parted sea, with walls of excited students pressing in on both sides, reaching out to touch his hand or pat his shoulder, cheering as he walked by, and chanting his name. Gordon really was Raila Odinga in that moment, and he tried to copy Raila's style, cool and calm, shaking hands and waving as he walked through the crowd. He also felt like Obama, smiling and pointing out individual people (whether or not Gordon actually recognized them), as he walked through the crowd and stepped up onto the stage to music mixed with cheering. It seemed like the entire university population had gathered there to see him.

In true Kenyan style, there were a couple minutes of obligatory dancing. Gordon again channeled his inner Raila Odinga and moved just enough, along with the other people on stage. The political style of dancing was to move just a little bit, to turn your shoulders to the beat, pump your arms, and stamp your feet, like exaggerated slow-motion walking. Then one of the team members began the introductory speeches. When it was time to introduce Gordon (even though everyone already knew who he was and why he was there), his team did not hold back. The speaker concluded his introduction in true grandiose fashion by saying, "Let us now call the person at MMU who has fought for all students, the one who has sniffed the teargas while fighting for our freedom to govern ourselves, the father of our democracy and our next president… Mr. GORDON OKUMU."

Gordon stepped up to the microphone at the center of stage, standing proud in a white button-up shirt and gray corduroy blazer, with blue jeans, and a black belt with a gold buckle. He had wanted to look good but not *too* fancy. He was still just a student after all. He had to strike the perfect balance of casual and professional, approachable and admirable, someone who didn't take themselves too seriously but still exuded confidence. Gordon launched into his carefully prepared speech that began by recapping all he had done for the university, from his part in the formation of the students' council to the drafting of the constitution and advocating for students' rights. He spoke loudly and proudly.

"Many of us last year around this time could have never imagined that we could pull off what we did today."

Students cheered and clapped and chanted his name.

"But this is just the beginning of what we will do in the year to come!"

There was another eruption of cheers and whistles and clapping.

He urged all the students to vote and to protect the vote, for Raila's stolen 2007 victory and the post-election violence was still fresh in their minds. It was like a wound that hadn't fully healed, but Gordon assured the crowed that their votes would *not* be stolen. He promised that this would be a free and fair election—he would make sure of it.

He paused for another wave of cheers.

"But—" he added, changing to a slightly more serious tone, "*If* we lose, we will not cause havoc. We will accept the outcome of this election, whatever it be."

Gordon strongly believed two things: First, that it was his duty as an elected leader to be a model for his voters. He wanted them to trust the electoral process, and he didn't want to do anything to discourage them from voting, to erode their faith in their newly formed democratic system at the university, or, heaven forbid, to make it *harder* for them to vote. Second, he would do all he could to ensure that there was no corruption in this election. As with the Kenyan national elections, when leaders didn't accept the results and called their supporters to mass action, this only led to violence, bloodshed, and more deeply entrenched tribal divides. Gordon wanted to bring unity, and he certainly, above all, didn't want to cause any student against student violence. There was no us vs them in his campaign and his vision for the future of Multimedia University. Though they were many individuals, together they would be united under his capable leadership as one student body.

*

After his triumphant campaign launch (which students were still talking about until election day and beyond), the campaign period proceeded as planned. Gordon gained momentum every day, and when the eve of the election day came, Gordon stayed on campus the day and night. There was no class on election day anyway to encourage students to vote. Gordon spent that day before still campaigning, making door to door rounds in the dorms, speaking to students, taking any and all questions. On election day, students had to have their paper ballot in the official box before the 5 p.m. cutoff. In the student center, Gordon sat at the table himself with the ballot box and watched each student slip their single paper in, so that there could be no stuffing this box or slipping in multiple ballots. The MMU radio and TV station completely devoted their broadcasts to the election. Even some Nairobi city news outlets reported on the momentous event.

After the cutoff time, the dean of students along with other university staff counted the ballots. Despite all of Gordon's reassurance, many students still feared rigging. It always happened in the national elections, without fail, and despite all efforts to outsmart corruption, people always found new ways to do it. Gordon personally didn't fear that the MMU election would be rigged though. He knew the ins and outs of the system—he basically was the system at this point—and he knew it had been heavily monitored and transparent from start to finish. Even the counting, which took around two hours, was watched in person by many people. After 8,000 and some votes, the faculty counters declared the official winner.

Gordon gave an acceptance speech right after the race was definitively called, and he declared that all students could have free meals in the cafeteria that evening—the cost would be covered by the students' council. He called this their *thanksgiving dinner* as a way to celebrate their victory, but he cautioned the students to behave and be orderly, even in their festivities. He didn't stay for the evening but instead headed home to his apartment to relax and rest. The evening wasn't very restful at first because he kept receiving calls. Some people just wanted to congratulate him and share their excitement, while others advised him already to start thinking forward, as this victory could lead to other victories. This success was a sure sign to keep pursuing politics—he was good at this and he was made for it. After the calls and adrenaline subsided, Gordon sat on his couch in disbelief—*did it really happen?* Maybe he was just too tired though, and he figured the satisfaction would sink in once he got some sleep.

3. The Campaign for Suna West

While Gordon spearheaded various initiatives during his one-year term as the 2011–2012 president of the MMU Students' Governing Council, the affairs of university politics began to seem trivial. He felt the pull toward bigger things, and he shifted his sights to the issues of national politics. Very quickly, he had become a big fish in a small pond, and he knew that he was meant for more and that he could do much more than manage the internal undergraduate drama of MMU.

All of the connections he formed throughout his time as president with other student leaders and even with national politicians certainly helped to broaden his horizons and give him a taste of the big leagues. In preparation for the national elections coming up in 2013, then-President of Kenya Mwai Kibaki wanted his protégé (and godchild) Uhuru Kenyatta to succeed him as the next president. President Kibaki wanted to increase appeal to the large and influential younger generation of voters, so he created a Ministry of Youth and invited many prominent young leaders to the statehouse in Nairobi. Gordon was among this group of important young leaders, and he got take part in the discussions with Kibaki at the State House, helping to explain what was important to the youth and what their main desires were. Gordon even got to shake Kibaki's hand and hear firsthand Kibaki's famously slow, lilting manner of speaking. He always sounded like someone in a video where the speed had been slowed down to 75 or even 50 percent, and where the pitch also got lower as the speed got slower.

After meeting Kibaki and learning more about his party, the PNU or Party of National Unity that was somewhat similar to the US Republican Party in its conservative values, Gordon decided to join the main opposition party, the ODM or Orange Democratic Movement. This was Kenya's more liberal, center-left political party. Kenya had many political parties now that the government had opened the flood gates to multiparty democracy, and basically anyone could start their own political party on whatever platform they wanted. There were lots of so-called *briefcase parties* that existed almost entirely in name and on a sole piece of paper carried in a briefcase. ODM, by contrast, was one of the established, legitimate, large, and popular parties. It was the party of Raila Odinga, whose official position at that time was Prime Minister. Raila had been a key part of the efforts to adopt a new Kenyan constitution and institute a multiparty democracy—all of which had successfully happened in recent years.

By the lead-up to the 2013 election though, many of the youth didn't even know what democracy meant, having grown up during Moi's oppressive single-party government. To combat this lack of knowledge and to better inform these youth who had just come of voting age, Gordon joined the Youth League of ODM and took part in promotions and discussions under the umbrella name, *Raila na Katiba*, or "Raila and the Constitution." Their purpose was to explain how Raila really was the father of Kenya's democracy, in the hopes of securing more votes for Raila as president in the 2013 election. They tried to position Raila as the face of the new constitution and western-style electoral freedom. Even though Raila was in his sixties, he was still the hero of the common man and especially the Luo people. He spoke without opening his teeth, mumbling and shuffling through a mix of Swahili and English words, but he always punctuated his speeches on the final word so that you could feel his enthusiasm and his fire burning inside.

Gordon also had the opportunity to meet a variety of other prominent national leaders. He was close to power, to *real* political power. He met the Honorable Martha Karua who was, in Gordon's eyes, the greatest leader Kenya would never elect. She was called Kenya's "Iron Lady," due to the fact that she was a serious, strictly principled, no-nonsense woman who cared about justice and uprightness above all else. She rarely smiled during her speeches and spoke without filler or fluff. Unlike other Kenyan politicians whose allegiances and priorities could shift as quickly as the wind, Karua's morals were unshakable. She admittedly attempted none of the charm or smooth-talking charisma that other politicians did (which was sometimes only camouflage for their corruption). Karua did not suffer fools or façades, and she had nothing to hide. She had famously even walked out of a public hearing with then-President Moi when he had refused to correct false public comments about Karua's opposition party or even give her an opportunity to comment. Her audacity and fearlessness in face of what could well have been a death sentence sent ripples of shock and awe through Kenya. She was perhaps the only, truly non-corrupt person in all of Kenyan politics, and Gordon admired her continual resolve to choose what was right over all else.

At one event, Gordon even had the opportunity to meet Dalmas Otieno Anyango, who just looked like a common man and of course didn't realize that Gordon had been the boy who had shaken his hand, all those years ago in Migori. Gordon also met the illustrious Miguna Miguna, a man with the same name twice, who served as Raila Odinga's political advisor. Miguna was known as much for his impressive intellect as for his aggressive and incorrigible nature. He would talk over anyone in any situation in order to always be and remain the smartest person in the room. He always had to have the last word, and there was basically no discussing with Miguna, only arguing, for he would steamroll anyone who contradicted or opposed him.

All of these new political acquaintances buoyed Gordon's hopes for his own political future. The more he brushed shoulders with Kenya's elite, the more he chomped at the bit to enter fully into that realm—these were the true movers and shakers. This was where real change could happen. Gordon had always felt that Kenya had all the resources and money for development and modernization, if only it wouldn't get stolen. Nairobi *really* could be one of the great capitals—not just in Africa but in the world—if it actually used its resources. Kenya had a staggering amount of money for a so-called third-world country, but no one would ever think so since that money was only ever used to build second and third mansions for politicians' children and to pay for their international vacations. The fact that the president was paid a salary, which was extravagant even by western standards, was a sure sign that this country had wealth.

All the money that came from the people needed to be used to serve the interests of the people—Gordon felt this so strongly he could hardly bear it. It ate him up inside to hear about projects that stalled and plans that dwindled because money mysteriously and untraceably disappeared. He'd watch news reports about yet another "investigation into corruption" that went nowhere, like always, for the people investigating were part of the very government doing the stealing. The highest officials in the Ministry of Justice along with all their subordinate cronies were appointees of the president. It was a tightly controlled, internally perpetuating, and seemingly untouchable system. It made Gordon sick to his stomach. He vowed that if he could gain enough power in the government, he would truly work to weed out corruption. ALL those corrupt people needed to face justice and answer for their crimes. What's more, it was time for Kenya as a country to prove to the world that it deserved to be taken seriously, that it could clean up the rotten mess festering at its core and put its house in order, once and for all.

*

In this line of thought, Gordon decided that he would run for parliament in the 2013 general election. The obvious choice would be to campaign for MP of the Westlands District in Nairobi, which included Kangemi and the areas like Loresho north of Waiyaki Way. As much as Gordon coveted this prime political district, Westlands was an expensive constituency and would require millions in campaign funds, which was simply far beyond Gordon's budget. Therefore, Gordon decided to run instead for MP of the Suna West constituency, based on the counsel of Professor Majany and his belief that Gordon would be *more sellable* to his home community in Migori county. Since the Migori constituencies were not as hotly contested as the Nairobi ones, Gordon would have a real chance at winning the seat.

During the 2012–2013 school year, in preparation for the 2013 election, Gordon began visiting Migori every weekend to establish his presence and build up his support base in the community there. He took the 12-hour bus ride every Friday, and returned to Nairobi around midnight every Sunday night. Gordon's political team would note down the important events happening that weekend in the community and all the info to remember about the families and their situations, so that Gordon could study before he arrived and appear well informed and invested at the events. He attended many funerals, sometimes up to five in one day. As his presence grew, he would be asked to speak at the funerals, to say a prayer over the caskets and to talk about the deceased and their family. In his speeches, Gordon always transitioned to assuring the community that in his future role as their representative, he would work to lessen hardships—there would be less water-borne disease, more access to medical care, less hunger, and more opportunity for progress.

As Gordon started visiting Migori more often, he knew that the first thing he needed to do was upgrade Grandma's living conditions. How could he, in good conscience, speak to other members of the community about working for their prosperity when his own grandmother lived in an old house, visibly suffering the effects of years of wear and tear? He would not appear as a powerful mover and shaker if he was still the grandson of someone with a poor house, or worse, if it seemed like he had abandoned his own grandmother and her house to the ravages of time. To remedy this, he used the salary he'd received as MMU students' council president to build Grandma a new house. There was no formal process for building in Migori, no need to obtain permits or permissions. Gordon just gathered some other guys and they undertook the labor themselves, for only about two weeks of concentrated construction. They built the new house right behind her old house, which they deconstructed when her new house was ready. They also built her a new iron-sheet kitchen hut.

This seemingly small gesture worked exactly as Gordon had planned and stood as a shining symbol to the bigger community of the great things that Gordon would do for *them*. The residents of the rural community were impressed by his enthusiasm and vigor; he made things happen. Community members began to seek out his opinion on general matters, referring to him as "our son in Nairobi," who had access to Prime Minister Raila Odinga and President Kibaki. Gordon was twenty-six years old and represented a breath of young, fresh air. The residents began to catch some of his excitement, saying, "He'll represent us for the next fifty years!"

When Gordon visited the rural country, he was as careful as ever and he never ate any food at funeral receptions or gatherings. He knew he had to be constantly vigilant because the more his notoriety grew and the more he gained the favor of the residents, the more he presented a threat to the incumbent candidate. The current MP running for reelection in 2013 was a much older man, who once spoke to Gordon to dissuade him from running and tried to earn Gordon's good favor by saying, "Your dad was my friend." Gordon found this appeal strange, and he couldn't help thinking, *I never knew that man. What was he ever to me?* By extension, the Okumu clan had never done anything for Gordon or helped him when he was in need. Invoking their name didn't strike any chords of loyalty or solidarity, but of course, the more Gordon rose in popularity, the more they wanted to claim him as *their* beloved son. Gordon instead based his campaign on being *the son of nobody*. He was one of the common people who had grown up poor and still took matatus and slow cross-country buses. He never had a personal driver or hired car when he was in Migori but instead got around by riding on the back of *boda boda* motorbikes taxis. He wanted to be living proof that greatness didn't depend on where you were born or who your parents were. The more that certain people told Gordon he was too young to run, the more he wanted to show them that he could do it. He had always been stubborn like that, and his political dreams mixed with his personal drive were a formidable combination.

Gordon's youth and vigor were definitely a plus, but they also made certain members of the community wary. There were established ways things were to be done, after all, well-trodden paths that you had to follow and traditions that you had to respect. Was someone so young and new to politics really ready to assume the role of representative? In the rural country, one of the unspoken requirements, simply put, was to be a *family man*. For how could you convince a community that you'd take care of them if you couldn't even convince a woman? If a man was married, and better yet, married with children, this was seen as a reassuring sign that he could represent the traditional, conservative community. They wanted someone who reflected and understood their values, ideally someone with a wife who did his cooking and cleaning and obeyed him dutifully.

Since Gordon was not married and didn't even have a fiancé, this was a distinct strike against him. It was a delicate line to walk, for during his term as student council president at MMU, Gordon specifically chose not to have a girlfriend. He felt like he was too busy to seriously devote himself to a relationship, and besides, politics could be a dangerous game and could get ugly. A significant other could become a liability, as they often became the prime target for kidnapping or bribery. If you confided in a boyfriend or girlfriend and allowed them into your inner circle, you also risked eventual scandal or slander. A politician's confidants were often bought by their political opponents and used as a weapon to erode the politician's credibility and destroy their campaign. Gordon just didn't want to deal with any of that.

As much as Gordon wanted to run for parliament in the 2013 election, the deadline for registering his official candidacy was approaching quickly, and he needed to temper his impatient excitement with a pragmatic view of reality—he didn't have the funds needed to run a full campaign and he hadn't yet completed the required paperwork to be a legitimate candidate. He decided that it was too soon and that he could wait until the next election in 2017. Anyway, waiting the additional five years would only help him rise in prominence and notoriety. During that extra time, he could further establish his presence, fine-tune his brand for the rural opinion, and continue building his network. He felt that he had nowhere to go but up.

In the meantime (as much as he had already mentally moved on), Gordon still needed to officially finish his university degree. The required final component to earn the degree was an internship during the 2013–2014 academic year. Gordon found a suitable position as a writer and editor with *The Seed Magazine*, the official publication of the Consolata Missionaries religious order. The magazine reported news about the Catholic Church in Kenya and around the world, along with updates about the evangelical efforts of the missionaries, and articles about edification in personal faith. The magazine described itself as "a great companion in the journey of faith and a guide to an attractive Christian lifestyle."

After Gordon's internship at *The Seed Magazine*, he graduated from MMU in 2014 and transitioned to a similar job as an editor for *The Catholic Mirror*, the publication of the Kenya Conference of Catholic Bishops (KCCB). Their office was located just north of Waiyaki Way in Westlands, right across from the office of *The Seed Magazine*. During his time there, Gordon helped KCCB redesign their newspaper, and he acted as their reporter at various events throughout Kenya. He enjoyed hobnobbing with bishops and cardinals and even the Pope's representative in Kenya. All the while, Gordon continued to build his political platform and look toward the 2017 election.

In September 2015, KCCB wanted to send reporters to the US to cover the World Meeting of Families, an international gathering of Catholics that is held every three years. This event was started in 1994 by the Roman Catholic Church as a way to celebrate the unity and sacred dignity of families and to ensure that they are modeled after the most holy family of Jesus and his parents Mary and Joseph. In Philadelphia, there would be attendees from over one hundred countries and most significant, the Holy Father himself, Pope Francis, would be there.

KCCB decided to send Gordon to the World Meeting of Families, as one of their reporters, along with one other employee. The two of them had to apply for travel visas, and Gordon handled all the paperwork and went through the interview at the American embassy. He was granted a multiple entry visa for the US, good for one full year. While the World Meeting of Families only lasted four days, Gordon planned to take the opportunity to stay for an entire month in the US. He wanted to travel a bit and see more of the great land of Obama, that Gordon had only seen on TV and in movies.

In Philadelphia, Gordon stayed with a Catholic host family that he'd contacted through the event website, and he met various members of their local church. While at the conference, Gordon got to sit off to the side with other reporters and take notes, then compose his articles and send them back to Nairobi to be published in *The Catholic Mirror*. It was exhilarating to be close to people he'd seen on TV and heard so much about, especially Pope Francis. The Pope had been recently elected in 2013, and he was not as tall as Gordon thought he'd be from the photos and videos Gordon had seen. The Pope was always bending and hunching though, so it was hard to tell how tall he truly was. The Argentinian man couldn't speak English and was very slow with his Italian, moving through the recognizable rising and falling intonation that rocked gently like a boat on the ocean. To Gordon, the man seemed compassionate and already well loved by Catholics throughout the world. If the Pope ever arrived late to any of his press conferences or engagements, people brushed it off and said that he'd only been delayed because he'd stopped to kiss babies and offer blessings. His papacy felt like a fresh start for the Catholic Church, and Gordon enjoyed the feeling, even as he tried to be a neutral reporter for KCCB.

When the conference was over, Gordon's first stop on his personal tour was New York City. He saw all the famed sights, like Times Square, Madison Square Garden (where his favorite WWE wrestlers, John Cena and The Rock still won their fights, night after night), and the 9/11 Memorial. Gordon stood on that ground where the World Trade Centers had been and looked into the two man-made reflecting pools. There was the large outer pool and a smaller, inner pool where the water continually fell into a seemingly bottomless black pit. Gordon was taken aback by how arresting the sight was. It was such a moving symbol of the life lost and the scars left on American history. He remembered back to that day when he had been a student in the Kangemi slum, without a TV or anything, and he had only heard from other people about the attacks. The other kids in Kangemi had just repeated over and over, "It looks like a movie. It's like a movie." At the time, Gordon didn't know what that was supposed to mean, maybe something about how it just didn't seem real. As he stood there on the spot where it had happened and watched the water disappear down into the blackness as so many people had in the devastation of that day, Gordon understood how real and how large the event was, and how profoundly it had rippled throughout the entire world, even to the dusty streets in the slum neighborhoods of Nairobi, Kenya. The waterfalls in the monument truly did depict "absence made visible."

Apart from the tourist sights and the memorial, Gordon's general impression of New York city was that it was just a big city, much like

Nairobi. Of course, it had fancier, newer, and bigger buildings, and there were times when Gordon was walking on the street where he felt like he couldn't even see the sky. Nairobi had skyscrapers and bustling streets full of taxis and pedestrians and buses, but you could always clearly see the sky. Apart from that though, the two cities were really not so different. After NYC, Gordon took a greyhound bus across the country to Sacramento, California, to visit Fr. Landon's parents. As Gordon looked around at the US during his cross-country trip, he only thought about Kenya and his political aspirations. He wanted to help bring Kenya forward so that it could rise to its potential. Nairobi could maybe even rival New York City someday. Gordon knew he had to dream big, for himself and for his fellow Kenyans. Even if no one else would dream that large, he would do it for them.

Throughout the touristic part of his time in the US, Gordon still took photos for *The Catholic Mirror* and of course for his own personal pleasure. Without thinking anything of it, he sent photos back to his friends in Nairobi and even posted some on Facebook (as people do). When he returned to Nairobi after his trip, he was met with an unexpected consequence of his travels—photos of him had been appropriated by various people and were now circulating on the internet. A specific photo from the World Meeting of Families caused a stir, and it wasn't even one that Gordon had taken (Gordon didn't know who had taken it). Pope Francis was in the foreground, and Gordon, in his capacity as a reporter, just happened to be standing in the background. To the average Kenyan eye, this photo showed that Gordon now had a direct connection to the Pope. People started saying that Gordon had gone to the US to fundraise for his political campaign—as other politicians, like Raila Odinga, often did—and that Gordon was friends with Obama. There were also photos of Gordon with various white people, which in the Kenyan popular imagination, became proof that Gordon must have loads of rich mzungu friends and donors. He basically had the support of the entire US government and probably knew many American billionaires. Who could now compete with that level of connection and wealth?

As another consequence of this entire situation, Gordon's unintended publicity made him a much more serious threat to his political opponents. Slanderous stories started to circulate about him in the media, and Gordon knew that the news sources had probably been paid to run false stories full of ridiculous and downright weird facts about his life. News articles about him surfaced out of nowhere, with interviews that he had never done, and they included photos of him in the US captioned with strange, fabricated tidbits about his background, family, and his life growing up in Kangemi. While this was annoying, Gordon didn't worry too much at the time, and it mostly served to reinforce his resolve. He knew that all this nonsense was a sign that his opponents felt threatened by him and that he stood a good chance of winning the Parliament seat. He remembered the proverb about how people only throw stones at the tree that bears fruit. The more he gained momentum and positioned himself for success, the more adversaries he'd create and the more resistance there would be. That was all part of the process, he figured, and it was actually a positive sign that he was going in the right direction.

Even other members of the ODM party took notice and discouraged Gordon from running in the 2017 election. They told him, essentially, to not *stir the pot*. He had already set himself apart by being so young, assertive, and openly non-corrupt. He could not be bought, which was a rarity indeed. His trip to the US now caused an even larger stir, and some people told him to just wait. Let the waters calm down. Don't stir things up unnecessarily. Don't upset the status quo. Gordon was even told by the serving MP for Suna West in Migori county that if Gordon didn't run, they'd give him some kind of job in the government as a consolation. Or, he could just wait one more term for the Suna West incumbent (the same man from the 2013 election) to have one more term and then surely, he'd retire.

As much as others claimed that the Suna West MP would only serve one more *final* term, Gordon didn't believe it, because there were no term limits. All he had to go on was that man's word and the claims of those around him, which couldn't be trusted. Gordon knew it would be shameful for an older MP incumbent to lose to a young newcomer, someone the age of his children, but Gordon didn't care much for this man's pride. He believed that if he was the right candidate for the job, people would understand that and vote accordingly. Just because someone has been doing the job for ages doesn't mean they should continue, and it certainly doesn't mean that they're *still* the best person for the job. Kenya needed new blood, new vision, new youthful vigor, and this was Gordon's time.

*

Shortly after Gordon's return to Nairobi, he met with a few people from Migori who had come to Nairobi to see him. They called themselves his friends, and they addressed Gordon with *Mheshimiwa* in Swahili, which means "honorable one." They met in downtown Nairobi on a Friday around 5 p.m. at the restaurant on the bottom floor of the Hotel Metro. Gordon didn't order any food and only asked for a cup of black tea with lemon. The waitress brought back the drink orders from the kitchen, and as Gordon sipped his tea, the men from Migori advised him not to run for the Parliament seat. They spoke about the character of the incumbent member of parliament, how he was a respectable old man who deserved to serve one more term (for no other reason than that he was currently serving a term). They didn't speak about the man's work or about Gordon's ideas for Suna West. Instead, they merely repeated that Gordon should, "let him have it." They wanted him to leave it to the current politician and wait for a future opportunity. "Now is not your time."

The meeting lasted about an hour, and then they went their separate ways. As Gordon headed toward Professor Majany's office to debrief (as was his habit after political meetings), he began to have a stomachache. The ache got worse and he felt bloated, like there was some strange expanding pressure in his abdomen. He hadn't eaten anything strange recently, so it shouldn't be indigestion or a food allergy or anything like that. The ache kept getting worse and it was escalating quickly. Gordon started to worry, and his intuition told him that this was not a normal case of indigestion or even food poisoning. When Gordon arrived at Majany's, they decided to go right to the pharmacy and ask if there were any over-the-counter medicines that could alleviate Gordon's stomach pain. When they explained Gordon's symptoms, the pharmacist said they should go immediately to the Kenyan equivalent of the emergency room at the hospital. Thankfully they didn't have far to go, as the ER was located in the same building on the floors above the pharmacy.

At the ER, they took all kinds of samples from Gordon, and the seriousness and urgency of it all made him feel more and more worried. *What was really going on here?* The nurses tested both a blood sample and a stool sample immediately in their own adjacent lab. This was a type of pared down lab that could only provide a simple toxicology test where a reaction with certain substances or a family of substances produces a certain color in a solution. When the nurses tested Gordon's samples, they turned the color that meant they were positive for some sort of poison.

The ER requested that Gordon be transferred to another hospital that could conduct more advanced tests to find out exactly what the substance was. There, the doctors took more samples, and as a means of immediate treatment, they gave Gordon an injection to induce what is euphemistically called a "bowel irrigation." The medical use of "irrigation" here implies the process of flooding organs or tissues with water to wash out harmful substances. While that sounds fine in theory, the reality is far less pleasant,

Mwendo wa ngarama: the difficult way

because what it actually means is copious and forceful diarrhea. While deeply unpleasant for Gordon, the procedure seemed (or at least felt) effective at emptying his system of the poison so that his body didn't have time to absorb much of it into his bloodstream.

The hospital wanted to keep Gordon overnight. But Gordon wanted to go home, so Prof. Majany called one of Gordon's cousins, Eddie, who came along with another friend to take Gordon back home to his apartment. The two guys stayed all night, talking, telling stories, even laughing, and generally trying to lift Gordon's spirits. Overall, Gordon just felt worn out by the whole ordeal, like a lion that's been rained on. Once the exhaustion receded, he felt truly fearful—for the first time—about his political safety. He had always tried to be careful with what he ate and drank, and he always met in public places where there were other people around, but obviously it wasn't enough. He had always had the mindset that, while it happened to others, it wouldn't happen to him. Obviously, he had been wrong about that too, and he'd now have to adjust his tactics.

He knew though that politicians in Kenya had to be careful—that was part of the package—and that many carried their own beverages with them to gatherings and wouldn't accept *anything* from any public place. Despite this, political assassinations in Kenya were not new and unfortunately not uncommon. While there were many different ways that your enemies could dispose of you, the point was always to do it in a stealthy way that couldn't be traced back to them. Murder hardly ever happened point blank in cold blood, so naturally poison was a method of choice. Gordon knew that real life poisonings in Kenya weren't any sort of spectacle. Subtlety was the point, and that made it all the more sinister. When people were poisoned, it wasn't like sensationalized depictions on TV and in movies, where the unsuspecting victim would have one spoonful of their soup, immediately cough, clutch their throat, and seconds later collapse face first onto the table, dead as a rock. In real life, the victim usually returned home before they realized anything had happened. Then they passed away during the night, drifting off to death in some mysterious way that would be labeled natural, or accidental, or even as suicide because—most importantly—no one had been there to witness it.

Gordon remembered the recent case of Raila Odinga's son, Fidel, who had been Raila's heir and natural political successor, poised to enter the national political scene in the 2017 election. In early January 2014, Fidel had been found dead in his home after a night out drinking with friends at multiple Nairobi bars. Even though a thorough autopsy was performed, the medical examiners claimed that the exact cause of death could not be determined. For many Kenyans, it was obviously a case of political assassination by some untraceable poison, but the news outlets concluded that it must have been common alcohol poisoning from too much heavy drinking. Gordon shuddered just thinking that he had almost suffered the same fate as Fidel.

Gordon reported his case to the police, and they recorded it in their paper Occurrence Book. What this meant was that they wrote down his case number, then tore off the carbon copy for Gordon to keep as his personal record, to show that it had been recorded. Then they closed the book, and that was the end of that. There was no further investigation. From then on, Gordon switched up his tactics and was *extremely* careful. He thought he'd been careful before, but this was a whole different level. He set the details of every meeting and chose to change locations and reschedule at the last minute, sometimes multiple times. He had to be as unpredictable as possible, sporadic, and spontaneous. He also brought other guys with him as bodyguards, and he became wary of any and all food or drink that was placed in front of him.

Throughout all this, however, he didn't back down with his campaign or political dreams. He was already facing persecution and he knew he'd just have to be stronger than ever because there might be more in the future. The news that Gordon was poisoned spread like bushfire in the Suna West constituency in Migori county, and this only strengthened Gordon's approval rating. His constituents saw him as the victim of a senseless crime, and when he didn't back down or give up, he seemed all the more fearless. The voters suspected the incumbent candidate or someone in his inner circle had done the crime (which was the logical assumption), and this only served to hurt the incumbent's approval ratings. The Suna West voters didn't want someone who played dirty and who cheated for selfish gain. So, for the moment, it seemed like maybe this was karma rearing its head in Gordon's favor, and he tried to use the momentum and to continue on and propel himself forward.

*

One night in December, Gordon was on his way back home from a meeting in an area just northwest of downtown. He was about to cross Waiyaki Way and head west toward Kangemi. He was driving a 1986 black Mercedes Benz, which definitely had problems but still looked good, and for Gordon, the image of status and wealth it radiated was worth the hassle. It was around 10 p.m., and he had one of his friends in the passenger seat. There were many other cars on the road. Suddenly they heard a loud BANG right behind them. Both he and his friend jumped in their seats—it was the recognizable sound of a gunshot. Then there was another shot, and this one sounded like it hit the back of the car. Gordon's heart raced, and he wasn't sure what to do, but he clutched the steering wheel and told himself to keep cool and just keep driving. He knew that he couldn't stop, even if he had a flat tire, because someone could be right behind them or waiting to ambush them. So, he and his friend pulled calmly into the first gas station they came to, which fortunately was busy, full with other cars and people milling around. No cars followed them into the gas station, and everything seemed normal, except that when they got out and walked around to the back of the car, they saw a bullet stuck in one of the back tires.

The sight of that bullet filled Gordon with a new kind of fear, and he stared for a moment at that small piece of metal as a cold heaviness radiated through his body. He started shaking slightly as various wild thoughts raced through his mind, and the most serious, most obvious one of all sunk in: that bullet had probably been meant for him, for his *body*. Or had the shooter wanted him to pull over, and then what would have happened if he'd gotten out of the car? Gordon didn't know what to do next, and he didn't want to panic, so he called Prof. Majany and told him what happened. The first thing Majany said was, "Don't go home. They might be waiting for you at your apartment." This made Gordon feel even worse. Majany wanted Gordon to come instead to Majany's faculty residence on the MMU campus. Gordon called a couple friends to come and accompany him, and they took a taxi to the MMU campus. They later had the Benz towed from the gas station. Once he got to Majany's house, Gordon also called Fr. Landon to tell him what had happened and ask for his counsel.

Fr. Landon's levelheaded advice was that Gordon should ease off politics, pure and simple. This whole situation was not worth dying for. Gordon, of course, didn't want to back down, and he especially didn't want to look like he was giving up. He couldn't give his opponents the satisfaction of winning, thinking that they had sufficiently threatened him to make him abandon the race. But—when he really stopped to think about it—wasn't that it, actually? What did it matter if he pulled out of the race, as long as he was alive? The whole thing seemed fairly black and white. As much as he didn't like the choice and he felt frustrated that he had to make that choice, it was a question of (maybe only temporarily) putting aside his political dreams in order to live, and to fight another day.

That should have been an easy decision, but it wasn't. Gordon had worked so hard to make those dreams a reality, and he was on the cusp of succeeding. He was so close that he even felt like he was *already* holding it in his hands. The ambitious, stubborn part of him didn't want to let go, but the practical part of him knew this his enemies would not stop. As usually happened in Kenyan politics, if someone wanted you gone, they would find a way. They had seemingly endless ways and tools and resources and people at their disposal. His enemies were many, and Gordon was only one. In this sense, he knew he had reached an impasse. If he wouldn't pull back the reigns on his campaign and his crusade for change, and his opponents wouldn't ease off their tactics to silence and remove him, who would win this deadly game of chicken? Gordon admitted to himself that the inevitable outcome was that someone would end up dead, and that someone would most likely be him. If it didn't happen right away, it would probably happen later. So, he had to decide now, before it was too late. As agonizing as it was, he knew no one could make this decision for him. He'd have to restrain his ambition and use his own right hand to pry the dream out of his left hand.

*

At the beginning of 2016, amidst all these conflicting thoughts and emotions, Gordon was called back to the hospital for a routine follow-up to make sure that everything was still fine. There he received the official result of the toxicology analysis: it was arsenic, the *king of poisons* and *poison of kings*. This poison had earned those titles due to its discreet potency—it was tasteless and odorless—along with its historical efficacy in many a royal and political succession scheme. It was also a popular and particularly literary poison, favored by authors like Agatha Christie, Arthur Conan Doyle, and even Gustave Flaubert, who famously had his heroine Emma Bovary commit suicide by eating arsenic. While Flaubert described the process of her death over the course of multiple pages of excruciating detail, suffice it to say that with a serious dose, arsenic can lead to death in a matter of hours.

This toxicology result reinforced the gravity of the situation and helped Gordon clarify matters in his mind. Together with Fr. Landon, they decided that the most prudent act would be for Gordon to voluntarily remove himself from the situation, completely, before anyone beat him to it. Fr. Landon's youngest daughter was about to get married at the end of February 2016, and this presented a good reason for Gordon to come to the US. The entry visa that he'd acquired to travel for the World Meeting of Families was still valid, so all he needed was the plane ticket. Once he was there, he would apply for political asylum. The Landon family graciously offered to host Gordon until he got back up on his feet, but since they were preparing a wedding, they couldn't offer to pay for his plane ticket. Ever since his trip to Philadelphia, Gordon had remained in contact with the family that had hosted him, and he reached out to them for suggestions or possibly to help with the cost of the ticket. They in turn spoke with their church community, and as had happened many times in Gordon's life, help appeared from an unexpected source right when it was most needed. One gracious good Samaritan, named Frank, from the church in Philadelphia offered to pay the entire cost of Gordon's flight.

When all the preparations were made and only communicated to a select few for safety reasons, it was then—and only then—that Gordon began to feel anxious about leaving. Asylum cases brought a restrictive finality, for once you applied, you could never return to the place you fled from. It was basically like you had to sever all ties with your country. As much as Gordon wanted his safety, he also wanted to still be involved with Kenya. This was his country and he cared deeply about its prosperity. Would his asylum mean that he would never be able to return to Kenya— never again for the rest of his life? All of his dreams, his friends, and his future were in Kenya. The whole plan filled him with a bittersweetness that mostly just felt bitter. He began to have doubts about whether his personal safety was really worth giving up *everything*. It would be a relief to not worry for his safety, but once that subsided, what would he do in the US? What would his life be like? He had absolutely no idea what the future would hold. He only knew, in the pit of his stomach, that it would mean starting over at the very bottom, once again.

Shortly before he was scheduled to leave, Gordon reached out to Fr. Ngugi at the Holy Family Basilica and asked if he could arrange a special Thanksgiving Mass in memory of Gordon's mother, since it was almost the anniversary of her death. Ngugi agreed and this time, they held a service in honor of Mary Auma *inside* the Basilica. Gordon drove in that same black Benz from Kangemi to the Basilica in downtown Nairobi, and he crossed Waiyaki Way for what could be the very last time. For the plan was that after the event, Gordon would simply disappear—mysteriously and untraceably.

Since Gordon was now a well-known face and rising political figure, people who had never cared for Mary Auma during her life suddenly wanted to pay their respects and express to Gordon how they had known her. They showed up at the Mass in plenty, something like four or five times as many people as had come for the original funeral, back when Gordon was only a teenager. Gordon's half-sister, Maureen, came and brought many members of her church, along with people in Kangemi who had known Mary Auma, and even Grandma came from up-country with some of Gordon's uncles and aunts. After the service in the church, everyone caravaned out to Langata Cemetery, just like before, only that in the past, there had been two pickup trucks with people sitting in the back next to the casket. This time, there were enough people to fill the Basilica's own bus and multiple cars. In the years that had passed, Mary Auma's grave had received a cement slab cover with a thin ceramic top layer, which looked smooth and clean. Each person in attendance got to ceremonially place a single red rose on the grave, and there were over a hundred roses in total. Roses completely covered the cement slab so that none of the gray was visible underneath, and the flowers even spilled over onto the ground on both sides.

While they were at Langata, Gordon's single packed suitcase was waiting for him back in the car. He stood beside his mother's grave, thinking about that suitcase and what it symbolized, trying to wrap his mind around the heavy reality that he might never be able to wear the Langata dust on the soles of his shoes again. This might be the last time he placed a flower on Mary Auma's grave, the last time he got to speak to his mother at her final resting place. He tried to remain calm and composed and had to hold back the water threatening to well up in his eyes. With all the other people around, he needed to not seem *too* emotional and not give himself away. Of the people there, only Fr. Ngugi, Grandma, and Maureen knew about Gordon's plan to leave. After they were done at the cemetery and the gathered family and friends started to dissipate and head back to the Basilica for refreshments, Fr. Ngugi reassured Gordon, saying, "Your mother is praying for you." Gordon nodded and cast one parting look at his mother's grave. He sent her a final farewell, and he silently prayed that he would see her again someday. He walked back to the Benz, and together with his cousin Eddie, drove to the airport.

When Gordon was on the plane, climbing into the clouds over Nairobi, he looked out the window, down over the streets and shanties and roads and skyscrapers that had been his entire world. He said goodbye to each one in turn, to the rusting roofs of all those shanties in Kangemi and all the places he'd lived and worked and studied and played soccer with friends. He tried to mentally let it all go and embrace the fact that he was headed toward a new horizon with an as-yet unknown and different future. Anyway—he reassured himself—he had started over many times before—with his mother in Kangemi, by himself at Grandma's in Migori, as an orphan teenager in the slums, as a seminarian in Arusha, as a student at Multimedia University—and now he could do it again, as a refugee in the US. He knew that wherever he ended up, Mary Auma would be there with him. He was still that boy who had amazed his mother by defiantly shaking the hand of the Honorable Dalmas Otieno Anyango, and who had never let poverty, class, tradition, or custom hold him back. He told his mother, in his heart, that no matter what, he would find his way in this new world and make her proud.

Thank you for making me resilient and teaching me how to dream. You gave me your courage and it has always served me well. Together we'll face this new adventure, lukumba lukumba.

Acknowledgments

It has been a long and winding road to reach this point. We couldn't have realized this project without the enthusiasm and encouragement along the way from so many family members, friends, and colleagues. It truly takes a village. Perhaps more than anything else, we are grateful for all of you who believed in this work as much as we did, even before we had much to show for it.

We want to first thank all those who read early drafts and versions of this book. Bingham, Carolyn, and Marketa, your initial feedback helped this fledgling story take its first steps.

Next, thank you to those who read the story in its entirety: Kathryn, Don, Samuel, Brenda, Susan, and Cheryl. Your willingness to be a part of this endeavor and your thoughtful comments helped transition us into the next phrase of the project. Your input made the writing better.

Thank you to Barbara for your careful editing, and Sarah for your eagle-eyed proofing. Amy—thank you for sharing your experience and being an inspiration.

A special thank you to Frank. Your kindness was the first domino that started a continuing, cascading series. Thank you for having the faith and ability to be the first!

We send a hearty thank you to Becky and Tom Zimmerman for your unfailing support and for always having ready opinions. Your feedback (on everything) has always been helpful, and you've provided much-needed perspective at critical moments. You helped us keep the fire of hope alive, and you have always been our biggest champions and cheerleaders when we felt discouraged or overwhelmed.

We're so grateful to the friends who've believed in the inherent worth of this project, the importance of the story, and in our ability to bring it to life: Nagore, Min, Megan, Crescent, Matt, Dale, and Melissa.

To Professor Bosire at the University of Oregon, thank you for your feedback on the translation of the *Dunia ina mambo* song lyrics.

We want to thank the church communities that have supported Angels of Africa and the two of us along the journey of starting the nonprofit and finding our footing. From the beginning, the members of Trinity Lutheran Church in Cottage Grove, OR have generously sustained the nonprofit, along with the congregation of United Methodist Church in Elk Grove, CA.

St. Mary's Episcopal Church in Eugene, OR and Christ Episcopal Church in Tacoma, WA have been our church homes throughout different times and some difficult periods. We continue to be the people we are and live the kind of life we do because we've had the experience of these inclusive and warm communities. Thank you for welcoming us when we were strangers, and for believing with us in our dreams.

We of course want to thank the Landon family for accepting Gordon, treating him like their own, and then welcoming Robin too. We are grateful to call you our family. To Jonathan and Rebeka—once again—thank you for befriending Gordon and helping him through big decisions and transitions. The story of this book would be very different if not for the role you've played. It still amazes us that Jonathan accepted a random friend request from across the world. Then you advised, trusted, and helped this Kenyan you'd never met, even to the point of welcoming him into your home as your own son. Your generosity has changed our lives, and we are forever grateful.

*

Years ago, on our very first date at an Italian restaurant in downtown Eugene, Gordon recounted his entire life story to Robin over dinner. Since then, we talked about writing it together, but there were so many priorities and responsibilities in the way. Now, finally, we have done it! It was a collaborative effort, and we are so thankful that life brought us together—because what are the odds?!—and that we get to share and sustain this life of laughter, languages, learning, storytelling, cooking, and above all, love. What a beautiful, blessed life it is, truly better than anything we could have asked for or imagined.

CROSSING WAIYAKI WAY

About the Authors

Robin has spent her adult life reading and writing. She holds a PhD in Comparative Literature from the University of Oregon and her articles have appeared in *Women in French Studies* and *Deleuze and Guattari Studies*. She previously earned a BFA in Drawing and Painting from Biola University and an MA in Italian Literature from the University of Washington. She has lived in Rome and Paris, speaks both Italian and French, and enjoys living a multilingual life. Currently, she works as a Technical Writer and as the Publisher for Angels of Africa Press. She and Gordon live near Seattle, WA.

Gordon grew up in Kenya speaking Luo, Swahili, and English. He enjoys living a multilingual life. He holds a bachelor's degree in Media Studies from the Multimedia University of Kenya in Nairobi, a BA in Global Studies from the University of Oregon, and a post-graduate certificate in Tropical Forest Management from Yale University. He is currently pursuing an MA in Public Policy from Oregon State University, and he works as an Environmental Investigator for local government. He founded the non-profit organization, Angels of Africa, and conducts community education and environmental development projects in western Kenya.

CROSSING WAIYAKI WAY

www.ingramcontent.com/pod-product-compliance
Lightning Source LLC
Chambersburg PA
CBHW030334010526
44119CB00028B/401/J